In Search of
QUALITY

4 Unique Perspectives, 43 Different Voices

New in a series by <u>Executive Excellence</u> Magazine.

Executive
Excellence
Publishing

Executive Excellence Publishing
3507 North University Avenue, Suite 100
Provo, Utah 84604-4901

Printed in the United States of America

10 9 8 7 6 5 4 3 2 1

Library of Congress Cataloging Publication Data

Shelton, Ken M., Editor
   In Search of Quality
   1. Quality   2. Leadership
   I. Title

94-62022
CIP

ISBN 0-9634-9174-1

Dedicated to the life

and mission of

W. Edwards Deming

(1900—1993)

Contents

Foreword

A Total Approach to Total Quality

by Stephen R. Covey

What powerful lessons in quality we are learning from being part of a global economy and marketplace! Business organizations face more intense, dynamic competition than ever before. This level of competition has made it so world-class quality and service is no longer an option—it is both the price of entry into the marketplace, and the only way to stay alive once you're in it.

Global competition teaches us that you can't fake quality or speed to market. No, you just cannot fake the culture of trust and empowerment that produces superb products and services in a time frame the market demands. In a sense, increasing global competition has taught us the same lesson nature teaches us on the farm—that you reap what you sow. The real insight is that natural laws or principles govern all of life.

I've gained many valuable insights into the principles and processes of Total Quality from this tremendous collection of articles on the subject. What emerges from the writings of the 43 contributors is a total approach to quality, coming from four unique perspectives.

I am a great believer in the power of viewing things both holistically and from many unique perspectives. If we are to achieve significant improvement in quality, we must work holistically. We can't just do a quick-fix to get people shaped up—improving their competency or communication—when we have misaligned systems. For example, we can take people into the wilderness for two days and have them do free falls off mountains to learn trust. But if they come back to misaligned systems, all our improvement effort is undone. Or, if we try to reorganize, restructure, or reengineer the company—or simply come up with a new compensation system or a new strategic plan—without having a foundation of trust, again our work is undone.

The same need for holistic thinking applies to the way we view our organization and its stakeholders. We have moved from the old days of owner satisfaction to shareholder satisfaction, to employee satisfaction, to total customer satisfaction. Total customer satisfaction was a dramatic break with employee and shareholder satisfaction, where people were looking out for their own piece of the pie. But executives can't be focused only on total customer satisfaction any longer. They need to make decisions that benefit all stakeholders. The new day is what I call total stakeholder satisfaction. And I define a "stakeholder" as anyone who has a stake in the success of the organization.

I sense a growing awareness among executives of the ecology of organizations and of the importance of all stakeholders. The CEO is like a symphony conductor, orchestrating all stakeholders, because their interests are all interrelated. The conductor optimizes the whole by suboptimizing the parts, directing them to give their energies toward the whole.

In recent years, the mind-set has shifted from a few people, such as owners or employees, looking out for themselves, to most people seeking to satisfy customers. But total customer satisfaction does not reflect the reality of the ecological nature of organizations, nor does it necessarily benefit all stakeholders. And so transformational leaders are starting to seek total stakeholder satisfaction through synergistic partnerships with all stakeholders.

To bring about total stakeholder satisfaction (the new mindset), leaders need a new skill set, and the skill set surrounds synergy. Synergy is not cooperation; it's not just working together. It's creatively producing better solutions than those we could have produced independently. This requires deep empathic listening and great courage in expressing perspectives and opinions in ways that show respect for the other person's view. Out of that genuine interaction come insights and learnings that are truly synergistic. Synergy can't be forced or manipulated. It has to come naturally from the quality of the relationship—the friendship, trust, and love that unites people.

If you can put the new skill set of synergy together with the new mind-set of interdependency, you have the perfect one-two punch for achieving the competitive advantage of total stakeholder satisfaction. When you have that mind-set of interdependency, and the skill set for building synergy, inevitably you create effective structures, systems and processes. These products of the mind need to be aligned with your mission. For example, if executive compensation is out of line, that deviation will disrupt the whole ecological balance.

Every organization is perfectly aligned to get the results it gets. If you want different results, you need a new mind-set and a new skill set. People who have the skill set but not the mind-set will never be able to pull it off, and vice versa. Both are interrelated. Each is necessary but insufficient.

What forces are driving the shift in thinking toward maximizing returns for all stakeholders? The primary driving forces are the demands of the global economy. The standard of quality is now so high that unless you have an empowered work force and the spirit of partnership with all stakeholders, you can't compete, whether you work in the private sector, public sector, or social sector.

Every leadership team I work with—in business, industry, prison administration, education, government, and health care—is being affected by the quality standards of the global market. Even if they're not competing in global markets, they're still affected by global competitive forces.

It's like throwing a big rock into a pond—the ripples envelop everything eventually. This economic ripple effect is now reaching every corner of the globe. And so executives are becoming increasingly aware of how interdependent we are. They haven't been aware up to this point, according to Lester Thurow, dean of the MIT Business School, because historically the U.S. has had five competitive advantages: the most capital, the best management, the best trained work force, the largest market, and the best technology. But within the last 40 years, those advantages have all disappeared.

When you're facing competitors who think more ecologically and interdependently, eventually the force of circumstances drives you to be humble enough to learn and change. That's what's driving the quest for quality, learning, process reengineering, and other initiatives. But many of these initiatives are not working because they don't go far enough. The mindshift was not great enough. As wonderful as total customer satisfaction is, it's not enough. The interests of all stakeholders must be dealt with in some orchestrated, harmonizing way, or you can't serve the customer.

The force of circumstance is driving us toward total stakeholder satisfaction. We're either forced by circumstance to be humble, or we can choose to be humble out of recognition that principles ultimately govern. To be humble and constantly learning is good. But it's better to be humbled by conscience rather than circumstance.

Preface

Raising a Standard

by Curt Reimann, Director of the
Malcolm Baldrige National Quality
Award for the National Institute of Standards and
Technology, Department
of Commerce, Washington, D.C.

I'M DELIGHTED to see this stellar collection of ideas on quality improvement compiled from the pages of *Executive Excellence* magazine and composed by some of the best and brightest minds on the subject in the world.

I'm also delighted that this book is dedicated to the memory of W. Edwards Deming. The Deming Award has been the standard of excellence in quality for many years in Japan.

When the Malcolm Baldrige Award Program started in North America in 1987, we were in the right place at the right time with the right idea. In its first few years, the Baldrige Award has captured the imagination of many leaders, symptomatic of a new season of competitiveness. The Baldrige Award has fast become America's premier symbol of excellence—for six good reasons.

1) There was fertile soil. There was a general awareness that quality in this country was not keeping pace with that of our best competitors—an awareness that we needed to improve quality to compete globally. The Baldrige Award gave us a vehicle to marshall our energies and to take positive steps toward renewing our commitment to excellence.

2) The Baldrige Award created a clear, tough, universal standard. Before the Award, there were many definitions of quality, and many tools for measuring quality. Communication was difficult—

adding cost and confusion to doing business. Through the Award, we tried to create a consensus, a common concept of quality. We also created an evaluation system to permit meaningful diagnosis and feedback. Because the Baldrige criteria are adaptable, many nonbusiness organizations benchmark against them. For example, thousands of leaders in schools, hospitals, federal programs, state organizations, and trade associations are using the Baldrige standards to support their work.

3) The Baldrige Award criteria integrate all the important quality concepts and themes into one comprehensive standard. For example, we show how the concept of continuous improvement pertains to all operations and functions within an organization. In effect, we weave all of the important quality threads into the tapestry of the Baldrige Award.

4) The Baldrige Award emphasizes high integrity and thorough competence. We were fortunate to attract to the Program many of America's best quality experts. Competence and integrity created a foundation of credibility needed for a high prestige Award.

5) The award-winning companies took seriously the charge to be quality advocates. They have spread the quality message very fast, very effectively, and very generously to many places and people. To date, the winners have given more than 15,000 presentations—reaching hundreds of thousands of organizations. This level of sharing, and its effectiveness, are nothing short of amazing!

6) American executives rallied around the Award and its high standards. They recognize that higher standards must be met to compete globally. In addition, executives find that the Award criteria are a useful and meaningful tool because they simulate real competition. Their use helps to pinpoint what needs to be done and accelerates the pace of improvement.

A Spring of Turnarounds

I see American business going from a winter of uncertain directions to a spring of dramatic turnarounds. Unlike the 30-year turnaround of quality in Japan, recognized by the Deming Prize, the Baldrige Award is helping to bring about a new focus on quality, and the start of rather dramatic business turnarounds.

I won't talk of specific companies, but I will say that we will see many more dramatic turnarounds—and some surprise winners of the Award. I'm amazed at the speed with which the message is spreading. That's because all sectors of the American economy are represented. And there's a lot of excitement and enthusiasm.

The Baldrige criteria of quality are reaching more boardrooms, as top executives are far more knowledgeable and articulate about quality. They now see quality as the essence of what a leader should work to create, not as something to delegate to a department.

The Baldrige quality criteria are difficult, explicit, concrete. When companies go through the process, they realize that they still have a long way to go. Often, their current performance is not even close to the standard. But we put the tools in the hands of leaders who, in the past, delegated and relegated quality to a department within the company. The new quality requires a different focus—quality driven by customer requirements. It's this concept of externally driven requirements that has captured the imagination of business leaders.

Leaders in education, health care, and government realize that they too must adopt the same standards as business—there can't be a double standard of quality. People are showing a new pride in producing quality products and services.

Government is playing the role of catalyst in the U.S. quality effort by bringing people together, aligning interests, and determining through consensus what the criteria should be. And the criteria continue to evolve as we learn from the lessons of the past and involve more and more people and organizations in the Award process and program. We are very encouraged by the momentum of the Baldrige Award. Nevertheless, we recognize that we still have a long way to go.

Many of the distinguished and articulate contributors to this book not only echo my sentiments—that we still have a long way to go—but many of them also point the way. Since the prevailing quality ethic is *continuous* improvement and competitive quality standards allow for no defects, none of us should be complacent.

Section One

The CEO's Perspective

To the CEO, quality is not so much about numbers, statistics, or inspections—it's more attitudes, beliefs, values, and lifestyles.

While CEOs are champions of quality, they are not engineers, technicians, or statisticians. They are concerned with the heart as much as the head and hands. They hope to achieve congruence among the motive, the mind-set, and the method of quality. Of course, they also want the results: improved quality in products and services and gains in productivity and profitability. That's not always what they get, but they remain committed to the ideal of quality as much as to any program or personality.

For example, consider the belief that serves as the foundation and focus of the quality initiative of the Xerox Corporation, as stated by President **Paul A. Allaire**: "We believe that management doesn't have all the answers. All people have ideas about how their work can be done more effectively; in fact, people closest to the problems often have the best solutions." As he says, "This belief has paid off handsomely."

Motorola Chairman **Robert W. Galvin** also talks about a set of beliefs—the counterpoints to his "10 heresies" of quality—and how these beliefs "govern our progress and our possibilities for the future." Ford Chairman **Donald E. Petersen** and **Lewis C. Veraldi**, vice president of quality, believe that the team approach has fueled the car maker's comeback. "We made quality our number one objective; we became customer-driven; we learned to control costs; and we rediscovered that our people create our success."

Douglas D. Danforth, former chairman and CEO of Westinghouse Electric, is champion of a new model of quality based on the reality that "we must do the right things right the first time."

Kenneth Iverson, CEO of Nucor Corporation, gives a no-nonsense explanation for their quality leadership: "Tell employees everything; base part of their compensation on the success of the company; make jobs meaningful; and be quick to try new ideas and technology." Procter & Gamble CEO **Edwin L. Artzt** makes a plea for all sectors of society to embrace TQM and "make it an integral part of the way we do business, educate youth, and run government."

Norman R. Augustine, president and COO of Martin Marrietta, says that the "secret of quality—indeed, the miracle of quality—is that "higher quality begets reduced cost." **James R. Houghton**, chairman and CEO of Corning Glass Works, writes that training is the key to "unleashing the force." **M. Anthony Burns**, chairman and CEO of Ryder, Inc., reminds us that investments in quality "result in tremendous rewards in terms of sales and profits through enhanced levels of customer satisfaction." **Bill Marriott**, chairman and CEO of Marriott Corporation, notes that the "principles of quality service" haven't changed much since his father founded the company. **Claude I. Taylor**, chairman of Air Canada, suggests that it's best to fly above the clouds where there are "no boundaries to quality." Finally, **Horst Schulze**, president of The Ritz-Carlton Hotel Company, points out that "excellence is a process."

From the CEO's point of view, every person ought to care about quality, if he or she also cares about the viability of the company. The philosophy of quality starts a commitment to excellence, to craftsmanship, to caring. Quality is both very personal and very universal. It's signing your name to your work and taking ownership of results. And it's building brand name, brand loyalty, and corporate identity.

Chapter 1

Quality Lost, and Found

by Paul A. Allaire,
President and CEO of Xerox Corporation

Xerox is an example of what happened to
much of American industry in the last
decade; now it serves as a model for recovery.

AMERICA is locked in a battle for global economic supremacy. And bringing representatives of management, labor, government, and education together to focus on issues of mutual concern is a much-needed part of the process of keeping American business competitive in a global economy.

Let me share three facts to make this point:

• As recently as 1960, the Japanese accounted for only 2 percent of the world's economy. Today they account for about 10 percent.

• When I graduated from high school, America controlled some 35 percent of the world economy; our portion today is about 20 percent.

• In recent years, we have gone from being the largest creditor nation in the world to the largest debtor nation.

These are fundamental issues for American society, with enormous impact on our way of life, our standard of living, and our ability to create meaningful employment.

The causes are varied and complex. Each of us probably has our own version of what went wrong. Almost all of us have pointed the finger of blame at someone else. We complain about the cost and interference of government regulation. Or the lack of able management and wise leadership. Or the high cost and the low productivity of the American worker. Or some mythical attribute of Japan Incorporated.

There is some truth in each of these, I suppose. But in my judgment, the root cause of our trouble is that we became arrogant and complacent. Because we were on the top of the economic pile, we assumed it was our birthright.

The Xerox Example

In many ways, Xerox is a microcosm of what happened to much of American industry. When Xerox introduced the first plain paper copier, the Xerox 914, in 1959, it created a new industry and launched the company into an era of feverish growth and success.

But after two decades of success, we became complacent and took our eyes off both the customer and the competition. We saw the Japanese coming at the low end of the market, but we didn't take the threat seriously. We believed we would always be successful, even as our market share began to shrink. After all, we told ourselves, this was our industry. We created it. We built it. And we owned it.

But by the late 1970s, the Japanese had almost put us out of business. Our market share was cut in half and return on assets slipped to eight percent. And customer satisfaction was eroding.

Fortunately, Xerox reacted in time. We started to take a good, hard look at what we were doing and how we run *our* business. And we started to take a hard look at the competition and how they run *their* businesses.

We were startled by what we found. We realized that our costs were too high—and not just a little high. In fact, the Japanese were *selling* their machines for what it cost us to *make* ours. We assumed that because they were low cost, they were poor quality. We were wrong! Then we tried to convince ourselves that they could not be making money. Wrong again! They were profitable.

That woke us up, and we went to work in earnest to close the gaps. We realized that to be a world-class competitor, we had to challenge everything we had done in the past. We had to change dramatically—from the way we develop and manufacture our products to the way we market and service them.

Quality became our basic business principle. Quality means providing our external and internal customers with innovative products and services that fully satisfy their requirements.

We involved the senior management team—about 25 people—to create a vision of where we wanted to go. We decided to focus on three priorities: customer satisfaction, market share, and return on assets. To be a world-class competitor, we had to change our culture. We had to implement a quality process.

The Results of Change

We've been at that process of changing the corporation and improving quality for about 10 years now; and, although we still have a long way to go, the results are gratifying. Let me give you just a few examples.

- We reduced our manufacturing costs by over 20 percent.
- We cut the time it takes to bring a new product to market by 60 percent.
- We substantially improved the quality of our products.
- We achieved a 90 percent customer satisfaction rating in U.S. operations.
- Customers rated Xerox number one in our industry for product reliability and service.
- Our profitability increased by over 50 percent.

We have regained market share without the aid of tariffs or protection of any kind, and without closing our factories or moving our manufacturing offshore. I say this only to illustrate that there is nothing inherently wrong with American business. We lost our way in the 1970s, but we have found it once again. And while we still have a long way to go, we are pleased to have our work recognized by the Malcolm Baldrige National Quality Award.

How We're Doing It

People sometimes ask me how we have reversed our slide and begun the long, tough road back. Believe me, there is no magic formula. Our incentive is a powerful one—survival as a successful business entity. We're doing this by involving all our people—union and non-union alike—in problem solving and quality improvement. The entire management team has a deep and real commitment to employee involvement. We've had to change just about everything we do and align all our processes to drive quality.

At Xerox we define quality as conforming to customer requirements—pure and simple. And when we speak of quality, we mean more than just product quality. We take the view that every person in the company has a customer for the work he or she does. For many people, the customer is someone inside the company—the person we type reports for or the person to whom we deliver parts.

Quality must work its way into the entire organization—into manufacturing, sales, service, billing, training, finance, and so on. Our quality policy sums it up well. It says simply:

Xerox is a quality company. Quality is the basic business principle for Xerox. Quality means providing our external and internal customers with innovative products and services that fully satisfy their requirements. Quality improvement is the job of every Xerox employee.

Xerox is hardly alone in this approach. Scores of corporations are finding that employee involvement in quality improvement is a powerful way to improve business results. And some of these companies are not in manufacturing. In fact, one of the leaders in quality is Florida Power & Light.

The movement has spread to government as well. We have hosted a meeting on quality specifically for representatives of the federal government. It was attended by senior executives of not only the Department of Defense, but also a variety of service organizations, including the Internal Revenue Service, the FBI, and the Social Security Administration.

This heightened interest in quality is not surprising. The Japanese have realized for years that you don't have to sacrifice quality for cost. In fact, quite the reverse is true. A focus on quality—on satisfying the customer and meeting customer needs—actually drives cost down. That clearly has been our experience.

Assumptions & Achievements

The focus on quality that we initiated four years ago was built on some very basic assumptions about the American worker:

• That management does not have all the answers.

• That all people have ideas about how their work can be done more effectively.

• That people closest to the problems often have the best solutions.

• That this almost unlimited source of knowledge and creativity can be tapped through employee involvement.

• That people are willing and eager to share their thoughts and participate in developing solutions to business problems.

Those beliefs have paid off handsomely. Today more than 80 percent of our work force is involved in more than 4,000 problem-solving and quality-improvement teams around the world.

• A manufacturing team in Rochester reconfigured their old computer system instead of upgrading it. They worked out a time-sharing arrangement with other departments that allowed them to cancel some leases on other computers. The team saved $2 million in overall computer costs.

• A service team compared its working hours with those of our customers, identified significant differences and shifted their work schedules to meet customer requirements.

• A group of keypunch operators set out to see if their work could be done more productively. They wound up recommending that their jobs be abolished and the work vended out. Then they found equal or better Xerox jobs for every member of the team.

And that's just the tip of the iceberg. Philip Crosby, the author of *Quality is Free,* estimates that the typical large corporation wastes 20 to 25 percent of its revenue by not having quality. For Xerox, that's more than $2 billion! We feel that we can capture a major portion of that.

Lessons for Others

When I look back on where we've been and where we're going and ask myself what advice I would give to others, I come up with four specifics:

First, senior management has to be committed to change. Without genuine, hands-on commitment, all attempts at quality improvement and employee involvement are doomed to fail. And that commitment must take the form of action, not rhetoric. Our expression for that at Xerox is that managers must "walk the talk." Their actions must demonstrate they are willing to listen to the ideas of employees; they are sincere in their efforts to change the work environment; and they are serious about their drive toward quality improvement and customer satisfaction.

Second, the commitment of union leadership must be every bit as strong as that of management. That certainly has been and still is the case in Xerox. In fact, quality circles were part of our manufacturing operations before we launched a company-wide strategy of quality improvement and employee involvement. Credit for that goes to the strong and enlightened leadership of the union that represents most of our hourly employees—the Amalgamated Clothing and Textile Workers Union. They understand that we must be competitive and that our union workers can provide significant help in that struggle. The Sloan School of Management at MIT has looked at our experience and summed up its success in one sentence: "The high level of trust built up over the years between labor and management in Xerox was clearly the instrumental factor in the company's success in employee involvement."

Third, it takes some initial investments. At Xerox, for example, we are in the process of giving every man and woman in the corporation six full days of training in problem solving, quality improvement, and team building. For us that means training 100,000 people worldwide. That's an investment of the equivalent of 2,500 man years. It's a big investment in both financial and human resources. But we're convinced it's one of the better investments we've ever made.

Fourth, it requires patience and discipline. Our experience has been that results don't come as quickly as we would like. There are some false starts. There are parts of the organization that lag behind others. There are teams that don't initially work on real business problems. There are managers, particularly middle managers, who see employee involvement as a threat.

One of the Japanese experts on quality and employee involvement likens the need for patience and discipline to that of the bamboo farmer. Once the bamboo seed is planted, the farmer must water it every day for *four years* before the tree breaks ground! But when it finally does, it grows 60 feet in 90 days.

That's true of employee involvement. It takes time. It takes nurturing. It takes patience. But when it finally takes off, its power is tremendous. We, like many other American companies, are proving this. It's a very powerful concept that can energize the total organization.

Education and Business Cooperation

Education and business must cooperate to increase the number and quality of college graduates entering the work force with quality management skills. Managing through this decade and into the next century will require well-educated, high quality managers in all disciplines, as well as managers educated in the application of quality techniques.

Academia must work more closely with their customers in business, government, and the professions to design and teach curricula that meet those customers' needs. Government has a chance to help both business and academia in these efforts through the National Quality Award program. Business must do a better job of articulating the need for quality managers in all disciplines and of supporting educational programs that meet those needs.

Most executives would agree that: *quality is a survival issue for the U.S. economy; neither government, industry, nor academia can do it alone; and we must all work together.* Even in the best companies, we must consider last year's performance a benchmark—and the task this year is continuous improvement! The successes in our business are all based on the assumption that no matter how good we are today, we can and must be better tomorrow. That's because our competitors are constantly expecting more.

American business is in a race with no finish line. That's true of the entire quality movement. Many of us have made quantum improvements. In some industries we have stemmed the tide of foreign infiltration of our markets. We must continue to set our expectations higher and higher.

As a nation, we are only beginning to fully understand the power of quality as a competitive weapon. We are just beginning to fully realize that we are faced with a never-ending spiral of increased competition and heightened customer expectations.

The race to quality has taught us that as good as we are today, we must be better tomorrow, not by a little but by a lot. Our global competitors are excellent. So are we. Let's not forget that continuous improvement, Yankee ingenuity, teamwork, and an inherent belief that things can be better are native American characteristics.

And let's not forget that our system of colleges and universities is the best in the world. But as good as higher education is today, it must be even better tomorrow. Here are some areas where academia could help business more:

- *Understand the needs of industry.*
- *Communicate what they are already doing.*
- *Graduate managers who understand quality.*
- *Embed total quality and participative management in the curricula.*
- *Adapt or add new courses.*
- *Internalize the importance of the customer in marketing graduates.*
- *Graduate a generation of manufacturing managers who can move freely among all phases of engineering and manufacturing and who are cross-functionally literate.*
- *Intensify the study of culture change.*
- *Perform research into quality tools and strategies.*
- *Form a partnership with industry to recapture global competitive advantage.*

I have a great deal of confidence in the ability of American business to compete successfully in the global marketplace. I don't subscribe to the conventional wisdom that our foreign competitors are superior. We still have the world's greatest financial resources, industrial capacity, and distribution system. And we have one other asset—the American people with their immense resilience, strength, and creativity.

But to be competitive, America needs cooperation and team-work among government, industry, and academia. Our people—the American people—can win, as long as the competitive environment is fair to all. That means that government, labor, business, and industry must support one another. We must break down "win-lose" barriers and create "can-do" attitudes and "win-win" strategies.

Chapter 2

10 Heresies of Quality

by Robert W. Galvin, Chairman of the Executive
Committee at Motorola, Inc.

I find that a lot of Old Testament truths
about quality don't work, and so I came up
with my own New Testament truths.

I RECOMMEND that all American business organizations decide to
go for the Malcolm Baldrige National Quality Award, the American
synonym for the Deming Award. The standards established for the
award are superior, and the award is judged by the premier quality
executives and academicians in the world. The decision to go for the
award could be employed as an economic strategy on an all-win basis.

Imagine what might happen if your organization would compete
for this award. If you are like our company, you may have to reach out
with more design engineering, research and development, or service
innovation. You might expect to change your methods and processes
extensively. You may have to invest in new tools, instruments, equipment, or other economic multipliers.

By instinctive calculation, I estimate that if by fiat this policy
were declared today, in just two years the growth rate of the gross
national product would rise an increment of one-half to one percent.
Why? Because our companies would reach out to do one of those
things with a new engineering method or tool. We would reach out to
you, then you would reach out to someone else with what you are
doing. We would all cycle ourselves up because we are engaging in
economic multipliers. To me, it's an automatic victory; and therein is
a strategy for economic growth which would position America to be
even more competitive in the world economy.

Ten Heresies of Quality

Now, let's talk about the heresies of quality.

What is a heresy? A heresy is a challenge to an old truth. I respectfully suggest that certain old truths hold us back in terms of what we potentially could be achieving. Some of us are learning, to our advantage, to challenge those truths and to generate new truths. I speak of old testaments with regard to quality, and what we have come to believe are the new truths.

1. *Quality is a department.* We all have quality departments. The old testament was that quality is a company, a department, or an institutional responsibility. The new truth is radically different: Quality is a very personal obligation. If you can't talk with humility about quality daily, in the first person, then you have not moved to the level of involvement of quality that is absolutely essential.

You must be a believer that quality is your personal responsibility. Of course, when one is interested in vast improvements in quality, it's consistent with another great objective, to be competitive. When we examined the issue back in 1980, when we had a renewal of dedication to quality, we also asked the question, "How do we make ourselves more competitive?"

I finally said one morning, "I think I've identified the key to being competitive. We've got to be competitive one person at a time, counterpart to counterpart. I must aspire to be as capable as Mr. Kobiashi, the head of NEC, one of our most distinguished competitors, our vice president counterpart to the vice president of Texas Instruments, each person's counterpart elsewhere."

2. *Training is an expense.* When I asked the question to myself, "Can I get there?" I had to say I didn't know how. I had to call in mentors, advisors, consultants, teachers, and trainers. So I went to my associates and said, "We've got to do it personally. We've got to have a tremendous amount of training; I need so much, you need so much, the best of our associates need so much."

And they said, "Good idea, Bob, but, of course, let's not take too much time because we're so busy, and we can't afford much money." Here's where leaders have to engage in acts of faith that key things are doable, even if they are not always provable.

I said, "Folks, I don't know how we're going to account for the cash that flows through this thing called training, but it's never going to cost us a penny." The old truth was that training is a cost, an overhead expense. The new truth is: Training is not a cost. We have convinced ourselves that like practical vocational training, we get our money back in the same accounting period.

3. *The up-front costs of quality are high.* Following one of my speeches, a man waited in line until everyone else had left. He said, "Galvin, you've made a point that quality is low cost, but what did you do about up-front costs? That's the big hurdle we all have to get over. You have to put a lot up front, and then finally you hope you make it back."

I'd been thinking about that question for some time. I looked around to make sure that nobody was listening, and then I said, "Sir, we never had any up-front cost."

He said, "That's incredible."

I said, "No, it's the truth."

We didn't know that when we got started in 1980, but we learned it later—and finally we got to feeling it and accounting for it indirectly. The cost of bad quality was extremely high. The cost of bad quality of a very ordinary company is upwards to 40 percent of sales! In 1986, after we were six years into our quality program, we estimated that our cost of bad quality was between 10 and 20 percent of our sales. We were doing about $5 billion worth of sales at this time, and so at least we had a $500 million cost of poor quality. Too much space for this, too much inventory for that, too many returns, too much warranty—it just goes on and on.

We then figured that in 1980, when we started to farm a little better, we were putting money in the bank that we didn't even know how to account for. So when we finally bought our first piece of instrumentation to improve our quality, we'd already effectively paid for it. As far as we are concerned, there is no up-front cost starting a quality program.

4. *Costs will increase if you decide to raise your quality.* We had a wonderful old-timer who was our quality manager in the 1950s. I once asked him, "Gus, why can't all die castings look like this when they're plated versus this?" He said, "Bob, you don't understand. There's a thing called a commercial quality." I was too busy with my other job to follow through with him. He said we would price ourselves out of the market if we tried to raise our standards to perfection on these die castings that went on the front of our car radios.

The new truth is this: You can't raise costs by raising quality. If you really have a quality program, then you change so many things from front to back, from the beginning to the end of your process or your service, that you can't raise costs.

5. *In running a quality program, keep data to a minimum.* That's the old testament. The new truth is: To be a problem solver, you can't have too much relevant data. Redundancy, of course, should be avoided. But we keep records on everything. We measure things left and right and down to the basics because we have to keep peeling that onion back one more layer at a time to get to first causes. The new truth to us is that you cannot have too much relevant data.

6. *An expectation of perfection is unreasonable.* The old truth was that to err is human and that some number of defects or rejects was to be expected. What is new truth? I went to grammar school at St. Jerome's in Chicago, and one day in the fifth grade Sister Mary Norberdette announced that she was going to give a test on Friday on the conversion of fractions to decimals and decimals to fractions—all the odd ones as well as the regular conversions. She said there was only one acceptable grade: 100 percent!

I went home and told my parents how unreasonable the nun was. I expected them to go over and set her straight—and guess whose side my parents came up on? We worked very hard because my mom and dad helped me a lot for the next few nights. I was one of the six or seven kids in the class who got 100 on that test.

She set the tone for what our company should have been, instead of what I accepted from Gus about those die castings. We now genuinely believe that perfection is operationally possible. We're proving it. It's happening in lots of our businesses. I assure you we've got a long way to go in many other places.

If you're in business, you probably have the same objective that we have—total customer satisfaction. Total. Everything. Perfection on delivery, perfection on reliability, paperwork exactly right. All these things are possible. Therefore, we might want to raise our level of expectation. Our expectation level was ground in a culture of the old testaments. Today our expectation is perfection.

One person heard me say this over and over again and finally came to me and said, "Bob, you ought to stop saying that. It's not believable." I said, " I can't stop because when your people buy our radios, they expect perfection, and all of our other customers are telling us that when you finally get your act together, we'll do more business with you." Incidentally, there's a corporate strategy there: The better our quality, the greater our share of the market.

7. *Quality improvements are made in small, incremental stages of 1 or 2 percent.* One of the very appealing and, incidentally, very

valuable testaments of quality today is that continuous improvements and refinements are important. The incredible thing about that particular testament is that people stop at that point.

To us, the new truth is that this is partially true. But, major step-function improvements in quality are both necessary and doable. We don't think about making a change in our processes regarding quality or savings of time anymore unless we think in terms of at least a 50 percent improvement. Sometimes, it's many times that. For example, when we set our first goals in 1980, we said, "Let's improve our quality 10 times, not 10 percent." In a few years we accomplished that—and then we improved five more times. Today, our objective is to improve 100 times more. When we get to that, we will have achieved what we call Six Sigma quality, measured in statistical terms at 3.4 defects per million. That's virtual perfection. And that is doable, but you must believe that radical change is achievable.

8. *If these things are going to be done, it's going to take a lot of time—it takes extra time to do things right.* Isn't that a truth that maybe our moms or our dads taught us, for special reasons. Well, the new truth is, "Quality doesn't take time, it saves time." A complementary old testament says, "Doesn't haste make waste?" Indeed, impetuous actions could cause us to trip over ourselves, but thoughtful speed makes quality.

The synonym for quality in our company is cycle time. We almost don't care whether a department opts to put emphasis on improving cycle time or improving quality, first versus second, because they each lead to the same result.

We used to take 44 days to process an order for a pager— mailing it into the office, checking the credit, buying the parts, making sure the specs were up to date, producing, repairing, scrapping, putting them back, counting them, into the shipping department,and finally shipping them out. Some of our people said, "This can be done very differently with much higher quality."

Today our system allows for an order to be entered by the customer at 9 a.m. It goes through the entire system and to the shipping department at 10:40 that same morning—less than two hours—and that's what I mean by radical change.

Everything isn't quite that radical, but when we consolidate our financial data, we close the books now in about 15 percent of the time it took us just a few years ago. These things are happening in the patent law department, in the personnel department, in the accounting department, and in the factory, in the laboratory, services, manufacturing, and design. People are now thinking in terms of doing things in virtually no time.

9. *Quality programs only fit manufacturing processes.* The new reality is that most people are in the service business and that the opportunities for improving service are just as dramatic. In fact, within Motorola, the department that is now making the greatest rate of change and improvement is our patent law department. They're doing remarkable, surprising things to improve quality and time of performance.

10. *Suppliers have no place in the quality process.* The biggest mistake that our company made when we started our quality program was our failure to bring our suppliers into the process early enough. Fifty percent of our costs are the things that we acquire from suppliers, and we weren't smart enough to engage them and involve them. We now involve our suppliers early and often because they are so much smarter about all the parts that we use than we are. They can teach us, and we can teach each other, and we can grow together. Before, we told suppliers, "You meet that price, and we'll do the rest in our own plant." The new truth is that if you're going to be a world-class purveyor of your product, you must also become a world-class customer. That's a paradox. There aren't very many people who have an objective of becoming a world-class customer.

We now practice this policy: if you want to be a supplier to Motorola, you have to go for the Baldrige Award. That message wasn't appealing to about half of the suppliers. Frankly, about 60 of them told us that we could take our business elsewhere. They didn't pledge to go for Baldrige, so we don't do business with them anymore. Now, incidentally, virtually all the rest are saying, "Thank you for rubbing our nose in it. We didn't realize how much we had to learn." Now they're getting better because they're aspiring to heretical standards.

Well, those are my heresies. They deal with personal obligations, expectations, costs, time, and other concepts. But the question remains, How do we do all of that?

Now, How Do You Do It?

To answer that question, I must tell you about Bernie Sergesketter, the manifestation of outstanding leadership. Bernie is one of AT&T's immensely talented senior officers. After we had won the Baldrige Award, Bernie called and asked, "Would you come and talk to our guys about quality?" I said, "Sure," and he started organizing classes for thousands of people.

When Bernie heard this idea about "quality is a personal obligation," he said, "I guess that means me." He started to list things that he
did that could be measured. He came up with a list of a dozen factors that
he thought he should start measuring himself. One was that he should be
on time, and another was that he should answer the telephone in two
rings—seemingly insignificant things. But he wrote those down, made
up a little chart, and kept data on each of these factors over time. He told
his co-workers that he was doing this, and asked them to help him. If he
missed on one, he asked them to challenge him.

When Bernie walks the hall, he is often asked, "How is your
personal quality?" He stops, takes out a sheet of paper, and says, "Let
me show you." Now, isn't that kind of silly? Not at all. Because
Bernie Sergesketter became a role model. Over 1,000 AT&T people
now carry their own personal quality records. I wouldn't want to have
to compete directly with AT&T if they spread this throughout the
whole system because they have embraced the personal responsibility of keeping records, analyzing, problem solving, understanding the
fundamentals, and raising their expectation levels to a highly person-
alized standard.

This is the theology of quality, and Bernie Sergesketter and others are helping lead us to that understanding.

Commit to Customer-Focused Quality

What we pragmatic Americans really want is this: "Tell me how
to, I want to get at the job." Motorola will make available everything we
have been presenting to thousands of business leaders since having won
the Malcolm Baldrige Award. Award winners are encouraged to respond
to other companies' interests. We have found it a privilege to share. The
more we present, the more expansive the demand for sharing.

Championing a customer-focused quality program is hard work,
but the results can be exhilarating. As you create quality processes,
your people will react. Your customers will respond. Word will spread
that doing business with your company is an exceptional experience.
Customer retention rates will rise, profits will increase, and employee
turnover will decrease.

Every organization has a secret weapon—its customers.
Customers can help businesses win the quality fight because the solutions are there for the asking. Companies need to listen to their customers. They must make the commitment to sincerely listen, react, and
then take that next critical step toward achieving the finest products
and services possible based on their customers' needs and expectations.

So, make a commitment to customer-focused quality and become a champion for change. Review the vision and actions of companies that have successful quality processes and begin to adopt those philosophies and processes that best suit your company. Share best-in-class practices with all employees and show how quality improvements will benefit your firm.

Please know that although we won the Baldrige Award in 1988, we are not perfect yet. In fact, the day after the announcement, I happened to ride down the elevator with two men. One of them said to the other, "Isn't it great; we won this award. Now we're going to have to work to deserve it." That is the spirit of good winners. We have a lot to do. We haven't seen all the results that are implied by some of these beliefs, but we think the beliefs are the platform for which we can aspire to the excellence that the award represents.

These are the beliefs that we think leaders need to know. We've been out talking to thousands of companies on quality, and we're now benchmarking what a large number of other very fine companies of our country are thinking. These are not beliefs accepted universally by everyone, so you're hearing the word from the heretic. You may disagree, and that's fine. Heresies should be debated, as they were in the church.

These are the beliefs that we believe govern our progress and our possibilities for the future. What is at stake is the battle for economic superiority. The outcome of this battle will shape our nation's future for generations to come.

Chapter 3

Ford's Quest for Quality

by Donald E. Petersen, Chairman of the Board, and Lewis C. Veraldi,
Vice President of Quality, Ford Motor Company

*Achieving world-class quality and improving productivity is the number
one priority of many companies today. Here is what we are doing to
achieve these goals.*

TRADITIONALLY, Ford and other automobile manufacturers
developed new vehicles in a "sequential" design process, meaning
that throughout the design of a vehicle, each activity does its thinking
and then hands off to the next activity. The designers do their thing—
design and then turn that over to the engineers. After the engineers do
their job, manufacturing is told to go mass produce the product. And
marketing is then told to go sell it. In the traditional system, you have
groups of specialists operating in isolation.

Consequently, what someone designs and styles may be quite
another matter to engineering, and by the time it reaches manufacturing there may be some practical problems inherent in the design that
make manufacturing a nightmare. The people who actually build the
vehicle haven't been consulted at all, and marketing may well discover two or three reasons why the consumer doesn't like the product and
it is too late to make any changes!

In automobile manufacturing, as in football, sometimes the ball is fumbled during the handoff. The result of this traditional process was a lack of teamwork, poor quality, redundancy of effort, and extreme inefficiency.

We changed the way we do business because back in 1980, Ford's image for quality was not very good. In addition, we were in the process of losing over $1 billion two years in a row. In this climate, we started planning replacements for our mid-size and large cars—these cars would become today's Taurus and Sable. The investment was estimated to be $3 billion, and we knew the old ways of doing business would not work.

In their class, Taurus and Sable were to be designed to compete with anything in the world—foreign or domestic—in fit, finish, ride, handling, and vehicle ergonomics. In short, they were to be designed with world-class quality and provide customers with a compelling reason to once again shop and buy American.

A Team Approach

As vehicle objectives were defined and redefined, we knew that upstream involvement and employee commitment were essential and that the existing organization wouldn't support our needs. Therefore, the sequential organization as replaced by a simultaneous team approach, "Team Taurus."

Team Taurus was organized to promote continuous interaction between design, engineering, manufacturing, and marketing along with top management, and the legal, purchasing, and service organizations. Overall coordination or direction is by a car product development group or program manager whose primary function is getting all of the team to work together.

The idea is that all these groups work simultaneously to bring our new car to market. Instead of being last to be involved, for example, manufacturing is involved 50 months prior to producing the first vehicles. The "downstream" people are factored into the program five years ahead of introduction. Thus, all activities have an equity, an equal opportunity for simultaneous participation throughout the entire program.

To ensure that the best ideas of the people who would be designing and building the car would be considered, our engineers developed a comprehensive "want" system. We visited the Atlanta Assembly Plant and spoke to the hourly and salaried personnel who eventually would build the car. We asked them to tell us how to design a car that was easy to build, and would avoid the design problems that had led to poor quality in the past. We visited the plant 50 months before Job #1 to incorporate their suggestions in the basic design of the product. Their suggestions, along with those of other groups, resulted in more than 1,400 wants being identified. Over half of these were incorporated into the product.

For example, the assembly workers told us that to achieve consistent door openings and tight door fits, a one-piece bodyside was necessary. So we reduced the number of components on the body side from 12 components to two. The doors are also one piece for improved quality and consistent build.

Just as important is the early involvement of suppliers, who are very critical members of the team. They are our partners, and their early involvement is essential to achieving our world-class quality objectives. On Taurus and Sable, we initiated two supplier programs: early sourcing and system sourcing. Early sourcing identifies a component source early and brings them upstream in the design process. The supplier is responsible for the fit and functioning of his components. System sourcing is a process where components which must be coordinated both in color and fit are sourced to one supplier.

An example of early sourcing is the Taurus subframe, which supports the engine and transaxle. It was sourced to A. O. Smith three years in advance. This allowed the engineering and manufacturing team to make 137 design revisions to improve the variable cost, reduce weight, and achieve an automated assembly.

By bringing suppliers into the process early, we could take advantage of their expertise. Prince Corporation, who supplies some of the sun visors, suggested several features which were added to the Taurus. These features included a dual visor system, a new pull-down visor mirror, and a new dome light, which will not shine into the driver's eyes at night. Masland Carpet, the supplier of the station wagon load floor carpet, suggested a method to ensure the carpet nap all ran in the same direction. The result is a uniform appearance for the load floor.

Early sourcing has another advantage. Prototype vehicles, which are built from components supplied by the production source, allow early resolution of fit and finish problems.

On a limited basis on Taurus, we initiated a process of system sourcing. The station wagon interior garnish moldings were all sourced to O'Sullivan. They were responsible for coordinating the fit and color match of all the interior garnish moldings.

Another aspect to system sourcing was the sourcing of the die models and tools for the interior garnish moldings to one supplier, Pro-mold. By having one tool supplier, we could evaluate the fits and coordinate revisions much more efficiently. The result—better fits and better quality.

Several new engineering processes were developed during the Taurus program. By far, the most extensive program to involve engineering was the Best-In-Class Expanded Image Program. The intent of the program was to focus more attention on details that affect the perceived quality of the vehicle, including the interaction between the vehicle and the driver/passenger.

To determine our objective, the team sought out the best vehicles in the world and evaluated more than 400 characteristics on each of them to identify those vehicles that were best in the world for particular items. These items ranged from door closing efforts, to the feel of the heater control, to the underhood appearance. The cars identified included BMW, Mercedes, Toyota Cressida, and Audi 5000.

Once completed, the task of the Taurus team was to implement design and/or processes that met or exceeded those "best objectives." I am proud to report that as we went into production, we had achieved Best-In-Class status on 80 percent of these 400 items. And that was accomplished with teamwork and paying attention to the details.

Finally, we continually asked ourselves the question "Why buy Taurus?" In other words, why should someone cross the street to shop in our store? We asked customers, dealers, buff magazine writers, service people, insurance companies, and professional drivers like Jackie Stewart, early in the program, what features they wanted. By the time we introduced Taurus and Sable, this translated into a feature list 32 pages long! These features included flush side glass for reduced noise, polycarbonate bumpers for rust-free life, and first-class seats for long distance riding comfort.

Where Are We Going?

We will take the "Team Taurus" approach to all new Ford Motor Company products. It has been put in place and endorsed by the top management of the company, who have signed a pledge of support for our new way of doing business. The team concept has been designated as the "Program Management" organization.

We have identified "program managers" who are putting their teams together to take new cars from concept to customer the same way Taurus and Sable were brought to market. Their assignment is to provide leadership for the planning, design, engineering, sales, manufacturing, quality assurance, and service for their product. I said "their product" because it is their product. The objectives for each vehicle will be the basis for measuring the performance for all members of the team.

The program managers have the responsibility for the "What" and "When" decisions of a program and for working with the line activities who retain authority for "Who does it" and "How the job is done." The program managers involve the line people as early or as far upstream as possible—in effect making them part of the team from the beginning, and involving them in the decision-making.

This up-front commitment by all activities is reflected in one of the tools we have developed for the program managers, a Timing Discipline Chart. The purpose of the chart is to get a commitment from all activities as to what tasks are required and when they must be performed. Each member of the team signs the chart. The chart allows each member of the team to see how his or her activity impacts other activities. For example, the chart shows the design events that must occur 26 months before production begins. In addition, managers use the chart to assess how the program is proceeding. If key events are performed late, they affect the quality and timing of the launch of the new product.

Program managers' scope of responsibility encompasses all aspects of the program. Each activity—design, manufacturing, sales—identifies one representative to work on the program manager's team. Each representative is responsible for coordinating the activities of his or her component and ensuring the objectives of the team are achieved. We look for a certain kind of person to be a program manager. He or she should be results-oriented, self-confident, excellence-oriented, decisive, have a broad view of the organization, and a sense of humor.

Now, we have made great strides at Ford by changing the organization and initiating new processes—but people are the most important element! Our colleges and universities have a role to play in helping us achieve our world-class objectives. We need more generalists. Technical specialists should be exposed to all facets of the business. All disciplines need a better appreciation of the roles of others.

Second, we need courses designed to improve the productivity, efficiency, and effectiveness of workers. To help companies be more competitive, people need a better understanding of how quality is achieved through statistical process control or quality function development. To be competitive worldwide, we must improve our manufacturing productivity and increase our level of engineering technology.

At Ford, the results of our new process are already being realized. The quality of Ford products has improved over 60 percent since 1980. For six years in a row, we have been first in quality among all domestic manufacturers. While we are pleased with our progress, we are not there yet.

Much remains to be done. We are developing new processes to reduce the length of time to develop new products, improve the flow of information, and increase the role of supplier to include design. We introduced the latest results of our team effort, the new Continental. This car is equipped with a unique combination of high-tech features not found collectively on any other luxury car in the world.

At Ford we have a single goal: to manufacture cars and trucks that are responsive to our customers' wants and exhibit world-class quality in every segment in which we compete. With the Taurus and Sable we are starting to see it. And this is just the beginning. The sparkle in the oval is getting brighter year after year.

At Ford, we've learned the hard way what competitiveness means. It means more than building a product and pricing it right. It encompasses product appeal and quality; costs and profits; the education, training and retraining of people; the use of technology; entrepreneurship; relationships among trading nations; and the role of government in fostering a competitive environment.

The International Challenge

Most people over 45 years old grew up with America's economic superiority an undisputed fact. Our technology was second to none and our products were outstanding. We saw ourselves as master salespeople—both at home and abroad. Until 1971, America registered merchandise trade surpluses every year during this century. Until that time, most people had never even heard of a trade deficit.

Now we're bombarded daily with horror stories of massive international imbalances. After the second World War, our nation envisioned and championed an open world economy. We assumed everyone would be eternally grateful and forever in our debt for promoting global prosperity. Now we seem to be forever in the debt of those we have helped. While we were fostering the world's economic growth, we fostered formidable global competitors and relatively diminished our own power.

Today's reality is that America's economic leadership is being challenged and tested as never before in history. Success—or failure—in setting our nation on the right path toward meeting the challenge of global competition will determine the quality of life and the standard of living for generations to come.

Here's what industry can do to improve its competitive position. Because we know Ford Motor Company best, we use our ongoing process as an example.

The automotive industry went through a lot in the 1970s and '80s: a web of uncoordinated regulations, inconsistent goals, two oil shocks, three recessions, an onslaught of foreign competition, and a gross imbalance in currencies which gave competing countries large, artificial cost advantages.

Our industry incurred the biggest financial losses in our history. Our response was to move back to the basics of competition—and a dedication to getting them right.

First, we made quality our number one objective. We committed ourselves to continually improving quality in every aspect—year in and year out.

Second, we became a customer-driven company. The customer became the focus of everything that we do. Either Ford is customer-driven or our products are not.

Third, we learned to control costs—sensibly.

Finally, we rediscovered that the most important factor in our success is people. The hard work, the teamwork, the commitment, the cooperation, the creativity, and the intelligence of Ford people made all of our achievements possible.

We believe Ford is well-positioned to face competitive battles. But I don't want anyone to think we have the competitiveness problem totally under control.

The charge now for Ford, and all of American industry, is to continue to improve the quality and value of our products and services. We must work "smarter" and become more efficient and more resourceful.

In this day and age of rapid technological development and

instant communication about market trends and consumer wants and needs, no country has a permanent technology or product advantage. The key to our success in the future will be our willingness to change and our emphasis on continuous improvement.

The primary responsibility for international competitiveness lies squarely with the businesses and industries of America, but no one can doubt that government policy matters a great deal.

Other economies know this. Our foreign competition is directly aided by coordinated government policies in their home countries. American industry needs the commitment of government to a policy environment that is supportive of our industrial competitiveness.

Competitiveness must be adopted as a national goal and elevated much higher on our national priority list. We need to institutionalize a process in which national competitiveness will be taken fully into account in the development of trade policy, tax policy, regulatory policy, and administration, and monetary and fiscal policy.

I also believe it should be part of government's agenda to foster a sense of global teamwork. The major trading nations of the world must work cooperatively to minimize what Peter Drucker calls adversarial trade—trade that creates serious dislocation in the importing country.

I listened recently to a Japanese business leader question why Japan should import American goods when the same goods are manufactured in Japan. This leader couldn't understand—or chose not to—that the United States could take that same position.

We must convince our trading partners that all will pay the price if the present level of imbalance is maintained.

The real long-term answer is for all global powers to accept a full partnership role in the management of world economic structures. The time has come for other countries to accept their fair share of the price of international economic stability.

As our government and the major powers of the world must work together to solve their problems, likewise cooperation and trust between the private and public sectors are essential. Government and industry must work cooperatively and bring new perspectives, new thinking and a shared sense of interest to our problems. It will enhance our competitiveness as a country.

Chapter 4

A Model of Quality

by Douglas D. Danforth, Former Chairman and
CEO of Westinghouse Electric

*Quality is the most powerful weapon we have
to gain or strengthen our competitive position
in the worldwide marketplace.*

MORE and more we have come to realize that the quality imperative is a survival imperative.

It's a realization that was slow in coming for many. In the years
after World War II, American firms could sell anything they could
make. But then many managers learned a quality lesson the hard
way—through head-to-head competition with foreign companies who
understood that emphasis on productivity and quality was the way to
succeed in the latter part of the 20th century. American industry, in
many areas, was losing market share—and in some cases, whole markets. This losing process has been going on since the 1960s. In that
decade, it was basic industries like textiles and steel. In the 1970s, the
technology and scope of the markets involved expanded broadly. Now
its high-tech areas—supposedly a U.S. strength—such as integrated
circuits, RAMs, and robots.

What's been happening?

There are many causes for our industrial dilemma. One of the
most significant is the emergence of a new and successful industrial
model, led by the Japanese. This has happened while much of U.S.
industry still operates under an old and outdated model. The old model
was pioneered in the early 1900s by Frederick Taylor under the ban-
ner of "scientific management." Henry Ford applied it successfully to
produce the Model T in 1913. The philosophy was to fragment tasks

or skills into their simple elements, analyze each element for efficiency, and give the jobs to the highest-aptitude employees trained for each task.

Meanwhile, after World War II, the Japanese began pioneering a different model. When the oil crisis hit in the 1970s, the Japanese were forced to make even more dramatic changes in their model to respond to cash-flow needs. The new model uses quality as a strategy. It operates with lower costs and investment. And it focuses on improving productivity rapidly. The results have been spectacular for the Japanese—and copied by other industrial nations. Let's compare the old and new models.

The hard fact is that the old model—the one followed by most of U.S. industry—no longer gets the job done. It's outdated, and most often, noncompetitive. It became clear that our industries had to regain their reputation and concern for quality. The nations with whom we were competing had shown that quality was a soft spot. American industry was vulnerable. We were suddenly in a competitive war different from anything we had ever faced. There was a battle to be won. Furthermore, it was a fight where our battle flag had to contain a single word: Quality. Quality was the only winning strategy.

To win required a radical change in how we think and work—not a fine-tuning of the existing system, but a new way of life. To fail, we only needed to do nothing—to continue to do what we had been doing.

To complicate the problem, the quality mentality we needed already was a part of everyday life elsewhere. A *Wall Street Journal* article illustrated how quality is ingrained into the Japanese way of life. It told of an American tourist who bought a compact disc player in a Japanese department store. Opening the gift at her Tokyo host's home that night, she was horrified to find that she had bought a display model—a beautiful case with no innards.

The American could hardly wait until morning to take the store to task. But before she could telephone the store the next day, the store manager called her. Discovering the error, the store's vice president had traced the American Express charge slip to the buyer's apartment in New York City, gotten the Tokyo phone number from the apartment sitter, and contacted the surprised American. A team from the store soon arrived. They brought a working compact disc player, a Chopin disc, a set of towels, a box of cakes, and sincere apologies. The author contrasts that testimony to quality service with a six-month battle she fought with a Manhattan department store. It involved a wrong charge to her account. Most of the battle was done by phone. And the author was still unsatisfied when she wrote the article months later. That's indicative of our challenge—to change dramatically the ways we think and act.

A New Model for Total Quality

At Westinghouse, our response to that challenge has been to work on our version of a new model. We call it total quality. It's my personal belief that total quality is the driving force behind value creation—and value creation is the key job of all management. For that reason, we have carefully woven total quality into the Westinghouse business strategy.

Let me illustrate. The corporation has followed a consistent business strategy for some years, one that places quality in its proper perspective for our people. I'm often asked what the elements of our corporate strategy are. I define them this way:

• Westinghouse is a diversified, technology-based corporation that competes worldwide. That's who we are.

• We manage our resources in ways that continuously build value for our customers, our shareholders, and our employees. That's the result we seek.

• We manage our operations to achieve total quality in everything we do. That's how we get the result we seek.

We are making progress. In the 1960s, quality was something with one-department ownership. In the 1970s, we focused on error-free performance. In the 1980s, we worked to make quality more all-embracing. Today, we're designing quality into our products and services, and the processes used to make and deliver them.

It's also our mission to get every Westinghouse employee to understand how comprehensive the total quality imperative is, and to adopt it as his or her personal commitment to our success. With the growing worldwide emphasis on quality, we have made total quality the driving force in planning and performance. We start with a definition. To us, total quality is performance leadership in meeting customer requirements by doing the right things right the first time.

That's a broad definition. It encompasses every facet of our business. It demands performance leadership—internally and externally—as a primary goal. It simply isn't good enough to be second best. Being number two is not total quality. In defining "customer," we also include our own employees—because they are both suppliers to and customers of each other in the internal operations of the corporation. We also insist that we do the right things right.

We all know from experience that it is perfectly possible to do a superb job on the wrong things—and fail miserably. The "right things" also focus management attention on performance requirements—on what it takes to be truly "world class" in every phase of our business. Finally, total quality emphasizes "doing it right the first time," the traditional definition of quality.

Zero defects, error-free performance—whatever we call it, it is still important. But it's inadequate by itself to address the total quality imperative. We must do the right things right the first time.

We portray total quality as a triangle.

• *First, results.* The basic result of making total quality a corporate lifestyle is a competitive advantage worldwide. We express that advantage in terms of our various constituencies—customer satisfaction, stockholder value, employee satisfaction, and public approval.

• *Second, measurement.* These are the measures we use to assess total quality performance. Two of them include the concept of value. The first, value-to-price ratio, is a measure of customer orientation. The second, value-to-cost ratio, is a measure of financial performance, which really addresses stockholder satisfaction. When these factors are expressed as targets, they become our requirement measurements.

• *Third, implementation.* Our "how to do it" segment consists of four imperatives: customer orientation, human resource excellence, product/process leadership, and management leadership. An organization that has total quality is driven by these four imperatives.

Conditions of Excellence

We characterize these imperatives by what we call the conditions of excellence—conditions that must be met to fulfill total quality requirements. We've classified the conditions by how they support our four implementation imperatives.

• *Customer orientation.* The customer is where it all starts. The key focus is on value. That means knowing what our customer needs and wants, and successfully translating that knowledge into the operating requirements of our business.

• *Human resource excellence.* This deals with motivation, participation, continuing education, and training. One of the major new challenges for our people is to understand that the big improvements will come from addressing the total system, rather than limited and functional subsystems.

• *Product/process leadership.* Products are whatever we deliver to the customer, either hardware or a service. Processes include everything we do to deliver them. This imperative dictates that we pay close attention to products and services, as well as processes and procedures, information, and suppliers.

• *Management leadership.* Implementing a total quality culture in an organization is neither simple nor fast. It requires a vision, a new orientation, and consistency—a new way for everyone to do his or her job. It also requires planning, communications, and accountability.

Successful change requires a champion of the new way who lives his or her convictions daily and ultimately causes, by example and persistence, a new system to be adopted. Leadership must stand back from the way it has traditionally done things and consider totally different approaches. That's top management's job. It's also the only way to achieve the quantum improvements required and make them permanent.

These conditions of excellence have helped us stay focused in Westinghouse. They are the conditions against which we measure ourselves, to get our arms around what we must do as a team to improve quality. It's our belief that the business that lives by these conditions is guaranteed to be in the running as a world-class competitor.

I believe that total quality is a global solution to the challenges facing us today. It provides a comprehensive and measurable road map for us to follow as we undertake the journey. And we need to make it clear to all our people that it is a journey. Total quality is a moving target, one that drives us to constantly improve, and then to set new and even more challenging goals. We must extend the quality imperative to every person who works for us—with the leadership coming from you and from me.

Chapter 5

Leadership for Quality

by Kenneth Iverson,
Chairman and CEO of Nucor Corporation

Nucor is the ninth largest U.S. steel producer,
but what sets us apart is structure, not size;
productivity, not privilege.

NUCOR manufactures steel and steel products. We operate seven steel mills on four sites. We produce about two million tons of steel, making us the ninth largest steel producer in the U.S.

But what sets us apart is quality, not size. All of our mills use the latest steel technology—100 percent of our steel is continuously cast. For more than 20 years, the price of our products has been equal to or less than the price of these products produced by foreign steel mills. For the last 20 years, we have not laid off a single employee for lack of work, and since 1965, we have operated profitably. Sales this year could reach $900 million, and return on stockholder equity may exceed 20 percent.

• *Structure.* Much of our success is due to our structure, programs, and policies. The best companies have the fewest number of management layers. In fact, one way to measure the size of a company is not by sales but by the number of management layers. The fewer you have, the more effective you can be in communicating with employees and making decisions. We have four management layers: the foremen, the department heads, the general managers, and the corporate executive team. We're very decentralized. The general managers make the day-to-day decisions that determine the success of the company. And we believe in reducing the number of staff. Staff people in marketing, engineering, or purchasing do not help you make better decisions nor do they accelerate decisions. Perhaps we carry it to extremes. With almost $1 billion in sales, our corporate staff consists of only 17 people, including clerical help.

• *Decision making.* We have strong loyalty to our employees. We believe that there are two successful ways to manage with regard to employees: Tell them everything, or tell them nothing. Both ways can be successful, but we believe in telling our employees anything they want to know about the company, unless it happens to be proprietary or it has to be secret for some very good reason.

I try to impress upon our employees that I'm not King Solomon. I use this expression: "Good managers make bad decisions." I believe that if you take an average person and put him in a management position, he'll make 50 percent good decisions and 50 percent bad decisions. A good manager makes 60 percent good decisions. That means 40 percent of those decisions could have been better. We continually tell our employees that their job is to let the managers know when they make those 40 percent decisions that could have been better. Because if they tell us, and if we examine them and agree, we will change our approach. Over the years, we've built enough trust with our employees that they don't hesitate to tell us when they think we've made a poor decision.

• *Incentive system.* All Nucor employees have a significant part of their compensation based on the success of the company. The most important incentive system we have is our production incentive system. We have about 75 groups of 25 to 35 people who are responsible for various tasks, and we establish a bonus that is based on a standard. If the employee group exceeds that standard in a week, they receive extra compensation based on their production over the standard. Very simple. There is no maximum. It is never changed unless we make a large capital expenditure that significantly changes productivity opportunities for employees.

The bonus is paid weekly, and in our steel mills, it is not unusual for that bonus to run 150 percent of base. It all goes to the employees who do the work, and they deserve every bit of it.

What's the result of this? The result is that the average integrated steel company in the U.S. produces about 350 tons per employee. We produce about three times that—or about 1,000 tons per employee. Our total employment cost per ton is about $60 per ton, including fringe benefits. The total cost for the integrated producer is about $150 a ton. That's why when we, or other mini-mills who have comparable programs, get into a product, the integrated producer moves out of that product.

• *No layoffs.* We have not laid off or furloughed a single employee for lack of work for more than 20 years. This is because most of our plants are located in small towns and rural areas. We think that rural U.S. has great untapped labor resources. People don't want to work in the cities. They go there to find jobs. Big corporations go there because that is where the people are. But if you establish manufacturing facilities in rural areas, you find that many people apply for work. We put a steel mill in the town of Jewett, Texas, that has 435 people. People said, "Where are you going to get 300 people to run this plant?" There were only 12,000 people in the whole county. We had more than 2,000 applications from people in Houston and Dallas who didn't want to live in Houston and Dallas. They wanted to live in this nice rural community that's about midway between the two.

And in small towns, we have to accept our social responsibility, because we are generally the largest employer in the area, and in many cases almost the only employer in the area. Accordingly, we can't just lay people off, because they have no place to go. So if we have a slow economic period, everybody works four days a week instead of five. But everybody still has a job.

You don't get good people if you lay off half of your work force just because one year the economy isn't very good and then you hire them back. If you do that, you aren't going to get the best people in the area. That's why we will not lay off people.

• *Employee benefits.* We have some unusual benefits for our employees. For example, we pay $1,500 a year for four years of college or four years of vocational training for every child of every employee in the company. We have about 400 children of employees enrolled in about 180 different learning institutions.

In case you should think that we are overly paternalistic, we also have some very tough rules. If you're late, you lose your bonus for the day. If you're late more than 30 minutes, or you're absent for any reason *including sickness,* you lose your bonus for the week. We do have four "forgiveness" days. We have some people who take those forgiveness days in January and February, and we have some people who haven't taken any for five years.

We try hard to eliminate any distinctions between management people and anybody else in the company. We all have the same group insurance program, holidays, and vacations. We all wear the same color hard hat. We have no company cars, company airplanes, company boats, executive dining rooms, assigned parking places, hunting lodges, nor fishing lodges, and everyone travels economy class. We think it is very important to destroy that hierarchy of privilege so prevalent and pervasive in many corporations.

• *Adapt to change.* A good manager must adapt to change. He or she must, in this day and age, readily accept new technologies as they develop. Because of the mobility required of executives, he or she also has to rapidly adapt to geographical and cultural differences. Children do this very well. But you find as you get older, it's much more difficult. You have to focus on the fact that "I am going to do it. I am going to make a change."

• *Communication.* We survey all employees in our corporation every two years or so. We ask them what they think of our programs and policies and ask a lot of other questions. It takes about an hour for them to go through all the questions. In one survey, virtually every hourly employee wanted better and more communication from the foreman. In American business, we don't train our foremen to communicate well with employees, often because foremen are hired for their technical skills, not their communications skills. So you end up with a manager who may be very good technically, but he can't communicate effectively with the employees.

Communication is terribly important. It ought to get more attention in business schools. Certainly, a big part of the quality of any communication is learning how to listen as well as how to say something.

• *Planning.* In some companies, planning is absolutely ridiculous, unrealistic, and sometimes almost fanciful. For example, consider the objective by a corporate office that says, "This company or division is going to grow by 25 percent per year." That's not planning, that's pearls cast before swine.

The short-term plans—such as the year's budget, the year's production—should always be a bottom-up plan. In Nucor, we say that we want a 60 percent probability that you will make the plan. It's not unusual for us to have a division come in with a budget for the year before. It doesn't concern us one bit because there may be some forces at hand. We may be past the top of the construction cycle. There may be some basic reasons why that's going to happen.

Long-range plans are different. Long-range plans should be the work of a corporate office putting together all of the projects that are underway, and all of the projects they think might develop in the company. I look at long-range plans as a guidebook. It also helps prepare you for what might be some unusual crisis in human or financial resources. It's not a Bible. It really helps you avoid difficult areas. I've never met a five-year projection in my life and never expect to. It's always different than the plan.

• *Productivity.* There is no quick fix. You can't decide to put in quality circles and expect to have a more productive organization overnight; in fact, about 60 percent of the firms that put in quality circles have abandoned them. There has to be an overall culture and philosophy in place to get the productivity that you are interested in. The Japanese system won't work here. There are certain elements of it that we can accommodate and incorporate. But basically, we're a much more heterogeneous society, and workers here have different expectations and different goals than Japanese workers. But let there be no mistake. Our workers today have a different attitude than did our grandfathers and even some of our fathers. To them, work was a place that they spent eight hours a day. They built their lives around their community, family, or religion.

Workers today expect more out of their jobs. They expect the job to be meaningful; they expect to advance; they expect to participate, particularly in those decisions affecting their work place; and they expect to understand how the company operates, where it's going, and how it expects to get there. If you don't develop programs that satisfy those needs and interests, you can be assured, in the long run, that your company will not be successful.

I am concerned by the attitude of many American executives who seem to feel they can't compete with foreign suppliers in such key areas as quality, service, and price. They blame their inability to compete on government subsidies, lower labor costs, or better technology, and then what happens? They reduce their capacity, source offshore, eliminate product lines, and pressure government for protectionism. My concern is that they are making bad decisions—decisions that are bad for their business and bad for our economy.

I'm convinced that we have the people, the ingenuity, and the skills to compete against foreign manufacturers in almost every industry. We need to automate and to develop our processes to the point where the lower labor costs of our competitors are more than offset by the higher costs of shipping their products into our marketplace.

And we need a dedication to new leadership and management styles. We certainly should not accept at face value the practices of the past, because many of them haven't worked. We need to try new ideas; we need to make new mistakes; and we need to be quick to accept new technology. If we do that, we can compete in quality with manufacturers anywhere in the world.

Chapter 6

Advancing TQM

by Edwin L. Artzt, Chairman and CEO of the
Procter & Gamble Company

*All sectors of society must embrace TQM to
make it an integral part of the way we do
business, educate youth, and run government.*

I HOPE to help make higher education the center of teaching,
researching, and practicing total quality—because America's competitiveness in years ahead will require a new generation of quality leaders and a replenished pool of new knowledge about how to apply total
quality. Consumers are spending their money differently; they are getting back to basics. They may not spend less than they used to, but
they're paying more attention to value.

Changing Values

I think there are other factors influencing this trend that go
deeper than the economic impact of the recession—and that will
remain even after the recession is over. The most fundamental change
is in personal values. For example, almost 90 percent of the people
surveyed in a study last year said their families had become their number one priority. Eight out of ten said they had become more "home-
centered" in the last few years.

They're redefining status. In a study by the Yankelovich research
firm, consumers said the things they associated with success in the '80s
are less important now. For example, 17 percent now say that wearing
designer clothing is a sign of success, down from 27 percent just four
years ago. And 20 percent now say that shopping in prestigious stores
is a measure of achievement, also down from 27 percent in 1988.

The bottom line—whether it's because of economic recession or changing values—is that consumers are changing the way they think about performance, price, and value. In fact, performance expectations are continuing to rise—eight out of ten in the Grey study say it's worth paying more for exceptional quality. But quality now has a stronger "value-for-the-money" component. What people are looking for, as the Grey report says, is "affordable quality."

And this isn't restricted only to consumer products. In fact, it goes beyond business and reaches into government, education, non-profit organizations—every institution that provides a product or service to the consumer. People want to know that they are getting what they pay for, whether that payment comes in the form of taxes or tuition or a charitable contribution.

In that sense, the need to deliver greater value is a national priority—which makes total quality a national imperative, because it's the only way we can meet the challenge.

A Set of Principles

Total quality isn't a formula we can follow blindly. It's a way of thinking—a set of principles that can guide our approaches to the way we work. For total quality to enhance our ability to compete, we must continually advance our understanding of it. We must ensure that we have new generations of quality leaders—young men and women for whom total quality is a way of life—who are capable not only of applying today's understanding of total quality but, even more important, who can advance tomorrow's use of it as well.

This will require changes in how we prepare these young leaders. It will require integrating TQ concepts across curricula and a commitment to ongoing, in-depth research of total quality.

This has been our purpose since David Kearns convened the first Total Quality Forum three years ago. We've made progress each year since, but I think our greatest progress has come just in the past 14 months. Last year, we had a "roll-up-your-sleeves-and-get-to-work" meeting. We'd had enough talk; it was time to nail down some firm, specific action plans to get total quality into our schools as fast and effectively as possible.

Four Areas, Six Councils

We laid out four areas that needed immediate attention. First, we agreed that we needed a definition of the core body of knowledge of total quality that is meaningful for practitioners, scholars, and teachers alike. Second, we concluded that curricula models and materials should be developed for teaching TQ at both the graduate and undergraduate levels. Third, we decided to develop strategies for accelerating faculty understanding of TQ. And finally, we said there needs to be a national research agenda for total quality.

At the close of last year's forum, we created the Leadership Steering Committee as a way to bring together top industry leaders and university presidents and deans who could provide the leadership needed to move the ball on these key national issues.

In January, we met and, after assessing the full range of issues on our plate, we created six working councils to conduct preliminary studies and make initial recommendations for action.

These councils were made up of 56 people—32 from universities, 16 from companies, and 8 from government agencies and professional and education associations. Together, these councils have made tremendous progress. The first council inventoried the core principles and practices of Total Quality. This was important because, despite all the years we've been using TQ, there isn't a standard definition of what constitutes Total Quality Management.

When I asked some of our people at P&G to tell me how they defined total quality, I received various answers: "TQ is the Baldrige Award." "TQ is customer satisfaction." "Business process management." "Short cycle management." "People empowerment and statistical data." This group had to sift through all these perspectives and come up with a comprehensive definition of total quality that can guide the many unique ways in which each of us approaches TQ.

Two other councils also had to sift through years' worth of accumulated TQ experiences. One was responsible for identifying what employers want new employees to know about total quality. The other was responsible for examining all the ways in which schools are currently incorporating quality concepts into their curricula—and, from that, proposing a best process for getting TQ into all our business and engineering classrooms.

Of course, it isn't enough just to determine what should be learned. There's also the issue of how it should be taught. The fourth council focused on analyzing existing processes for building the understanding and skills of faculty to teach total quality. They also surveyed more than 900 deans of business and engineering schools on new options for faculty development.

Our work doesn't stop in the classroom, however. We need today's business and engineering schools to help advance the practice of total quality. We need an ongoing body of research.

There is a broad range of quality research already underway today, and a need for a great deal more. This has been part of the work of the fifth council—the Total Quality Research Council. The recommendations made by this group give us—for the first time—an overall direction for TQ research projects. This will not only accelerate the practice of total quality, it will help us provide breakthrough approaches for the future.

Finally, I want to point out the work of the University Practice Council, the sixth council. These seven members, all drawn from colleges and universities, identified the ways schools practice total quality. Many colleges and universities are leading TQ practitioners in their own right. They provide valuable models that can be reapplied. But more importantly, this council's work indicates that students benefit from *experiencing* TQ in action—not just learning about it in classrooms.

Taking Action

The work of these councils represents enormous progress. Now that we've completed our initial studies, we are ready to adopt and implement recommendations for action. The Leadership Steering Committee has already agreed to take action on four recommendations that require national leadership.

• *First, we're committed to broaden company participation in the TQ University Challenges.* Bob Galvin, chairman of Motorola, came up with an idea that has proven to be one of the most innovative, effective means of enlisting faculty leadership in total quality. He invited several universities to send faculty to visit Motorola for a week and study his company's quality practices. The response was so overwhelming that Bob enlisted IBM, Milliken, Xerox, and P&G to join Motorola in hosting challenges of their own. In total, partnerships have been formed with eight universities; more than 600 faculty members have participated so far, and most of them have said we should expand this concept.

So, we've begun a CEO-to-CEO contact to encourage other companies to participate. Our goal is to put at least 20 new partnerships in place each year. We have representatives from 14 other companies here to learn more about these partnerships and to consider hosting universities themselves over the next year.

• *The Steering Committee is also committed to stimulate research on total quality.* To support the research, we will raise $9 million through private and public sources over the next three years. I encourage you to adopt some of the innovative research methods. In particular, I want to urge university researchers to get closer to business, working collaboratively to develop research proposals. I'm not talking about consulting arrangements; I'm talking about research. This involves sharing more data and techniques than we're used to, but the idea here is to stimulate and try unconventional ideas.

In three years, we'll step back and review the success of these various approaches and, if we're convinced they're working, we'll raise additional funds.

• *We hope to create a resource directory for total quality.* In fact, the American Association of Collegiate Schools of Business has already committed to do this, and we'll be inviting an engineering organization to get involved, as well. The directory will include case studies, bibliographies, and teaching notes. This will give educators fast access to information about total quality, and even more important, models of best practices that can be reapplied.

• *Finally, we're committed to see that these conferences continue.* Motorola hosted the fifth Total Quality Forum, and we're developing an administrative structure that will enable the work of the councils to continue.

These commitments reflect our belief in the soundness of the recommendations—and in the fundamental importance of our colleges and universities taking the lead in teaching, researching, and applying total quality. I can't overstate the importance of this. The link between our nation's economic health and our colleges and universities is indisputable. And at a time when our economic future rests so firmly on the education of our people, we must ensure that this link is strengthened.

Chapter 7

The Secret of Quality

by Norman R. Augustine, President and COO of
Martin Marietta Corporation

Higher product quality and productivity
reduce costs and increase competitiveness—
but it all starts with quality leadership.

FEW subjects provoke philosophical speeches, slogans, banners, and flag waving so much as the subjects of quality and productivity. However, once one cuts through the fog it turns out that there is a great deal of meat to be found; it is just that much of it has been corn-fed too long.

Not too many years ago, the "Made in USA" label was considered to be a symbol of desirability. Similarly, the descriptor "Japanese copy" was a pejorative term. But times have changed.

Most if not all businesses would obviously prefer to produce a higher quality product—one which does what was promised, and does it every time—but they are often curiously inhibited by the presumed high cost of achieving such a degree of quality.

The Simple Truth

The truth, ironically first discovered some years ago by an American, W. Edwards Deming, and exported to Japan when American industrialists wouldn't listen to him, is this: *higher quality begets not increased cost but reduced cost.* This is the miracle of productivity and quality.

A few years ago, for example, one Motorola facility was producing television sets averaging 1.5 defects per set, despite employing seven inspectors for every 25 workers—a very low "tooth-to-tail" ratio. When the facility was taken over by Japanese management, however, the defect rate dropped to 0.05, the number of inspectors was reduced to one for 25, and costs dropped as well. The work force was basically unchanged.

Similarly, a few years later at a Sony plant in San Diego, product quality was not achieving the expected level despite a ratio of one inspector per 15 workers. U.S. management was again replaced by Japanese management but no change was made in the work force. Soon, with a ratio of one inspector to 50 workers, the plant set a worldwide record for Sony production—200 consecutive defect-free days.

Quality and productivity, like much else both good and bad, start with management. A highly illuminating study of the cost of quality has been reported by professor David Garvin of the Harvard Business School, who has conducted an in-depth examination of the U.S. and Japanese room air-conditioning industries. Restricting somewhat the basic data collected in his assessment, one can produce a graph revealing various levels of quality to the cost of achieving their levels of quality.

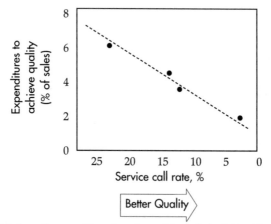

The conventional wisdom would argue that as more and more resources are expanded to achieve high quality, the cost line in the figure should veer upward to the right. But the observed trend is exactly the opposite, sloping downward to the right. That is, the higher the quality that is achieved (within limits, undoubtedly) the lower the total cost. So much for the conventional wisdom.

Garvin observes that "The shocking news, for which nothing had prepared me, is that the failure rates from the highest-quality producers were between 500 and 1,000 times less than those of products from the lowest. There indeed is a competitive problem worth worrying about." He goes on to explain that with regard to the lower "costs of quality" assignable to the more demanding high-quality manufacturers, the reason is clear: "Failures are much more expensive to fix after a unit has been assembled than before, and field service costs are much higher than those of incoming inspection." Simply stated, it costs less to do the job right the first time.

Augustine's First Law of Counter-productivity can be stated as follows: *It costs a lot to build bad products.*

The knee-jerk reaction of a bureaucracy trying to solve a problem is often to hire more auditors to try and catch the wrongdoers. Similarly, the instantaneous textbook solution to achieving better quality has far too many years been to hire many quality inspectors. Unfortunately, it is simply not possible to "inspect in" or "audit in" quality. Quality must be designed in and built in from the beginning.

Shining Examples

Relevant to this conclusion is the experience at one large U.S. manufacturer with one of its Quality Circles, a now well-established concept wherein groups of employees meet to seek to better the products they produce. This particular Quality Circle conceived a superb idea involving the use of special optical instruments for inspecting electrical connectors the company had been purchasing in large quantities. A resulting savings of $817,000 per year at a single plant was projected.

When questioned as to just how many of the connectors received for suppliers were defective, the answer indicated a 40 percent rejection rate. Although the new inspection technique proved very effective, the real problem was that the supplier was building shoddy merchandise—and the purchaser was tolerating the practice. That was the problem that needed to be attacked. The principal task at hand was not one of more efficiently finding the bad parts (although that in itself was useful); rather, it was one of producing fewer bad parts in the first place.

Quality Circles have proven to be a very effective means of attacking problems. As usual, this breakthrough in business methodology seems rather obvious in hindsight: Who could possibly know more about the work being performed than the workers themselves? But the process is not easy. One General Motors manager has described the four stages of an employee Quality Circle as "griping, groping, grasping and growing."

At the Martin Marietta plant in Michoud, Louisiana, where the large orange fuel tank is built that helps loft the space shuttle into orbit for NASA, quality circles were established which led, as expected, to substantial cost reductions. An unexpected benefit was an accompanying 58 percent reduction in employee grievances, a 45 percent drop in lost time, and a 59 percent decrease in hardware nonconformities among those individuals participating in the quality circles. This plant recently received an award from NASA for the quality of its products.

Bureaucracy: The Great Impediment

Perhaps the greatest impediment to the achievement of high quality and productivity is burgeoning bureaucracy. Every job and every externally imposed regulation needs to be challenged on a basis of value added, the "Where's the beef?" test. The value added can of course be measured in terms of intangibles as well as tangibles—such as quality of work life. But absent such a disciplined cost-benefit analysis, a corporation or even an entire economy can descend into a businessman's never-never land, such as that which *The Wall Street Journal* attributed to Portugal a few years ago.

A classic article by Barry Newman sums up what sounds like the ultimate well-meaning but nonproductive society:

Nobody gets fired in Portugal unless the boss has a very good reason. That is the law set down a decade ago after the radical left took over the government. Bosses hate this. They want to consolidate, modernize. They are aching to fire people. Lucky for them, the radicals who wrote the law to protect jobs forgot to write a law to protect salaries. So Portuguese bosses have devised a new way to increase cash flow. They don't fire workers; they just don't pay them. And yet almost everybody keeps on working. How come?

Well, according to the law, if somebody doesn't show up for work just because he isn't being paid, he could get fired. A worker could become officially unemployed if his company goes out of business. But Portuguese companies try to avoid that. If a company shuts down it has to pay severance. And it loses the state subsidies designed to keep people working. If you lay people off you have to pay them. It would be very expensive.

According to one Portuguese employee, Frotuoso Santarem, who has been paid only nine months out of the last eighteen, "We're used to working, so we work. If I left or the yard closed, I'd have to look for a job." And Mr. Santarem does gain one advantage. His company used to subtract 15 cents from his salary for a midday meal. As long as he doesn't get paid, the company can't do that. He gets a free lunch.

That's why America must take productivity and quality, seriously. Everyone knows there is no such thing as a free lunch.

Chapter 8

Unleashing the Force

by James R. Houghton, Chairman and CEO of Corning Glass Works

Our commitment to Total Quality required a deep commitment to total training to unleash individual creativity and initiative.

ONE comment, made by an instructor from Corning's Quality Institute, illustrates what is probably the most valuable insight resulting from our ongoing company-wide quality training: "Take away the coveralls and suits and ties, and I can't tell the machine operators from the department heads."

At Corning, training for quality has been the most ambitious effort of its kind ever undertaken. The fact that education and training is a very important and powerful strategic tool is even more apparent to us today than when we started, and I'm convinced that our situation is not unique.

We've known, but only now come to understand, how little separates the production work force from the salaried work force. Barriers that have long existed between payroll groups are being broken down by our practice of mixing all payrolls together in quality classes.

Quality training has also helped us liberate a force we knew was there, but seldom did anything to unleash. This force is the creativity and initiative of the individual. Our approach to quality training has highlighted and encouraged the wealth of talent that exists at all levels of the organization.

Why and how such a massive training effort was undertaken by Corning—a Fortune 200 firm located in upstate New York, with roots going back to 1868—provides a lesson in competitiveness, survival, and change.

In 1983 Corning found itself beset with many of the problems experienced by large U.S. manufacturing firms. Customers were tightening requirements and asking for performance levels that we were not accustomed to seeing. Costs were rising, even after we responded to a wrenching downturn in 1982.

Employees were asking for more involvement, or at least more satisfaction from their work. Finally, imports were threatening us as never before and, in some cases, were actually taking market share.

A Commitment to Total Quality

When I became chairman in April 1983, I quickly realized that something had to change. Working with a new management committee, I reached a decision that started us on the path of what we came to call Total Quality.

• *Begin with a vision.* Looking back, it is now clear to me that we really did not know what we were asking for at the time. We had a rather dim vision of where we wanted to be in five years or so, but we did not know how we were to get there.

To learn more about how to get there, we visited several other companies, such as IBM and Milliken Corporation. We listened to a lot of people, both here and overseas, and we learned what Juran, Crosby, Deming, and others had to say. We decided finally to design an approach that made sense to Corning.

• *Identify some guiding principles.* With the help of consultants, some basic quality principles were developed especially for Corning, focusing on the meaning of quality, the importance of error-free work, the role of prevention, and finally the use of cost of quality.

We realized that determining the approach was the easy part. Implementing it—with 28,000 people worldwide—was the real challenge.

• *Provide training for all employees.* We decided to use awareness training for all employees, worldwide, as the vehicle to convey our new set of tools to the organization. Today the decision seems obvious, but at the time there were other options.

Even within the training option, we considered the alternative of giving very specific skill training to selected employees. For example, we could have concentrated on statistics in the manufacturing area as the sole thrust of the quality effort. Or we could have used an increased emphasis on the unit results as an approach. Or at the very minimum, we could have relied on bands and banners and tried rhetoric and speeches as a way of encouraging our people to pursue quality.

We made training the centerpiece of our Total Quality strategy for three basic reasons.

First, and most important, the content of the quality material was new to the organization. Much of it did not match past experience. Total Quality brought with it a new set of words, which could be threatening if misinterpreted. It demanded changes in behavior that were not easy to understand by just reading or listening to someone else's description. We felt that all of these content characteristics could be best dealt with through training.

Second, we already had a good training facility and skilled people who had a history of delivering complex and varied education and training tools to the organization. Moreover, most employees already used internal and external training as a means of personal development.

Third, we could see that training and education would become increasingly important to us. At that time, our Korean joint venture was already several generations ahead of us in quality. The fact that they had a significant mandatory training requirement was not lost on us. We knew that training, all kinds of training, was by necessity going to become a much more important part of our ongoing activities.

• *Build quality into performance agreements.* By January 1984, we established an infrastructure and gave several executives the charge to implement Total Quality as part or all of their job descriptions. These executives, led by our Education and Training Department along with some front-end consulting help, put together our Quality Awareness training.

Phase One deals with basic principles of quality as well as some plans for implementing the quality process. Participants actually start their quality planning in the classroom before returning to their units.

I, along with two vice chairmen and three group presidents, attended the first class, which started on a Friday afternoon, continued through Saturday, and finished late Sunday. The fact that we—the top management of the organization—were spending this kind of time in quality training was made visible to the rest of the organization. It became very difficult for people to say they did not have time to attend sessions that were scheduled during normal working hours.

Training as a Change Agent

Some key decisions made quality training a very powerful change agent.

• *We made the training mandatory for everyone in the company.*

We wanted everyone to get the same information, no matter how experienced they were or how long they had been with the company. We stressed that it was especially important for the supervisors to have quality training in common with their subordinates. If people said that they already knew the material, our position was that they must still take the course because we wanted to be sure that everyone learned the new vocabulary and had the same knowledge base.

• *We established a Quality Institute.* A physical facility was built, and all course materials, communications, and directives from senior management were funneled through the Quality Institute. Initially, then, the Institute, its people and its offering were the center of the Total Quality effort.

• *We used a cadre of permanent instructors and made them part of the institute.* An alternative, and a popular one in many other companies, is the "waterfall" technique. The top person trains his or her staff. The staff in turn then faces the next level and trains them, and so on, with each level training the next level down through the organization. We felt that using permanent instructors would do a great deal to insure that the same message was heard by everyone in the organization.

• *We selected experienced and successful middle managers to be the instructors.* These people were respected for what they had accomplished and for the practical wisdom they had picked up along the way. They knew Corning, its people and its practices. Instructors were assigned to the Institute for a two-year period, with the agreement that they would return to their home divisions at the end of the assignment.

• *We next trained these newly selected instructors how to teach.* They became perhaps the best prepared people ever to enter new jobs. They went through several weeks of intense training, not only to learn course content, but also to determine what would be included in each day's session and how it would be taught. We even hired a consultant to teach platform skills and to teach the instructors how to keep the class interested in the material, how to deal with conflict, how to make a special point, and how to use voice and eye contact to maintain classroom control. By the time they started, these managers had been trained to be outstanding teachers.

• *Finally, we prepared and supplied course materials.* A manual was prepared and issued to every attendee. Instructors had guideline materials that anticipated the kinds of questions they would receive from the attendees. Emphasis points were highlighted. Standard overheads were developed and reduced copies were placed in the instructor's guides, next to the material being explained.

Lessons Along the Way

Overall, we have been very pleased with the results of Quality Awareness training. We've confirmed the strategic power of training, and we've started to unleash the most powerful force we have, the initiative and creativity of our people.

To date, some 25,000 people have taken Phase One Quality Awareness training. We have translated the basic course into Spanish, Portuguese, German, French, and U.K. English. Along the way, we've also learned the following lessons.

• *Top management must set the tone in advance.* Not only must management make it clear that it is necessary to attend the training, they also have to convey *why* it is necessary. People who came to class understanding why they were there and what was expected of them upon returning to their workplace related immediately to the material and exhibited a willingness to "dig in." Those who lacked an adequate endorsement from their leadership generally took longer to settle in.

• *The effectiveness of the training increases dramatically when people attend in teams with their boss.* Having everyone hear the same thing at the same time helps to eliminate barriers.

• *Real-world examples work best.* Examples that relate directly to people's experience and to their workplace were most effective. Generic examples were less effective. And examples that related to home life weren't nearly as powerful as real-life stories from Corning Glass Works.

• *Start from the top down by work unit.* If top and middle management goes through the training first, there may be a lapse of several months before the last of their colleagues gets through the course. We found that it's best to go top down by unit. Get a whole unit trained and underway before starting the next unit.

Moving on to Phase Two

We have now moved on to Phase Two—mandatory training in Communications and Group Dynamics, Problem Solving Skills, and Statistical Tools. These courses have already been translated.

Encompassing the whole effort, I set a goal for the entire corporation that five percent of time worked will be spent on training aimed at meeting job requirements.

I am absolutely confident that people are willing to do a quality job. What remains is management's responsibility to make sure people are trained and that they have the necessary tools to do a quality job.

Chapter 9

A Value-Added Vision

by M. Anthony Burns, Chairman, President, and
CEO of Ryder, Inc.

*In service and manufacturing companies, the
time and attention given to quality result in
big rewards in profitability.*

WHAT do Burger King, J.C. Penney, American Express, Marriott
Corporation, AT&T, and Ryder System have in common? We're all
service companies which have strategic visions about the direct bottom-line benefit derived from a focus on quality.

Despite reports of a renaissance in American manufacturing
(thanks largely to a dollar-driven export boom), the U.S. economy is,
and will continue to be, largely dependent upon the health of the services sector.

There's no doubt that the services sector, which contributes
roughly 70 percent of our GNP, is learning lessons from its manufacturing counterpart. Inattention to detail and sloppiness in handling
customers are just as much an Achilles heel to service providers as
faulty design, high failure rates, and shoddy workmanship used to be
to manufacturers. At Ryder System, it has been our experience that
quality is the most important way a service company differentiates
itself from the competition. But unless concerted efforts are launched
to improve both productivity and quality in services, America may
soon witness a market position decay similar to what we experienced
in manufacturing during the '70s and '80s.

The global consumer—whether of services or goods—is growing
increasingly quality conscious, and has an expanding number of options
to choose from when purchasing a good or service. As competition
heats up in services, the highest quality provider will be successful.

Ryder System, for instance, is a highly decentralized company made up of diverse business units located throughout the world. All of our businesses, however, provide specialized services and despite the wide spectrum of highway transportation services, aviation services, and insurance management services which we offer, all of our employees must share certain management precepts if we are to succeed in the highly competitive global environment. Obviously, one of the most important of these is a commitment to quality.

Key Attributes

We define quality as "meeting and exceeding customer requirements," aiming for zero defects" and "doing the right job right the first time." Based on studies of employees' attitudes toward quality, as well as research on quality programs at other companies known for their quality innovations and leadership, we have identified a number of key attributes of quality.

We believe the following should be part of the business plan of every service company that expects to successfully compete in the future.

• *An unqualified commitment to quality from top management.* For quality to become formally woven into the fabric of a firm's corporate culture, top management must be involved from the outset. Quality goals and objectives (including measurements and timetables) should be integrated into annual operating plans and subsequently evaluated for success.

• *A shared commitment to quality by employees.* This can only happen if they understand what the company expects from them in terms of quality performance, and what the costs of poor quality are.

• *A customer-focused attitude.* Successful service companies foster a consultative relationship with their customers, regularly meeting with them to discuss their needs and problems and recommending possible solutions based on mutual consensus. They use market research techniques to offer their customers advice for new or improved services, and they constantly provide their customers opportunities to assess service, cost competitiveness, billing accuracy, convenience, frequency of customer contact—even cleanliness of facilities and courtesy of employees.

• *The company's highest level of executives should be actively involved with customers.* Corporate and division officers should be assigned to make periodic visits with certain accounts to demonstrate the company's high level of commitment to the customer.

• *Constant revision of quality goals and objectives.* Customers' needs and wants are never static. By regularly sitting down with customers to set specific target goals which can be effectively measured and establishing "zero defects" checklists with customers and potential customers, service providers can ensure high levels of customer satisfaction and long-term relationships.

• *Leadership training in quality.* Employees at all levels must have hands-on opportunities for quality improvement training. At Ryder System, officers attend a "Quality through Leadership" seminar which identifies 36 leadership practices viewed as critical success factors in Ryder System companies.

Management should attend quality awareness training sessions. At Ryder, they meet with such quality experts as Tom Peters, George Labovitz, and Phil Crosby. A number of executives have even attended Phil Crosby's Quality College, in some cases accompanied by key customers.

• *Quality training programs for the rank and file.* Employees at all levels throughout the company should regularly attend quality training programs to define problems and areas needing improvement; analyze data to determine the root causes; develop solutions to keep the problem from recurring; and create, execute, and monitor implementation plans to ensure long-term success.

• *Rewards for "quality heroes."* Superior achievement should be matched with superior merit raises and opportunities for advancement.

By defining quality, establishing its attributes, and developing measurable objectives to gauge success, we've achieved some notable successes in quality. For example, in one of our aircraft service locations, where getting the job done right the first time is the key to profitability and customer satisfaction, rework and rejected items have been drastically reduced by implementing a quality team approach. The team is in charge of interviewing new hires, nominating team leaders, identifying and helping solve problems and recommending changes to enhance quality and productivity.

It's likewise in our Automotive Carrier Division, which transported 5 million new cars and trucks last year, or 33 percent of U.S. new vehicle sales. Few new car buyers appreciate finding scratches or missing parts after they drive their new cars home. By setting specific quality enhancement programs, we've reduced vehicle transportation damage rates from 3.9 percent in 1981 to less than 1 percent today at a direct cost savings of more than $10 million annually.

"Quality is free," says the old adage. But we've found that it really isn't. The time, attention, and efforts needed to focus on quality assurance require resources of many different kinds. But, for Ryder System at least, these allocations have resulted in tremendous rewards in terms of sales and profitability through enhanced levels of customer satisfaction. Other service providers should take note of the strategic advantages inherent to an obsession with quality—and the risks associated with refusing to acknowledge its value.

Chapter 10

People Create Quality

by J. W. (Bill) Marriott, Jr., Chairman and
President of Marriott Corporation

*The competitive edge in the hospitality busi-
ness, as in any service business, is people.
People make or break quality.*

W E'VE been in the hospitality business for many years, and over
time, we've learned a few things about how to treat people. Basically,
we believe that you have to treat people fairly, and you have to treat
them as if they're your most important assets—because they are. You
need to motivate them, train them, care about them, and make winners
out of them.

The competitive edge in this business is people. I try to communicate that I care about our people and that I think the role they play
in the organization is an extremely vital one. I try to drive out fear. No
manager can be fired unless he or she has been warned in writing three
times. In performance reviews, we applaud strengths, pinpoint areas
that need improvement, and determine what assistance is needed.

If the people on the front line of our business do not feel that
they're being treated fairly by their manager or their boss, they can go
above his or her head right on up to my office. I've learned to consider the concerns Marriott people have about working conditions or pay
or any other problems they have.

There can't be a double standard in how you treat your guests
and how you treat your employees. We know that if we treat our
employees correctly, they'll treat the customers right. And if the customers are treated right, they'll come back.

To treat people right, you have to make some hard choices about
what you value. We have learned that diversification is not always

desirable. When we sold our Great America theme parks, two chains of restaurants, and our Howard Johnson manufacturing distribution operations, we decided to dispose of operations that didn't fit with our established businesses. We discovered that we didn't belong in the theme park business because it was basically the entertainment business. Coming up with new attractions every year was just too capital intensive. We sold the restaurants to concentrate on our major fast-food operations and hotel development.

Many companies have to learn by trial and error who they are and what their real mission is. I'm not sure we must always learn by sad experience, but most of us do learn that way. I suppose it's because we're not smart enough to figure things out in the first place.

Regarding the mission of Marriott Corporation, we've decided that we're going to stay in the business of feeding and housing people. We think there's still plenty of room for growth in those areas. I'm confident that we can continue to grow by sticking to what we do best and by looking to the long term. I've tried to develop a deep understanding of the ultimate benefits of giving up some short-term interests for long-term gains.

My father established a strong foundation for the company, largely by taking good care of the employees. But he demanded a lot out of everyone. He demanded perfection in execution. He was very interested in the details of the business and very concerned about giving value to the customer.

I learned from him that if you really want to know how things are going, you need to get down on the line. You need to get a first-hand feel as to whether people are up or down, if they're motivated, and if they care. You need to see the condition of a place. You can't really know what you need to know if you sit behind your desk all the time. We did a series of ads emphasizing that point: "I have to make sure we do things right... it's my name over the door."

For many years I flew more than 250,000 miles a year to inspect our operations personally. I visited more than 100 hotels each year, inspecting the kitchens and usually eating three nights a week at company restaurants. When I'm on-site, I'll ask both guests and employees what they like and don't like. I also ask myself, "How is the general condition of the place? How do the Marriott people look? Are they happy? Well groomed? In uniform? Pleasant? Is the kitchen clean? How are sales? Is the manager on the job? Is he or she taking care of things?"

Personal involvement in the details gives you the basis for planning. If you know your business and if you understand what's going on out there, you won't be led along by strategists or theorists who don't know the real world in which you operate.

In our business, if you lose sight of details, you can lose sight of the entire business. If a person comes to our restaurant for a hamburger and gets it overcooked or cold, he isn't coming back. If a person checks into a guest room and finds spots all over the carpet, he's going to wonder what kind of a place he's in—and he's not coming back.

We figure that our employees make ten million personal contacts a day, from answering the phone to opening the front door. They have lots of chances to excel, and lots of chances not to excel. In the people business, every employee—from waiters to maids to truck drivers—must be able to get along pleasantly with others all day long.

How do you manage to be fair and nice with people and yet demand excellence from them? The answer is tough-minded management, which basically says that you treat people right and fair and decent, and in return they give their all for you. We make sure that Marriott people have the proper training to do a quality job and that they know what is required of them. For example, there are 66 steps to go through in making up guest rooms, and we require every employee working in the guest room areas to learn and follow each one of these steps. If all of the employees follow all of the steps, then every guest room is made up perfectly. If they don't follow the steps, then we'll have inconsistency. A chain cannot be inconsistent in quality.

If the chain is going to be recognized for excellence, it must be consistently excellent—in Saudi Arabia, Jordan, or New York. It's tougher to achieve excellence in some cities and countries than in others. It's tougher, for example, to run a quality hotel in the United States than in most foreign countries because the quality of labor in many of the foreign countries is higher.

We look for motivation and people skills in the people we hire. We then spend $20 million a year to refine these skills through intensive and extensive training.

A good employee is one who has the attitude that he or she can and will take good care of the customer and shows genuine enthusiasm in doing so. Marriott employees have to like people. They have to enjoy serving people. They also have to be a little thick-skinned because not everybody is going to be happy upon waking up in the morning and coming to breakfast. Not everybody is going to be happy when checking into the hotel at 11 o'clock at night after being on the road all day.

We also look for good character, especially in managers. We all know of some business scandals that have almost ruined companies. But I think these scandals are making business executives more cognizant of the importance of honesty and good character in managers. Managers who are rich in talent but poor in ethics often get themselves and their companies fouled up.

I ask of myself and all our employees that we try to maintain balance, enthusiasm, and perspective in life. My dad always told me to take time to smell the roses. He said that if I devoted all my time to business, I would get stale, tired, and irritable. That's good advice, and these days I take more time for smelling roses.

Basically, there are four parts to life: family, church, community, and business. I'm heavily involved in each part, and try to take care of my responsibilities in each area to the best of my ability. If I do, I have balance in my life.

I think the things that make for success today are the same things that have made for success throughout the centuries: hard work, dedication, commitment, creativity, sensitivity, an ability to teach and motivate and listen to people—to forge a team to get the job done— and, of course, an ability to make an excellent product that is of value to the customer. It's also important to keep current, to stay ahead of the changing times, to be willing to change yourself.

If there's a secret to making smart investment decisions, it's getting lots of practice and learning from each experience. We're very different from a manufacturing company that may only make a dozen entrepreneurial business decisions a year. We make a dozen entrepreneurial decisions a week. That's one of the fun things about this business. To make smart decisions consistently, you have to have a thorough understanding of your business products and people. Lacking that, you will make bad decisions.

When I was made executive vice president of the company in 1964, my father sent me a letter of advice. I think his 15 points are still relevant:

1. Keep physically fit, mentally and spiritually strong.
2. Guard your habits—bad ones will destroy you.
3. Pray about every difficult problem.
4. Study and follow professional management principles. Apply them logically and practically to your organization.

5. People are number one—their development, loyalty, interest, team spirit. Develop managers in every area.

6. Decisions: People grow by making decisions and assuming responsibility for them.

7. Criticism: Don't criticize people, but make a fair appraisal of their qualifications with their supervisor.

8. See the good in people and try to develop those qualities.

9. Inefficiency: If a person is obviously incapable of doing his job, find a job he can do or terminate him now. Don't wait.

10. Time management: Have short conversations—stick to the point. Make every minute on the job count.

11. Delegate and hold people accountable for results.

12. Let your staff take care of most details. Save your energy for planning, thinking, working with department heads, promoting new ideas.

13. New ideas keep the business alive. Encourage all management to think about better ways and to give suggestions on anything that will improve business.

14. Don't do an employee's job for him or her—counsel and suggest.

15. Think objectively and keep a sense of humor. Make the business fun for you and for others.

Chapter 11

No Boundaries to Quality

by Claude I. Taylor,
Chairman of the Board of Air Canada

Every executive must build the resilience to adapt to the demanding changes dictated by the quality imperative.

As a Canadian writing to American business leaders about quality—with the question of free trade and tariffs between our countries so much in the news—I feel a little bit like Daniel in the lion's den. However, the point of my message is that there are no boundaries to quality, especially between our two countries—and especially in view of the rapidly developing global economy.

Politically we are classified as Canada and the U.S., but geographically we are North America. That gives us far more in common than we have differences. In fact, one-fifteenth of all trade conducted in the world is between Canada and the U.S. And the Canada-U.S. bilateral air agreement, for example, contains more "items of understanding" than any other air agreement in the world. Canadian and American industries are so interlocked that we stand to benefit from sharing our knowledge.

As one of Canada's largest service companies, with 12 million customers last year, we at Air Canada realize that our products are so customer-sensitive that quality must be our primary consideration, at every operating level, if we are to be world competitive. Every customer sees our product in a very real way and identifies with it. If we fail to meet our commitment to on-time performance for you, or if we fail to meet our high customer service standards, you will choose another airline when you next travel—and rightly so.

The Primary Objective

Meeting the needs of the customer has to be our primary objective because the competition is just too fierce. We can't be satisfied with what we think is good; customers will tell us by their indifference that, despite our definitions, we don't measure up to their standards and their needs.

Every seasoned executive could tell a story about a corporation producing a product or a service in search of a market it never found because people just didn't want it. In other words, customer satisfaction has to be the basis of any business strategy that is going to be successful. The question to be asked is, "How do you guarantee customer satisfaction?"

As we are painfully aware, the days are gone when North American industries competed only against each other in relatively secure markets. Today we are part of a truly global marketplace. Not only are we fighting for customers in Europe, Asia, and Africa, but we are also struggling against foreign competition within our own national boundaries.

If we are to succeed, our products have to appeal to a wide range of global customers. These customers must know that whenever or wherever they purchase a North American product, they can expect a standard of excellence based on a common denominator with which they can identify. And the common denominator that can be relied upon to appeal to Canadian, American, European, Asian, or African consumers is quality.

We all know the story of Toyota's successful entry into the North American market after their first failure. One of the major reasons for their success: Toyota guaranteed that for the money, it was selling one of the best quality cars available. Toyota determined what the consumer was seeking and met the needs of the market. Today they are the leading import nameplate in car, truck, and combined sales for the eighth consecutive year.

When it comes to the consumer, there are no boundaries and no nationalities to quality. Simply put, if foreign competitors can be successful in North America by producing top quality, then it stands to reason that we can effectively compete internationally by producing even better quality.

I offer you the following example only because it is one I know best. In 1985 Air Canada introduced service beyond London, to Bombay and Singapore. We realized that in serving Asia we were competing against some of the world's best and most prestigious airlines. To compete successfully, we realized that we would need to demonstrate a strong commitment to quality. The result: two years later we are now increasing the number of flights on the route.

North American industry certainly has the technology, the people, the modern plants, and the knowledge. But do we have the commitment? We often hear about the need to move from 97 percent quality to zero defects; and it's not that we don't have the skill or technology to do it. I suggest it's the commitment we are lacking in North American industry. And yet quality is fundamental to the future success of North American industry if we are to compete in the transnational economy. Whether you are in a service-based industry—and to one degree or another we all are—or whether your emphasis is on production, it is essential to identify those factors which our customers see as underlying their perception of value.

Think from the Outside In

At Air Canada, we have learned that the key to building and providing quality in our products is to think from the outside in—from the customer's view—rather than from the inside out. Last year someone in Air Canada met face to face with every one of our 12 million customers. We know that we must create and reinforce the customer's perception of value in our products.

We have also learned that there are ways to communicate value other than the medium of purchased advertising. It is the perceived value of our product, at the moment it is being used, that will generate the perception of quality, and in turn, conditions for future growth.

If we are to be successful, we know that everyone in our organization must be committed to consistent, high-value performance. And this means more than top-down leadership. Every member of the team must understand that the time to do it right is the first time—and every time after that.

We also realize that customer definitions of quality create a constantly moving target. The way we monitor that target is by tapping the best resources at our disposal: our customers and our employees.

This is exactly what we did at Air Canada when we launched our executive class service on our major American routes. The introduction of this service followed two years of research. We wanted to design a business product conforming as precisely as possible to the wants and needs of the business customer. Five different studies were conducted with more than 600 business travelers. Workshops and interviews were then held with 100 business travelers to find out what they perceived as the most important features of business travel. And when it came to the question of in-flight service for the new product, we went to the flight attendants—ones who deliver the in-flight product and who observe firsthand the customer's response to the product. By involving our flight attendants we made sure that they had the right tools to do the job and that our customers would be getting what we had committed ourselves to deliver.

The moral to this story is that our customers are important, but it's our people who deliver the service. If for any reason they do not feel committed, then Air Canada has a very big problem. We want our employees to be aware of the effects of meeting the criteria for that absolutely necessary degree of excellence, as well as being aware of the consequences of not meeting it.

Every industry has its own unique perspective on meeting consumer demands. The president of a furniture company told me recently that compared to his industry, airlines have it easy. We have a customer for an average of three hours, but people generally keep their sofas for ten years. He said that when it comes to putting quality into a product, his problems are basic. "I have to ensure that my product will stand the test of time," he said. "It must have durability and comfort at a good price, or I don't have satisfied customers. The problem is that they won't tell me what was wrong but they will certainly tell their friends."

In an industry, the worst thing you can have is dissatisfied customers who don't say anything to you—all they do is walk across the street and buy their products from someone else; you never see them again. To prevent this from happening, we have tried in Air Canada to build into the culture of our organization the resilience, the capacity to absorb the demanding changes the quality imperative dictates—and to adapt to them. We also have to ensure that, in producing a product which the consumer perceives as having value, we do it efficiently and cost effectively.

With the intensely strong international cost competition, keeping our costs competitive can give quality-leveraged companies in North America a competitive advantage—and it may be the best opportunity some of us have for improved return on investment.

There was a time in North America when quality control and quality improvement were thought of as almost one-dimensional concepts.

They were terms of the assembly line, the factory—necessary as a form of measurement of the production process. But those days are over. The ongoing search for quality must reach every facet of our business if we are to prosper—indeed survive—in the international arena.

The task facing North American industry, Canada included, is to take the quality imperative and:

- use it within our corporations to inspire people
- build it into our operations to reduce costs and
- ensure that within the domestic and international marketplace our consumers come to know that North American quality is inherent in every one of our products and services.

No boundary should be left uncrossed in the ongoing search for quality. The job before us is not easy, but it can be done. It must be done.

Chapter 12

Excellence in Process

by Horst Schulze,
President of The Ritz-Carlton Hotel Company

Once you get your people to catch the vision,
they will be able to resist the temptation to
sell out.

ALTHOUGH we were voted the best hotel company in America in 1987, for the second time, we knew that we were not good enough because we were not satisfying all of our customers—all the ladies and gentlemen whom we served. Many customers clearly told us that they had problems in our hotels, and at that time we had several more hotels under construction.

Knowing we were not fulfilling our mission, we searched for benchmarks and asked, "How can we improve?" We knew our traditional way of achieving a certain level of excellence, but we didn't know how to improve from there. For many years in our industry, we only looked at the bottom line. The old question was, "How do you manage to improve the bottom line?" And the answer was that you raise prices a little bit, and take a little bit out of the product. We knew that we couldn't manage that way any more.

The Search for Quality

We also knew that manufacturing was making great strides using total quality management, but we didn't understand it. There was no model for it in our industry. I wondered, "Who can we learn from?" I started in the hotel business when I was 14 years old. Most of what I did was instinctive, because I had done it forever. But I also adopted the defects—the mistakes of the past. I knew that we couldn't keep doing things the same way we did 90 years ago. There had to be a new approach.

We looked at companies like Xerox and Motorola, and saw that they had a "process" approach. We learned that they design quality into the product at the start, rather than try to inspect quality into the product at the end when it's too late. Some things, however, applied only to manufacturing, not to service.

In 1988, we heard about the Baldrige Award, and we talked with the Baldrige people to learn more about it. They showed us the application, explained it to us, and suggested that we use the application as a guideline. Slowly we realized that this was not just for manufacturing. A process is a process.

The Baldrige criteria afforded us the chance to analyze our processes. As we surveyed our customers scientifically, we started to understand our business processes for the first time. We asked our customers, "What do you want?" and "How do we live up to your expectations?" We found that we didn't even pay attention to many expectations. Once we knew our customers' expectations, we searched for the process that would allow us to meet or exceed those expectations by delivering "defect free" customer service.

By studying our customers, we learned that we were full of defects that were accepted in our industry. For example, in our first study in 1990, we asked, "Did you experience any problem?" We found that 30 percent of our customers experienced defects.

We knew that getting to where we wanted to be would not be easy. Sooner or later when you embark on the reengineering journey, you encounter some black holes where you don't know where you are, and you feel that everybody around you is against you. No executive who begins this journey and gives up on it after three or four years will ever live to tell a positive story. Only those who stick to it and are committed to it will find the light at the end of the tunnel. I knew it was the right journey, but it was still very painful. More than once I felt like stopping.

To make this journey, we had to invest some dollars. We added three positions in each hotel: a quality manager, a repeat guest coordinator, and a training manager. Some investors question why we added those positions. In a recession, prices don't go up, so your traditional way of making more money doesn't apply. And you're not efficient yet, because your systems have not been implemented. In the meantime, your owners and investors are unhappy with you. Your management is also unhappy with you because you're forcing them to learn and teach new approaches. At the same time, the customers don't see any improvement yet. So you have no results, only agony and cost—and all this works against you.

During the dark days, what pulled us through was vision—my vision and that of others around me—and the constant focus on that vision. I think that's the essence of leadership. Leadership doesn't go away. In fact, only leadership can pull you through that tough time. You have a vision, you are committed to the vision, and you do the things that it takes to get there. But to keep focused on it, to keep people energized behind it, and to not be sidetracked by excuses and by superficial effects is hard.

It would have been very easy for me to say, "We have 30 hotels. I have three optional employees in each hotel. I can dismiss 90 people tomorrow. That saves a few million dollars and shows everybody what a hero I am." It was very tempting to do that.

But when you have a clear vision, you resist the temptation to sell out. You think, "What I will spend in four years on this effort, I will save in one month later, and from then on it's a benefit." I knew that. But it was still hard to explain to other people.

At the top we kept focused on our vision because the entire management team of about 10 people all came here to fulfill a dream. We made a decision to take this direction. This challenge was the only one left. They're not only colleagues in this quest, they are all dear friends.

The other day, one of my vice presidents said, "You know, maybe our biggest accomplishment in ten years is that we're still good friends." He mentioned that I did what I had to do— re-energize them, and keep on re-energizing them. What was hard, however, was to re-energize myself every day. At one point, I put Post-it notes all around to remind myself not to give up—to do the right thing, not the convenient short-term thing or what seemed right to others, but do the right thing for the long term and to be ethical about it.

We were trying to live by the values we teach, but it was very difficult. We were different in an industry where people were often cynical. People were sending me articles from management magazines that argued, "Quality doesn't work." People were making fun of us in speeches, and newspapers were writing that the Ritz-Carlton had problems. It was very difficult.

We made it through that time by being united behind our vision. We held weekly meetings with the corporate officers, and we had monthly meetings with all the vice presidents. No meeting was held without talking about our credo, our values, our beliefs, our vision. We asked, "Where do we want to be? How do we get where we want to be? Can we get there any other way?" Everybody had to admit that there was no other way. I told everybody: "If you know a better way to assure that we will continue our improvement and become defect-free, tell me and I will give up anything I have."

This may sound ridiculous, but I said, "I'm a history buff, and I remember when Martin Luther was asked to rescind what he was preaching relative to reforming the Church at the time. He was threatened with discipline unless he would take back what he was teaching. He said, "Here's the Bible. If you prove to me that I'm wrong, I will take everything back. If you cannot, I cannot. Do you understand? I cannot do it. Otherwise, God help me."

Historically, unbelievably strong people stood for what they knew was right. So I said, "If you can show me where I'm wrong, I'm willing to change. I'm open to it. I accept it. I want to discuss it. I want our actions reviewed. I want us to come to consensus. But if you cannot find a better long-term solution to be the finest hotel company and to deliver defect-free customer service, then we go on the way we are. If we find a better route, we will take it."

Whenever we got together to discuss a new program or the opening of a hotel, we talked about our vision first. We relentlessly pointed to the vision and how to get there. I insisted that we commit to each other: "When we leave this room, we will advocate what we have decided. We will not change our minds." The central task was then to keep on teaching the process to both outsiders and insiders. Teaching what quality management is all about—giving examples, bench-marking, and showing and telling again what we learned.

Today's Picture

In 1994, only 6 percent of our customers experienced defects. Still, that's too high, and so we're in a continuous improvement mode. We know that in 1995 we'll be around 3 percent because we're constantly improving the process. We now understand how to analyze defects, find root causes, and eliminate problems for good by improving the process.

Today we know exactly what our defects are; we know how we measure up against customer expectations; and we know where we're improving. We are not looking any more at the bottom line. We're looking at the things that get us to the bottom line.

Not only do we study how the process can give the customer what the customer wants, we study how we can deliver the product so it costs us less. We improve the bottom line by improving the product and by becoming more efficient in delivering the product.

Over the last four years, customer satisfaction has jumped from low 80s into the high 90s, and employee satisfaction soared from the high 70s to the low 90s. So, customer satisfaction went up; employee satisfaction went up; and efficiency improved dramatically—all because we managed a process. Our basic values have not changed. Only now we have processes to ensure that we live our values.

In the next few years, we will move to the "six sigma" level of quality. That basically means no more mistakes, zero defects! To reach that level, we're moving toward individualized product development, understanding the individual customer better and delivering what that individual customer wants. That is the future—but it's here today.

What we have created will only be seen over the next two years. The industry can't even fathom it. It is mind-boggling. When you go to "six sigma" quality, when you go to individual marketing, when you know your guests, then you will have no more customer defection. We are in such an incredible position today because we reengineered our processes to support our vision.

Defining Quality and Service

Quality is consistently and efficiently giving your guest what the guest wants and expects. Quality is not a chandelier. Quality is being extremely reliable and consistent.

Service is different. I can give you efficiently what you want. You want to check in, you want to have a room, you want everything to work, you want to be on time, and so on. But now I can take it a step further by doing it with caring and sincerity.

Suppose I go into a bank to change $10, and the teller greets me with, "Yes," not "Good morning, sir." I say, "I want to change $10," which she does. She gives me my correct change. But I want something more. I want the teller to understand my value as a customer— to understand it intellectually and emotionally—and to treat me accordingly. That's the service aspect, the caring aspect that comes on top of the product. The product is giving the customer correct change. But if the teller then adds, "Sir, I'm happy to give you the change, and please have a wonderful day," then she has served me. Then she's delivering both quality and service.

I've been told, "It can't be done in Florida; it can't be done in Atlanta; it can't be done in Australia, Spain, or Mexico." But that's just a bunch of baloney. I tell everybody, "It can be done." In Australia our hotels just won a national customer service award. We were inspected in Cancun, Mexico, for a national quality award, which makes me particularly proud. And our hotel in Spain won the European Quality Award.

Quality helps everybody. You should want your business to help your community and your industry. You do that best by setting a higher standard and opening yourself up for benchmarking. That's our role as a business—to add value to all stakeholders.

One of our values from the very beginning was "we want to be the best for all concerned." We identified "all concerned" as the investors in the company, the employees, the guests, and the community. And when we made decisions, we asked if these decisions would truly benefit all concerned. We found that good decisions benefit all concerned. When you have all your stakeholders in mind, your decisions will benefit all concerned.

We conduct a survey every three months to identify what our customers want and expect. Today, for example, they want access to fax machines, they want speedy delivery, they want to keep in touch using the latest technology. So one aspect of continuous improvement process is to be on top of the latest technology. But we've learned that most guests don't want fax machines in their rooms—they simply want to have office capability in the hotel.

Service is not just about speed and technology. People want to feel well. It's all about people, about one-on-one contact with other human beings. And guests measure value and quality by those moments of human contact. The "moments of truth" are still the measure that most people use to evaluate service.

We sense that our guests want to have the product tailored to them. Customers want what they want in a hotel. If they want to be on the top floor, they want to be on the top floor. If they want six pillows, they want six pillows. They want the service to be tailored and individualized to them, and they don't want to explain it all the time. They want to come in and have it their way. That expectation of a product tailor-made to the tastes of the individual is more and more the future in the service industry. You can't just say, "Okay, we'll study the market, find what the market wants, and give it to them." Our customers want absolutely hassle-free service. That's why it's essential that we work defect-free. They want a reliable product, on time, all the time, made to suit them individually.

I like to think in terms of customers, guests, and non-guests. Customers are decision-makers. Guests are the people who stay with you. Non-guests are people who haven't yet stayed with you. I make this distinction because from our studies we know that the "customers" who have a meeting planned at one of our facilities have 42 different additional demands than the average guest.

Our focus is to keep the customers and guests we have. Again in this area, we battle another tradition—not to care about losing customers if the competition lost even more. For example, if we lost 30,000 customers a year because of defects in our service, we were supposed to feel okay if the other guys lost 32,000. That's a horrible attitude. We said, "We need a process to ensure we keep our customers. Every employee needs to clearly understand how we keep our customers." So we set a simple, clear, and precise objective: "We will keep every customer." We think if we can meet this first objective, we will meet the second—to win new customers—because to a great extent that objective is met by satisfying customers to the point they become sales persons. The key to winning more customers is to first satisfy current customers.

Five-Step Improvement Process

To improve competence in the core skills that drive our business, we use five processes.

First, we have a *selection* process. We don't hire people, we select people. At the very beginning, we need to know if the person has the talent to become a competent and committed employee who can meet the demands of our customers. Our selection process is designed to ensure that we have the right people. Often in this industry, people get hired simply because there's 100 percent turnover, and managers don't have much time to select people—they're just happy that somebody walks in the door. Our turnover is about 25 percent, and so we can afford to select employees carefully. Careful selection costs more money on the front end, but it saves dramatically over time because it reduces turnover.

Second, we have an *orientation* process. When employees come into our organization and industry, we orient them to our values, our vision, and our mission. We don't just shove them into the job. We orient them first to our values because these are the foundation, the core of who we are—and that won't change. During orientation, they understand who we are, why we are different, what our vision is, what our goal is, what our thinking is, and what our mission is. They must understand these things before we let them loose.

The third process is *certification.* New employees are taught what they need to know by the people who work in their various departments. After they have been taught, they have to pass a certification test, which tests their values and their knowledge. If they don't pass 100 percent, they have to start all over until they pass 100 percent. Every hotel reports whether or not they're 100 percent certified. About 99 percent of our employees are certified. We measure everything. And managers are paid in accordance to how they live up to their measurements. If their employees are not all certified, they do not get their bonus. They can only reach the highest pay rate once everyone is certified.

A fourth process is on-going *teaching* or *continuous learning.* All employees go through a learning process *every day*—not once a week, not once a month, every day for 15 minutes. This on-the-job training best fits those employees who have little formal education. We can't teach them in a classroom style, because that's intimidating to them. So we have 15-minute teaching sessions. On every shift in every department, people get together, and the designated teacher for the day teaches the message of the day. The message comes from my office, and the same message goes to all hotels.

Whenever we detect a new need of the customer, we teach employees how to meet that need for 10 days in a row, every day. We may say, "Gee, we've had a number of complaints because we didn't have enough smiles, or because we aren't greeting our guests properly." So at the same time in all hotels all over the world, the same thing is being taught at the same time.

Fifth, we have a *reorientation* process. Once a year our employees get reoriented to who we are. These ongoing teaching efforts are rather sophisticated. Our strategic planning process involves every employee. We work on company-wide approaches to reaching objectives. The hotels get the objectives, but they work the hotel approach into the objective. For example, dishwashers get the same objectives, but they must decide how to accomplish them. So we are totally aligned—in objectives, strategic plan, and mission statement—each hotel department to the last employee.

Keep It Simple

I find this all so simple, and yet the quality people in this country are trying to make it so difficult. But what they're doing is frightening people away from quality.

When I went out in 1987 and objectively looked at our level of customer satisfaction, I came back totally depressed. I said, "I'll never reach this dream of zero defects." But I was wrong. We can reach it. It's no quick fix, but it's not that complicated either. We need to make quality easy and simple to understand.

I have mixed feelings about our situation. On one hand, I'm happy that we're the only ones in the industry who took early action, because it gives us such a competitive advantage. Most people don't even understand how far ahead of the competition we are. In the next two years, the difference is going to be mind-boggling. On the other hand, I'm sorry when I feel that way, because it's my industry. And it's my country. As a country we can't afford not to be competitive.

We need to help make our industry and our nation more competitive. We need to make sure everyone wins from the decisions we make and the actions we take. We need to find a way to look at our business the way our customers look at it, and not make quality improvement so complicated.

Section Two

The Manager's Perspective

To the manager, quality is a clear mandate, often one that comes from both above and below, inside and outside, with a "do-or-die" post script. The good news is that when it's a matter of do or die, quality at least gets serious attention. Many managers start looking around in earnest to benchmark what they're doing against the best of class.

The manager is the one who has to "make good" on the promises of the CEO and "make it right" for the customers. Managers must find a way to get from here to there—from the current reality to the imagined ideal. The quality initiative might be driven by customers, suppliers, government regulators, even competitors, but the end must always be the same—continuous improvement, as measured in sales, satisfaction, perceived value, fewer defects, reduced costs, lower cycle times, and higher returns.

Frank McCollough, senior manager of Sales at Federal Express Corporation, invites us to think of quality as value. **William F. Hayes**, executive vice president of Texas Instruments, contends that we won't know how we rate unless and until we benchmark against the Baldrige criteria. **Roy S. Roberts**, manufacturing manager at Cadillac Motor Car Division of General Motors, wants to "once again become the world standard by which all others are judged." **Peter A. Gallagher**, senior vice president of AT&T Universal Card Services, notes that quality and competitiveness go together and that "the cornerstone of quality is benchmarking."

Marilyn R. Zuckerman, director of Quality Planning at AT&T, and **Lewis J. Hatala**, CEO of The Partners in Discovery Group, write about "an All-American approach to quality" based on the unique American quality archetype. **Bruce Gissing**, executive vice president of Operations at Boeing, asserts that world-class companies are redis-covering quality and "dare to compare their processes with the best in the world." **Robert W. Schrandt**, vice president of Customer Service, and **John P. McLaughlin**, national Customer Administration manager of Toyota USA, drive home the point that quality service boosts cus-tomer satisfaction, which in turn boosts repeat sales and profits. **Al Tolstoy**, vice president of Bell Cellular, reports that the benefits of con-tinuous improvement are real: "Nothing can stop people who believe they make a difference."

Robert L. Stark, executive vice president of Hallmark Cards, says the stark truth of quality is that "those who wait too long to respond to the challenge of continuous improvement have to scramble for survival." **Stephen B. Schwartz**, senior vice president of Market-Driven Quality at IBM, relates that "market-driven quality is not something we just do on the job, it's our way of life." And **Barry Sheehy**, principal of The Atlanta Consulting Group, and **James D. Robinson III**, former CEO of American Express Company, say that unless we "stay the course" we won't get the results we desire and we'll start cursing our quality programs.

Ultimately, managers must see quality in terms of process, a journey, with allowances for both incremental and quantum, leap-frog improvement. Faced with raised bars and stringent competitive stan-dards, mangers must jump higher, faster, and farther, and yet maintain a sense of balance and equilibrium, in spite of all the pressure to "do it now." For this reason, the manager who makes quality happen every day for the customer is the real hero.

Chapter 13

Beyond Quality

by Frank McCollough, Senior Manager of Sales at
Federal Express Corporation

*When total quality is viewed through the eyes
of customer value, some cherished beliefs
about quality are challenged.*

W HAT lies beyond quality? To some people, it is unimaginable that
in certain situations quality is meaningless, if not a waste of time and
money! This blasphemy, if true, might shatter the favorable connotations that surround the word quality.

But I would argue that quality may have no meaning, or cost
savings, if it is not tied to value. Whether you agree or disagree, some
of the paradigms you have built around quality may be validated, others constructively challenged by my thinking.

I ask you to consider two examples.

• *Billboard.* As I travel the country as a senior manager of sales
for Federal Express, I am barraged with advertising that touts the
virtues of many products and services. The use of the word quality in
advertising has reached epidemic proportions. One interesting billboard shows an eagle with huge, bronze-blazoned words: "Quality
Above All." In the lower right-hand corner, the sponsor of this ad
reveals itself as a large tobacco company.

I am curious how people who see this sign might define quality—
in terms of 3.4 defective cigarettes per million, or in terms of unparalleled taste, or in terms of elapsed time before they become victims of
the surgeon general's warning? For those who do not use tobacco, the
highest level of tobacco quality is meaningless and worthless.

• *Rocking chair.* With the birth of our first child, my wife and I
spent many nights rocking our son to sleep or simply comforting him

through the traumas of infancy. The rocking chair we have is an old one. It creaks; it is really not that comfortable; and it needs to be refinished. The quality of that rocker is relatively poor, but it has immense value because it is the same one my wife's grandmother used to rock her children to sleep.

Quality as Value

I use these two examples to show that quality is better defined in terms of the value it provides. The concept of value is not new, but to more fully understand it, study the following grid, the basis for the quality/value analysis (QVA).

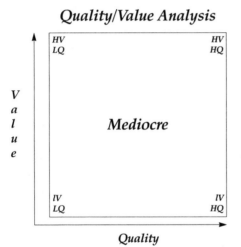

Quality/Value Analysis

QVA is a tool that can be used to better understand the relationship between quality and value as perceived and experienced by the customer. In the case of the tobacco company, High Quality and Low Value positions are occupied by nonsmokers. The rocking chair story reveals a Low Quality and High Value position.

When a company examines all of its products in terms of this grid and based on input from the ultimate customer, customer satisfaction can be increased and company costs driven down.

When the quality of a product reaches a certain point, the value of that product does not increase. Attempts and efforts to raise quality above this level result in no increase in value—it's the point of diminishing return.

For example, manufacturers of stereo equipment have attempted to distinguish their products by claiming that they provide better frequency response. In some cases, this resulted in frequency ranges that go beyond the range of human hearing. While much expense was associated with marginal improvements in sound quality, these advancements provided no increased value for many of today's audiophiles. It might be argued that to meet anticipated needs and keep ahead of the competition, such differentiation must be done. The message is still the same. A company must know at what point the economics of quality result in diminishing returns.

The reality and perception of both quality and value ultimately affect customer satisfaction. Quality can be either relative or absolute. The quality of a manufactured part may be measured against a statistical ideal or level of absolute perfection, or against past levels of quality output. It may also be compared to the competition.

The value of products and services is comprised of intrinsic and extrinsic combinations. The cut, clarity, and weight of diamonds, for instance, correlate to the extrinsic value of the gems and are measured with a price tag. Diamond quality can be measured against scales of perfection or compared to that of other stones. Through comparative or absolute standards, the extrinsic value is determined. However, variations in diamond quality do not necessarily correlate to the intrinsic measures of personal value and meaning that are assigned to these precious objects.

QVA is a process to improve customer satisfaction. It can be used in many situations by a variety of people. One way to increase customer satisfaction through QVA is through quality partnerships. First, customer and supplier get together and define who is the ultimate customer. The ultimate customer is usually the end user of a product or service. Secondly, QVA is also a way to explore and define the balance and impact of quality on value, and vice versa. Ways to increase value, reduce costs, and improve quality may develop as a result of customer and supplier focusing on the ultimate customer needs, requirements, and expectations in terms of quality and value.

QVA challenges some traditionally held beliefs about quality and, when fully explored, reveals that in certain situations quality may be meaningless, of no value, and not worth the cost.

I invite you to use a quality value analysis to ensure actions are taken to positively correlate quality and value in a meaningful, worthwhile, and cost-effective way.

Chapter 14

The Baldrige Process

by William F. Hayes, Executive Vice President of
Texas Instruments

*There's nothing like a healthy dissatisfaction
with your rate of quality improvement to
motivate and unify your company.*

How do you know where your company's total quality efforts rank? How do you measure your company's progress from one year to the next? At Texas Instruments, we are using the Malcolm Baldrige National Quality Award criteria to track our progress—even now, more than a year after our Defense Systems & Electronics Group (DSEG) won a Baldrige Award.

TI began benchmarking against the Baldrige criteria in 1989, when each of our businesses did an internal assessment of processes and procedures. But while that assessment was helpful, we knew it could only carry us so far. We knew that to find out where we stood, we had to step onto the playing field and open ourselves to the external scrutiny that comes with applying for the Malcolm Baldrige National Quality Award.

So, in 1990, DSEG submitted its first application for a Baldrige Award. We reapplied in 1991, and again in 1992. Each time we went through this process, we learned more about ourselves.

Feedback Accelerates Improvement

From our first application, we received the kind of feedback we needed to help move us to the next level in our total quality process. DSEG was committed to using this feedback and the Baldrige criteria to drive our rate of improvement.

Right away, we learned that we had some significant areas for improvement. With customer satisfaction, for example, we found that our processes were ad hoc. We had spots of brilliance here and there, but we were not sharing them with one another. We quickly put together a customer satisfaction improvement team to define and deploy a systematic process for achieving and measuring customer satisfaction.

We also learned that while we had continuous improvement strategies in place, they were not world-class. We did not have goals that significantly challenged the organization to improve. So we put together a team to identify the most appropriate metrics. We set a cycle time stretch goal to achieve two-times-theoretical performance, and a quality stretch goal for defects of Six Sigma, or no more than 3.4 defects per million opportunities.

We were reminded of the importance of our people's ownership and understanding of our quality strategies. A participatory leadership style and open exchanges between top managers and tiers helped facilitate teamwork and empowerment. And we learned the value of benchmarking, of measuring ourselves against the best companies to understand what we needed to do to become world-class.

In 1991, we submitted our second application for the Baldrige Award, and this time, we qualified for a site visit. Feedback from the visit taught us that while a small group of us understood what we were trying to accomplish, we had not yet fully deployed our vision and our goals throughout the organization. That assessment was right on—and there's nothing like a little humiliation from a group of outsiders to identify the areas where we need to improve.

But that's what it took to further unify our organization around a comprehensive total quality strategy. Tiers at every level became more involved than in previous years. We made sure everyone understood what we were doing, and we narrowed our metrics to those that we felt were most important to our objectives.

Winning Drives Improvement

We submitted our third application in 1992 and won a Baldrige Award in the Manufacturing category. Winning the Baldrige Award didn't mean we had achieved total quality. It meant that our organization was finally on the right path for continuously improving. Our Baldrige feedback provided insights into our strengths and weaknesses. Our strengths, for example, were in leadership and teamwork. However, we were just getting started in deploying our quality and cycle-time goals. We improved our customer satisfaction process significantly, reducing the number of areas for improvement in the Customer Focus and Satisfaction category from 19 in 1991 to 3 in 1992. In all seven categories, we reduced our areas for improvement from 89 in 1990 to 35 in 1992.

By the time we won the Baldrige Award, the areas that were initially identified as significant areas for improvement had become our greatest strengths. We attribute this change to the way the Baldrige criteria helped accelerate our rate of improvement.

Winning the Baldrige Award is a great honor. But having gone through the process three times, we can say that it makes you humble and more self-critical. We actually feel less worthy to win the award now, because we see that we are still far short of our standards for world-class quality.

Winning a Baldrige Award is not a culmination but a beginning of continuous improvement. After all, the purpose of any quality strategy is to improve customer satisfaction to sustain competitive advantage. As companies get smarter, maintaining that advantage gets harder. So we are forced to find better, more efficient ways to manage our processes. And for us, that means managing by the Baldrige criteria.

This deep understanding of quality is helping us achieve continuous improvement and giving us the sustained, competitive advantage we need. Our challenge has now become: Are we winning the new defense programs that are being awarded? Are we executing the programs we have as well as we can? Are our customers happy?

Since winning the Baldrige Award, we've seen significant increases in our productivity. Our cycle time last year improved by 25 percent on major defense programs. Quality, as measured in defects per million opportunities, improved by 30 percent. And we maintained consistent profit margins despite the reduced revenues associated with the general decline in the U.S. defense budget.

The benefits of the Baldrige process go far beyond standard measures. The process drives more valued relationships with our customers and helps sustain our competitive advantage. We continue to win programs because our customers recognize that our quality program brings them value. We have trained more than 800 customers and suppliers in six sigma methodology alongside our DSEG employees, and through that, strengthened long-term relationships.

If total quality is truly a part of our culture, winning the Baldrige Award is a gratifying confirmation that we're on the right path. It does not mean we have arrived.

Would we encourage other companies to measure themselves by the Baldrige criteria? Yes, because they are a non-prescriptive guide for improvement. The Baldrige process is a way for you to look at yourself through a world-class set of criteria.

Do we need to win the Baldrige Award a second time? Not necessarily. If we're going to be competitive, winning it two times isn't what's important. The important part is knowing where we're going and what we need to accomplish. Our goal for 1995 is to achieve six sigma quality levels and two-times-theoretical cycle times. That's only one year from now, and we're not certain we're going to make it. But we are attacking barriers at a ferocious rate. We are benchmarking our progress. We are re-engineering our processes. And we are improving the way we do things.

Road Map To Competitive Leadership

Early in our quest for quality we learned the importance of understanding exactly what we are trying to accomplish. We learned that if we are doing something to gain recognition or win an award, we are doing it for the wrong reason. Awards are appropriate in their place, but the real value comes from improving a situation or making a difference in the way we do things.

We chose to live by the Baldrige criteria—not to win the award, but as a way to improve our processes. The Baldrige criteria provided the road map we needed to build a more competitive company. We applied for the award to accelerate our rate of improvement in the process.

While we're not yet where we need to be, DSEG is much better off than if we had never applied. If we hadn't had that first dose of healthy embarrassment, we would always have rationalized, "Well, maybe next year." This experience has proven valuable in our company-wide quest for quality, and as a result of our success, each of TI's other businesses has developed an internal continuous improvement process based on the Baldrige criteria.

I'm convinced that DSEG progressed at twice the normal rate of change by continuing to apply formally for the Baldrige Award. The internal assessment was necessary to get buy-in, but it took the external assessment to drive real improvement. It's a healthy embarrassment—but it's worth it. Put yourself at risk, and learn from the feedback. Your organization will most definitely benefit.

Chapter 15

A Winning Approach

by Roy S. Roberts, Manufacturing Manager at Cadillac Motor Car Division

In our quest to become a quality company, we changed our way of doing business, focusing on culture, people, and financing.

Before winning the Malcolm Baldrige National Quality Award, Cadillac underwent several quality improvement efforts and created an approach that helped us win the award.

• *Customer satisfaction.* Consider that 167,000 applications were sent out, 97 returned, and only the 12 highest-scoring applicants received a site visit. Thirty percent of the overall score was based on the company's approach to satisfying customers. This means that to win the Baldrige Award (and to survive in today's marketplace), you have to put your customer first. We've done this at Cadillac for the past six years, and it has really paid off.

For example, J.D. Power & Associates, an independent research firm, has a consumer survey that measures satisfaction with the total ownership experience, product and service, for one year. In 1985, Cadillac ranked 16th on their customer satisfaction index. By 1990, we ranked fourth; and we have been the top-rated domestic automaker for four years in a row.

The improved satisfaction is a direct result of higher quality products. We have seen a 67 percent reduction in the number of problems experienced by our customers, and our warranty expenses show it. Our success can also be attributed to our dealers, rated the top domestic service group for four years in a row. In J.D. Power's rating of overall customer handling (a reflection of the dealership experience), owners of our top-selling DeVille and Fleetwood models gave us the industry's first-place score. Cadillac is ranked second overall, one point behind the leader in all categories.

• *Customer loyalty.* Our commitment to customers has paid off in owner loyalty. Cadillac's repurchase log has improved 23 percent in three years. We now have the highest owner loyalty of any car in the world, foreign or domestic. Customer loyalty has helped us retain our leadership as the number one luxury car maker in America for 42 years in a row.

Achieving this has not always been easy, especially when we took our focus off of the customer in the early 1980s. We reacted too quickly to fuel shortages that never materialized, and to emissions and fuel economy standards that did. In responding to these factors, we failed to listen to our customers, and compromised our standards for quality and styling. But we learned from our mistakes, renewed our commitment to our customers, and regained our share of the total industry in the face of a 20 percent increase in competitors—newcomers such as Acura, Infiniti, and Lexus.

Three Keys to a Quality Program

How did we accomplish such a turnaround in such a relatively short period of time? We changed our entire way of doing business. These changes can be summarized by three strategies:

• *Changing our corporate culture.* We focused everyone in the organization on quality and customer satisfaction. We needed everyone's input and ideas—this required a cultural change that valued teamwork and employee involvement as sources of competitive advantage. We empowered people at every level to take responsibility for making things happen. We created an environment for listening to our employees, customers, and suppliers. We turned the organizational chart upside down. We put leaders at the base, and emphasized that their role was to lead, not to manage.

These changes did not happen overnight. They took the commitment of our top executive staff.

The major catalyst for change came in 1985 when we implemented simultaneous engineering, a team-based process for developing and continuously improving our products. It enables us to break down the walls between the focus areas within our company. Team members come from every function and include hourly and salaried representatives.

We began to reach out to and involve our suppliers, dealers, and labor partners in the simultaneous engineering process. In fact, 75 percent of our teams include representatives from our supplier community. These teams work together during the life of the product, and are responsible for the quality, reliability, durability, cost, timing, and technology of the program. Some suppliers even have resident engineers at our facilities.

We ask our suppliers to take on more responsibility for product development in our process. We have regular conferences with key suppliers—our "partners in excellence"—to develop new programs to benefit both partners. And we help our suppliers improve their own competitiveness by implementing a corporate initiative known as "targets for excellence," a supplier assessment and development program conceptually similar to the Baldrige Award.

We have also changed our relationship with our network of over 1,600 dealers, our primary interface with the marketplace. In the past, we rarely asked them for their input; now, we share our future plans with them, listen to their feedback and implement their suggestions. They bring their knowledge of the market to the simultaneous engineering process through a number of methods. One example is a program called "listening post" dealers. Selected dealership service departments provide immediate computerized input concerning product performance to our engineering team.

The United Auto Workers union has also been a part of our effort to change and improve our culture. They are more involved than ever before in the running of our business. Although joint activities have been going on at Cadillac for decades, in 1987 General Motors and the UAW agreed to implement a joint quality network. This established a consistent quality improvement process for Cadillac (and all of General Motors) by directly addressing how the two organizations should work together.

At Cadillac, the concept of partnership has expanded into everything we do in manufacturing. The resulting changes prompted an hourly employee to describe his 26-year tenure with Cadillac this way: "The first 20 years we were awful; the last six have been fantastic." We have seen some dramatic results from this increased participation: improved morale, a flood of good ideas for improvement, and a direct impact on quality and productivity.

For example, we have nearly 600 work teams involving nearly 5,000 people. One example is our "grow-the-business" team, made up of skilled and non-skilled hourly people as well as salaried people. We have empowered this team to look at ways to grow the business through continuous improvement and the end-searching of business. One team bid on a 1990 project and worked with simultaneous engineering teams to improve the design for the product. The total annual savings of their design was $52 million. They won the bid and secured 154 jobs for their plant.

• *Constantly focusing on people (employees and customers).* As Cadillac's culture has changed, we have placed increased value on people. We implemented a "people strategy" to integrate our human resources into the quality process and maximize their potential to contribute in teams.

The people strategy is administered by cross-cultural teams made up of hourly and salaried employees. Seven-member strategy teams work on enhancing aspects of our human resource system—choosing, researching, designing, and implementing features that make up their own work lives. One new process emphasizes ongoing coaching and counseling and replaces the traditional merit pay performance appraisal system. Over 60 percent of our employees now serve on at least one team—a 600 percent increase since 1985. These are not teams focused on "touch-feely" types of things—they address issues that are real and impact the business.

We constantly focus on the customer to define needs and then to translate those needs and expectations into products. In 1985, we knew we needed to support our customers and commit to fixing their every problem. We designed a problem resolution to isolate the cause of problems and prevent them from reoccurring. This process reduced the communication levels between the customer and the problem-solver from six to just two. Our engineers now get better information about customer concerns, increasing their ability to analyze problems and develop solutions.

We also improved our responsiveness to problems by giving dealers greater latitude in administering warranty policies. Our dealers make their own judgment calls in warranty disputes—we all know that when a customer walks away happy, everyone wins.

We even have UAW workers from our plants calling customers directly and asking them how they like their new automobiles. Most of our customers are surprised to get this call. They do not expect this kind of concern from us. That is the best part—giving customers more than they expect. Teams of employees also visit dealerships to talk to customers and dealership staff, and then share that feedback with the entire plant in order to help us focus our quality improvement efforts.

Cadillac is concerned with internal customers who use our goods and services to do their jobs within the company, and external customers who purchase our products. Our focus on the internal customer prompted us to reconsider manufacturing requirements and capabilities throughout the entire development process. The place to attack quality is not at the operator level, since he or she has little control over the manufacturing process. Instead, try to simplify the design for ease of assembly. A simpler process improves overall quality.

Our assemblers, plant operators, and simultaneous engineering teams work together to evaluate the feasibility of future models. Once a year, a simultaneous engineering team and the entire executive staff spend a day working on the assembly line to gain a better understanding of the requirements of the operators. Our focus on the internal customer has enhanced cooperation and teamwork and has certainly contributed to our cultural change.

Our other goal is to meet and exceed the expectations of our external customers. We use a market assurance process to identify customer needs and requirements and integrate the desires of the customer at every phase of vehicle development. We conduct extensive market research and use the resultant data to define our customers' desires. Input from customers tends to be fairly vague; a customer may say a car should "feel good and make people notice me." Our job is to translate that information into technical specifications our designers and engineers can use.

More information comes from vehicle clinics, where we show prototypes of future models to potential customers and dealerships in order to get feedback. We are conducting this kind of research earlier in the development process than ever before. We also conduct research to monitor product quality and customer satisfaction levels. We also monitor independent surveys before and after the sale.

• *Taking a disciplined approach to financing.* At Cadillac, our business plan is our quality plan, the method by which we will continuously improve our products and services. We involve every employee in the company in our planning process. The executive staff sets the direction, but people at every level define the goals and action plans to help Cadillac achieve its mission. This plan is used by everyone to help set priorities—it is not a document just for management. It is shared with employees, suppliers, and dealers, and helps keep us all focused on our quality objectives. The business plan and the process used to develop it are as subject to continuous improvement. We improve it every year to enhance its effectiveness for those who use it.

We have a regimented product program management process known as "four phase." Four phase is a road map used by simultaneous engineering teams to develop and continuously improve our products. The process places a heavy emphasis on identifying all of the success factors at the earliest phase, long before the automobile prototype is built. By following the detailed steps of this process, we have shaved nearly a year off the lead time needed to bring a product to market.

These three strategies have put Cadillac quality and customer satisfaction back on track. Our quality results highlight this; a key measure of our process capability is assembly hours per car. Since 1986, we have seen a 58 percent improvement in productivity at our Detroit Hamtramck Assembly Center!

We are proud to be the first automobile manufacturer to win the Baldrige Award, but our pursuit of excellence is far from over; there is no mountaintop. Our goal is to once again become the world standard by which all others are judged.

Chapter 16

Quality Means Competitiveness

by Peter A. Gallagher, Senior Vice President at
AT&T Universal Card Services

*At AT&T Universal Card Services, we believe
that the Malcolm Baldrige Award has played a
big part in the success of our company.*

M ANY companies are discovering the power of Total Quality
Management principles, and the result is boosting competitiveness
and renewing the focus on the customer. Integrating Baldrige principles into a business will drive that business toward the needs of the
customer.

We structured our business with the Baldrige Award criteria as
the foundation. We launched our business just three years ago, in
1990, using the Baldrige philosophy as an entry strategy. We took to
heart the major tenets of the Baldrige criteria and focused our attention on not simply satisfying the customer, but delighting the customer
by exceeding the customer's expectations.

We believed that we could not delight our customers without
delighting our employees. Therefore, we made taking care of our
employees the first order of business, treating our employees as our
customers. We realized that the best competitive weapon we had was,
and is, our people. We created a culture and a values system with quality as the foundation and customer delight, employee delight, and continuous improvement as the central focus.

As a result of our adherence to the principles and the discipline of the Baldrige template, we have rewritten the ground rules for success in the credit card business. We now have more than 16 million cardholders. We are growing at a rate of 300,000 new accounts every month, and our business has skyrocketed. We are now a multi-billion dollar business with more than $6 billion in receivables. Today, Universal Card is the second largest bank credit card in terms of number of accounts. We achieved profitability ahead of all schedules; in fact, we achieved our first one million accounts in just 78 days!

Our employee opinion surveys tell us that our employees (associates) believe that Universal Card Services is a great place to work. They rank us above all other bank card operations and above other high performance companies. The outside firm that conducted our survey described the Universal Card results as "results made in heaven."

The Quality Journey

The road to success has not been easy. From the start, we were aware that customer delight, associate delight, and quality are moving targets. Each time we raise the bar, the customer or the competition raises the bar as well. Holding the course requires constant commitment to the Baldrige criteria.

We offered a uniquely customer-focused approach. The quality process was not compromised to meet business demands. We survived the early challenges because of strong quality processes that were built into the business.

Throughout our business, we have established real and measurable standards by which the company's performance is judged not just once a month, but each and every day. We check ourselves against 110 quality measurements of various segments of the business, and a portion of everyone's compensation is based upon meeting or exceeding these quality indicators. As we achieve our quality indicators, each employee, up to and including the CEO, earns "a piece of the pie." Thus, each associate has ownership in making quality an integral part of his or her job, and teaming to achieve our goals is encouraged.

• *Listening.* We saw an opportunity to create an explosive growth company by startling customers with service that went far beyond what they had come to expect. We felt sure that we could understand the real desires of customers, not just their minimum needs, better than any of our competitors. We applied the same concepts and practices to understanding and delighting associates.

Listening is the key to creating a powerful competitive advantage through delighting customers and associates.

We listen obsessively to our customers, our associates, our partners, and our competitors to identify our quality goals and opportunities. Listening is a structural element of our business that is very sophisticated, extremely controlled, tracked, and measured. Among the many tools we use to listen to our customers and to understand their needs and desires are the following seven: 1) monthly customer satisfaction research that determines the factors that influence customer selection and use of credit cards; 2) monthly telephone interviews of a random sample of our customer base drawn from carefully segmented sections of our cardholder population; 3) customer responses received over our 24-hour-a-day, toll-free help line; 4) customer correspondence (including the more than 2,000 letters of commendation a month); 5) marketing focus groups held around the country; 6) customer panels at which our executive team spends a total of more than 200 days per year; and 7) call monitoring by not only telephone inquiry team leaders, but by every associate in the business. Each associate is encouraged to listen to customer calls for at least two hours each month to stay close to those issues affecting our customers and to encourage ideas for improvement. These sources and others drive our business to constantly improve our products and customer services with the goal of delighting our customers.

We listen to our associates with the same zeal with which we listen to our customers. We continually ask associates to evaluate how we are doing and what is important to them. We use the same tools to listen to our associates as we use to listen to our customers, including surveys, focus groups, associate panels, and suggestion programs. We have an annual employee opinion survey and a monthly opinion survey. The results of both surveys are communicated to all associates along with how well we stack up against our previous results, our competitors, and high performance norms. Our goals and plans for improvement are communicated as well. Because associate delight is a critical element to our success, the employee satisfaction indicators generated by the two surveys are reported regularly as a key measure of our business.

• *Benchmarking.* The cornerstone of quality is benchmarking. To maintain our position as a provider of world-class customer service, we benchmark processes that are world-class. We look within the credit card and financial services industries, and we also identify world-class processes outside of our industry. By identifying key processes, rather than focusing on individual companies, we broaden the scope of our benchmarking efforts.

We define benchmarking as the art and science of improving our performance by identifying, analyzing, and selectively replicating world-class processes or practices within and outside of our industry. We involve those employees most closely associated with our key processes in the benchmarking. We use a Steering Committee to help prioritize those benchmarking activities that will have the greatest potential impact on our key measures and objectives and provide the greatest opportunity for improvement. This committee serves as a clearinghouse and as a facilitator.

Adhering to the Baldrige principles is not enough. Our success also depends on the quality of the services provided to us by suppliers and partners. We partner with our suppliers to instill total quality management principles in their businesses, and to establish the same rigorous measurements, continuous improvement goals, and focus on customer delight that we establish for ourselves. We also listen to our suppliers to understand ways in which we can improve and be better partners.

By providing an incentive to suppliers and partners to integrate the same quality management principles into their businesses, the Baldrige success story spreads.

• *Delighting customers.* Customer delight is our overarching goal. Our motto is "Customers are the center of our universe." Our obsession with customer delight includes our unabashed customer advocacy whenever billing disputes arise that involve a transaction on a cardmember's account. When a cardmember has a problem with a billed transaction or service, we send any necessary documentation he or she requires, along with a prepaid envelope to forward it on to the merchant. If that fails to solve the matter to the cardmember's complete satisfaction, we will take whatever further action is needed. Successful interventions that result in delighted customers are an everyday occurrence, and customer delight "heroics" are rewarded with official recognition and the respect of co-workers.

We even focus on delighting customers who have let their accounts run into payment problems. We have named our Collections Department "Customer Assistance." Their motto is "Make Them Happy, Make Them Pay." Customer Assistance associates work with delinquent customers to keep the account, maintain the customer's dignity, and solve the problem. There is constant communication with the customer about the options available. We routinely survey customers whose overdue accounts have been settled to understand how we performed during the process and how we can improve our service. Nearly 90 percent of customers from whom we have successfully collected would recommend us to a friend.

Our recipe for customer delight is simple. We strive to give unmatched service and the best value. We listen and care when customers tell us what is important to them, and then do whatever it takes to surpass their expectations.

• *Delighting and empowering associates.* Delighting associates is at the heart of our company philosophy and culture. In fact, we feel that Human Resource Development and Management should be given even more weight and attention in the Baldrige application.

Our Associate Delight strategy focuses on the whole employee, taking into consideration family life, work life, and individual well-being and development. Integrated into our business and culture is a system including: 1) Continuous learning through education, training, skills development, and experience; 2) rewards and recognition, including a number of peer-nominated awards and team awards; 3) attractive compensation packages; 4) involvement in the business, including one of the most active employee ideas (suggestions) programs of any business; 5) recruitment and staffing initiatives; 6) employee well-being and morale initiatives covering health and fitness, safety, child care, employee/family events, work environment, family leave, and even telecommuting trials; 7) employee communications; and 8) state-of-the-art technology.

Our management philosophy supports and encourages empowerment, responsibility, and innovation. Our associates feel empowered to do whatever it takes to delight customers and other associates, and they take that responsibility seriously. Those who live the corporate values and demonstrate this commitment are rewarded by their peers and the company. They are also rewarded with a feeling of ownership and involvement in the business, and a sense of control and satisfaction.

We are such firm proponents of the Baldrige principles that we strongly recommend that the Baldrige Award be extended to other vital areas of interest in America such as education and the public sector. Much can be achieved by adapting the Baldrige criteria to the special requirements of the education and public sector arenas. Some states have begun to establish their own version of the Malcolm Baldrige

Award and have extended the award criteria to education, health care, and the public sector. And some government agencies have begun to explore the application of Total Quality Management principles in their operations. In our home state of Florida, the Governor has established the Sterling Award, based upon the Baldrige template, to address the health care industry, education, and the public sector, as well as the traditional services and manufacturing categories.

The Malcolm Baldrige National Quality Award has helped restore America's confidence in its manufacturing and service-based companies. It has helped put us back on track by focusing our attention on delivering quality and delighting customers. We believe passionately in delighting and empowering employees as a critical component of success.

Chapter 17

An All-American Approach to Quality

by Marilyn R. Zuckerman, Director of Quality Planning at AT&T, and
Lewis J. Hatala, CEO of The Partners in Discovery Group

Many companies commit to a quality process, only to lose momentum because of a poor fit between the quality program and culture.

W HAT'S missing in so many failed attempts at teamwork, empowerment, and quality improvement is the knowledge of what makes us tick as Americans and what really motivates us.

Quality means something different to Americans than it does to people of other cultures. An American is not motivated by the same things that excite a Japanese worker. Americans are stimulated by challenges, doing the impossible, "going to the moon"—all emotionally stimulating. Americans are unique; the emotions associated with quality in America are the source of energy that drives Americans to excel.

Some years ago, the AT&T Network Systems quality leaders wanted to understand why the quality renaissance they believed in so deeply was not taking root. They had benchmarked the current best practices and tried to install them into the mainstream of their business. They faced what medical doctors face when trying to revive someone's life with an organ transplant and the patient's body has rejected their good work and heartfelt intentions.

Undaunted by this rejection, the pioneers launched a study of quality in America. Their findings are documented in our book, *Incredibly American—Releasing the Heart of Quality.*

American Archetype of Quality

A unique blueprint informs the American idea of quality, a pattern of unconscious memories and powerful emotional experience that helps to explain why people resist or ignore many thoughtfully designed quality initiatives. The quality archetype reveals how Americans feel about quality in every aspect of their lives and suggests how emotions, rarely acknowledged or accommodated in the workplace, can become a force for achieving organizational breakthroughs in quality, productivity, and customer satisfaction.

The American archetype of quality cannot be avoided or neutralized. Ignoring it invites disaster, but an understanding of how to work with it can help achieve success. The study revealed a consistent archetypal pattern that helps to explain why some quality approaches succeed and others fail.

The most important finding from the study is that the first imprint of quality is negative and has a strong emotional component. The imprint structure, or archetype, is depicted as a field of forces created by elements pulling in opposite directions. The basic quality archetype creates a field of forces or tensions between actions and feelings. On one axis,

action tension moves between not doing what others expect or want and doing what others expect or want. The forces are further intensified by the tension between our feelings of embarrassment and negative self-worth and our feelings of pride and positive self-worth.

The first time we "learned" quality was when we did not produce what others expected or wanted and we felt very bad about it. Because this structure is buried deep within us and is out of our conscious awareness, we may inadvertently try to stimulate desired behavior using messages that conflict with the basic logic of the archetype. In the case of quality, the theme "Do it right the first time" will backfire in America. The basic pattern of the quality archetype says we don't do it right the first time. Of course, the desired outcome is correct, but this message is more likely to motivate us to not achieve that result.

In the transformation process, represented by the quality arrow, we move from this initial undesirable state to the time when we do produce what others expect or want and feel good about it.

The Pattern: Three Phases

Early in life, Americans tend to have a powerful emotional experience which imprints them with the meaning of quality; to the emotions and connotations that become unconsciously linked to the word. The pattern of the quality archetype, and the pattern of this formative, childhood experience, both consist of three phases.

Phase 1. Crisis and Failure: A child faces a problem, attempts to do something about it, and fails, experiencing much emotional pain.

Phase 2. Support: The child receives encouragement (mentoring) and guidance (coaching) to try again.

Phase 3. Celebration: The child's (champion's) efforts and success are recognized and celebrated along with his or her supporters. The intrinsic worth of the person is validated by this experience.

This basic imprint pattern is the same for everyone. Americans very rarely achieve and sustain quality unless they experience all three phases of this pattern. There are important roles at each phase and if we are to realize the benefit and power of the archetype, all of these roles must be experienced.

The process is transformative by virtue of key roles played at different points in time. These roles are essential for quality improvement. While cyclical and repetitive, for descriptive purposes, we can say the process begins with Phase 1. The Champion's initial crisis is triggered by a figure who lies at the heart of the archetype: the Lawgiver. In Phase 1 the Lawgiver communicates a crisis, an urgency of need, and, in so doing, creates pressure and forces movement. At the same time results are demanded. We Americans have a propensity toward action, and faced with the demanding Lawgiver we move. The greater the demand, the bigger the crisis, the faster we move. We do so with good intentions, feeling hopeful and challenged.

The Lawgiver issues the challenge, applies the pressure, makes the demands that must be satisfied. Whether an institution, a set of circumstances, or a force of nature, the Lawgiver is the component that creates the sense of urgency necessary to begin the process. In business, the Lawgiver may be customers, competitors, market forces, the economy, and other forces that establish the criteria for survival and success.

In Phase 2, the struggling Champion is supported by **Mentors** and **Coaches**. The former offer emotional support and encouragement, while the latter help build tangible, real-world skills.

Somewhere, early on in the process, the Champion stumbles and falls. At this juncture the second, most critical role must be played —that of the "mentor." The mentor provides support in ways that help us accept the reality of our situation and release our guilt at having failed. By caring about us and helping us renew our sense of purpose, the mentor helps us move past those negative feelings to try again. When there is no mentor, we risk losing people, temporarily or permanently, who, falling, either seek safety and never risk again or, worse yet, seek revenge. When we're ready to try again, the "coach" supports us by working with us to develop skills, insisting on practice, setting deadlines, and coaching the champion(s) toward a breakthrough success by building on smaller successes.

In Phase 3, we must celebrate our champions. The successful individual or team is characterized as the **Champion**, one who has overcome the adversity and celebrates at the end of the journey. The celebration here is not a party, it is more a ceremony—a ceremony that recognizes and relives the entire journey and not just the accomplishments of the champion. The ceremony is emotional. It reaffirms our worth, creates a memory and refreshes our energy to meet the Lawgiver once more.

In another related finding, quality for Americans resonates positively when associated with breakthrough, challenge, new possibilities, and doing the impossible, but it resonates negatively when associated with perfection, standards, specifications, and control.

Implications and Questions

We invite you to look at the pattern as a way of better understanding your leadership role. It challenges you to reflect on your own story and discover the pattern that underlies your experience of quality; consider the implications of the pattern; and try some experiments to learn how to work with the pattern and use the insights gained to help others learn and apply the information.

There is a uniquely American way to do quality and any improvement efforts are destined to fail if they are not aligned with what works for Americans. Americans are challenged by breakthrough. A crisis has positive potential, for it plays a key role in motivating people toward breakthrough.

The American quality archetype provides a lens through which leaders can analyze their current quality initiatives, whether it's the quality system as a whole, or a particular organization or process. In addition to its use as an analytic lens, the archetype reveals the secrets of engagement—how to excite, energize, and renew all those involved in the effort.

As an analytic lens, ask yourselves the following questions:

• Who or what conditions serve as Lawgivers? If the answer is the boss, beware. Putting the boss in the position of Lawgiver puts him or her in an adversarial position with respect to the people. What other conditions or forces can serve as Lawgivers?

• Do you accept and acknowledge crisis and failure? How can it be harnessed and channeled into releasing the emotional energy of the people into a state of high performance?

• How are dreams expressed? Are they expressed? Are they valued or are they passed off as "just another kid's dream"? Are they emotionally linked to the business vision?

• How are mentoring and coaching done for the different groups of people in the organization? Who mentors the leaders?

• Do you celebrate and give recognition? How can you interject more celebration that is of the intrinsic type—giving from the heart in ways that touch another's heart?

• Who are the champions? How do you tell their stories? When their stories are told, do you tell the whole story, the Phase 1 and Phase 2 episodes, not just the Phase 3 experiences when everything works right the first time?

We think of Phase 1 as the time to *generate emotional energy.* Emotional energy flows from the tension that exists between the crisis and the dream—in other quality language, the gap between the current state and the desired future state. The conventional quality language is accurate but it is not fully engaging. Emotion is required to achieve engagement. Engagement that builds commitment is based on full engagement, the head, heart, and hands. Attempts to engage that are only "head" too often yield compliance only, not commitment. It is next to impossible to sustain compliance unless you institute punitive measures. This builds fear, and fear is the enemy of quality. Dr. Deming's 8th point, *Drive Out Fear,* is the cornerstone of the human side of quality.

Phase 2 is the time when we *stimulate innovation.* In Phase 1 our creativity is often directed toward covering up mistakes, creating alibis or finding someone or something to blame for the fact that things did not go right the first time. If we are supported by mentoring and coaching when things are not going well, we are more likely to continue to try again. The emotional energy from Phase 1 drives us towards more constructive creativity—where real innovation can occur. Here we build on an idea, confident that the first idea is simply an element of a solution. If we keep going we will find solutions that are more than continuous incremental improvement, but are breakthrough ideas yielding discontinuous change.

Phase 3 is a time for *encouraging renewal.* A celebration that tells the whole story of someone's accomplishments—what it took to achieve the results—is a renewing experience for not only the recipient, but all those in attendance. Renewal prepares us for a new challenge—gets us ready for facing another struggle where, once again, we feel the tensions between a new crisis and another dream. Celebrations do not have to be elaborate. They must be sincere and heartfelt.

Raising the Bar

As the archetype suggests, the quality process is not a circle; it's an upward spiral. Celebration is followed by another Phase 1, another crisis. But, having learned from their struggle, people never really return to the same place. They face the next challenge armed with the confidence and insights of the earlier ones.

This is the power of the American quality archetype, and of the business leader who understands and applies it. With clear challenges and effective support and reinforcement, the three-phase cycle of the American quality archetype generates its own momentum. It remains the Leader's role to keep raising the bar, to listen for the distant roar of change, to make the Lawgiver real and communicate the sense of urgency so as to enlist everyone in the organization, and trust and encourage their desire to achieve the dream. Business success is achieved by developing people that are fully engaged with their work: head, heart, and hands.

Chapter 18

Rediscovering Quality

by Bruce Gissing, Executive Vice President
of Operations at Boeing

We need to rediscover some things about
quality as a competitive strategy to have
world-class companies and leaders.

A SUCCESSFUL continuous quality improvement program integrated with your strategic business plan could make your company the envy of the industrialized world. It could also make your company profitable beyond your wildest dreams. Impossible, you say? If you start today, it could happen by the end of the decade, perhaps sooner.

Today's consumers demand perfection. When we learned that cars and radios and waffle irons weren't supposed to break all the time, we raised our standards—a little bit at first, and then more and more. And when we learned from the Japanese that cars could be practically flawless, well, we decided that "flawless" was the new standard.

We now insist on cars that don't rattle, banks that stay open on weekends, and fast food that is both healthy and wrapped in environmentally acceptable materials.

Expectations of quality are contagious. Finding flawless reliability in cars and VCRs breeds the expectation of quality in toasters and flashlights. In the mid '80s, consumers began to say they'd gladly pay extra for products that were well-made (20 percent more for a car and 40 percent more for a dishwasher, says one Gallup poll).

Today, that mood has changed again. Now, we expect our products to be well-made. We are no longer impressed by a "money back guarantee." We don't want our money back—we want goods that work. We get annoyed when stores offer us a service contract, asking us to pay a substantial amount of money so that if the refrigerator or the TV doesn't work, they'll fix it. We don't want it fixed—we want it not to break! And in our global economy, the expectations of consumers are growing worldwide.

But by definition, "quality" doesn't just mean good workmanship. It also means anticipating and even exceeding the customer's needs. Companies need to find better ways to attract and hold customers, to be the "preferred provider." Businesses are finding it more difficult to ride on their reputations; even a dominant market share may not protect a company for long. Maintaining quality isn't enough. Products, methods, and processes once considered superior may be judged as substandard by tomorrow's customer.

Today, the company that decides not to "reinvent the wheel" risks losing business to the company that develops a better wheel. The folk wisdom used to say: "If it ain't broke, don't fix it." Now, the folk wisdom says: "Since it ain't perfect, try to improve it, make it more reliable and less costly to produce, and have it ready when the customer wants it."

As customers have changed their attitudes, so must businesses change their paradigms to meet the needs of customers. Companies that have been very successful and confident sometimes believe that if they can just ride out this "quality" fad, they can continue to do business as they have in the past.

Rather than reinvent the wheel, they blame the customer's fickle tastes, and hunker down to await the return of a "rational marketplace." The poor fools. Companies like those are at terrible risk, and they don't even know it.

It's hard to think about changing things when business is good and the cash and profits are flowing. But that, of course, is exactly the time to position your company for the inevitable future. There is a saying around the farms and barns of America—"Fat cats don't hunt." And sometimes, fat companies think they don't have to improve.

To survive and prosper today, all companies will eventually have to toss out many of the concepts and beliefs they once held. Old assumptions, standards, measurements, definitions of success, and systems of reward—they all must go. A lot of these beliefs and definitions have to do with quality.

A century ago, Ivory soap made its reputation by claiming to be "99.44 percent pure." Today, shoppers would be skeptical about a product that claimed to be 56/100ths of a percent *impure*. What's in there anyway? Gravel? Pencil shavings? Today, 99.44 percent isn't pure enough.

Malcolm Stamper, Boeing's vice chairman until last year, told a story about the early days of buying airplane parts from the Japanese. The contract called for no more than three defective parts per hundred. The first shipment arrived, and when our guys opened it up they found 100 perfect parts. On the bill it said: "Three defective parts, per contract agreement, will be shipped separately."

We thought that was a pretty funny story at the time, but only in recent years have we come to understand what that attitude meant for American industry.

Today, Motorola is trying to achieve Six Sigma—3.4 defective parts per *million*. Motorola's paradigm has shifted dramatically, and so has their success at building reliable products. Their high quality standards, as they once saw them, simply weren't good enough for today's market. And in fact, in today's world, no standard ought to be considered "good enough" for long. Any standard that is "good enough" implies a limit to what we can do, and a limit on what we dream of achieving.

If we hold onto the old paradigm, we are the prisoners of our current limits and of our current expectations. Once we embrace the new paradigm, we are only limited by our imagination, our effort, and our desire to move forward.

Quality as Competitive Strategy

Quality can be endlessly improved and "reinvented." Quality can be an old idea, stretched to fit a new situation, or it can be a new concept that solves an old problem. Here's what I mean when I say "rediscovery":

• *Rediscover that quality goes beyond the shop floor or the manufacturing bay.* Many companies make improvements in the shop and even in the quality of the product, and then clap themselves on the shoulders and a declare a victory. These companies haven't begun to enjoy half the benefits of quality—quality in the office, quality in sales, quality in shipping, quality in distribution, and quality in service. In some "manufacturing companies," only 20 percent of the employees actually work on products. The rest work in offices and staff functions, cheerfully wasting time and money and wondering why it takes so long to get things done. Many techniques of quality improvement in manufacturing can be translated into improvements in the quality of the company's business functions.

• *Rediscover that quality improvement reaches beyond the company itself.* Quality includes a genuine involvement with the customer—asking questions, anticipating needs. Your customers are quite likely to have some very good ideas about products or services you can provide. You may not like everything you will hear from your customer, but in today's environment, you can't afford *not* to listen. Quality also means involving the suppliers, helping them reach the standards you set, and helping them improve as you improve. Quality also means involving your employees with both customers and suppliers so that they know how your products will be used out in the real world, just as it's important to let your supplier know that there are real people in your company, using *their* products.

• *Rediscover some techniques and concepts that are simple, straightforward, and very effective.* These include the idea that: 1) Training always will be the key to improving quality; 2) Industrial engineering principles are still very valuable in quality improvement; 3) Process control and the simplification of processes work best at the lowest practical unit level; 4) No quality improvement initiative can succeed unless the CEO wants the program, initiates the program, pushes the program, and is personally involved; and 5) People have brains, and the people who do the actual work in the company know more about its processes, problems, and solutions than anyone else. The people who form the base of the "knowledge iceberg" are those who are the most valuable in every quality improvement program. Listen to them; let them help improve *their* company.

• *Rediscover the fact that achieving quality is hard work.* We have all indulged ourselves in the myth that quality improvement is available in pill form, or the result of a three-day seminar. That's not the case. The hardest part of a quality program is convincing people that you really mean it. Achieving quality requires dedication, repetition, and continuous effort. Changing the attitudes of workers is not easy or fast. Everyone ought to acknowledge this fact right at the beginning—it cuts down on heartbreak later on. Also, let's dispel the myth that middle management stalls most quality programs. Middle managers can't stall a quality program when senior executives set the agenda, sign the paychecks, and control the priorities and expectations.

World-Class Companies

The superstars in the use of quality improvement tools are often called "world-class companies." Many of these are Japanese firms, but American companies are growing in number—Motorola, Xerox, Corning Glass Works, Aetna Insurance, Hewlett-Packard. They're not all necessarily big or well-known. Until it won the Baldrige National Quality Award two years ago, Globe Metallurgical was practically anonymous—two plants, 240 employees.

By contrast, my company, Boeing, is very big. And most people believe we're very successful—we are a consistent world market leader, and we have been for 35 years. Do we think we are at the end of our quest? Of course not. We continuously see opportunities to improve, and once we make those improvements, we use them as platforms for viewing more opportunities. It's never-ending, no matter what your business.

When I study world-class companies, I note that three characteristics consistently show up in all the evaluations:

• *They establish a vision that describes how they will achieve concrete goals and objectives over the next five years or so.* These goals often test their limits and stretch their capabilities. To outsiders, the goals may look more like wishful thinking or dreaming, rather than rational business decisions.

When these companies achieve their goals, they are sometimes seen as having performed a miracle—what was previously thought to be impossible; naturally, gaining that kind of reputation only adds to their strategic advantage. This practice, often called "Management by Policy," generally targets better problem solving, more efficient planning, increasingly simplified processes, and better human resource management.

• *They insist that their employees be process thinkers.* Each person knows which processes in the company are important, and which steps in a given process are critical. Employees know their role in the process, and how their role fits with the roles of other people in the company. People in these companies know that results come from processes. They know that to improve the results, you must continuously improve the process.

• *They spend a great deal of time measuring defects and cycle time.* Their objective is to reduce both, simultaneously. They know that one cannot be reduced at the cost of the other. Measurement of these two vital signs is critical to the productivity and success of the company.

Is this your company? Are you satisfied with where your company is today? Could you find something your company could do better? Do you know what it will cost if you continue doing business the way you are? Are your managers part of the solution or part of the problem?

World-Class Leaders

To compete as world-class companies, we'll need a different kind of manager and leader. Here are nine requirements for the executives of the future. You might want to give yourself a grade.

• *They are personally committed to quality and process improvement.* One way or another, managers have to experience and transmit the commitment and passion for quality improvement. This enthusiasm can't be delegated, but fortunately it is contagious.

• *They fully understand the important processes of their company.* They know that as the processes are refined and improved, the people and capital used to build and operate those processes will increase in value.

• *They know that process management is central to their overall success.* They know they can't succeed without process management. Before we can make meaningful changes to the process, first we have to really understand it—and then improve it with a passion.

• *They focus on tangible process measurements.* Companies that set goals and objectives without plans and definitive measurements are just dealing in slogans. And slogans, coffee mugs, and banners without realistic programs don't produce results—they just make workers skeptical.

• *They believe that teamwork and empowerment are necessary for success.* Teams cannot succeed without the authority to solve problems. And individuals acting alone—however they are empowered—can't accomplish what a team can. At Shenandoah Life Insurance, self-managed teams improved the ratio of employees to supervisors from 7-to-1 to 37-to-1 while improving service and reducing complaints and errors. Empowerment breeds ownership and dramatically alters traditional roles of manager and worker—managers focus their efforts on planning and training, while workers modify and improve the processes.

• *They dare to compare their processes to the best in the world.* It's not enough to benchmark against yourself or your industry. Your company's finance department should compare itself to a world-class financial institution and your shipping department to the best overnight express agencies. Search out the best in a given discipline—and then try to beat them.

• *They are involved and available.* They spend more time where the action is, and less time in their offices. They are highly involved. The CEO of a very successful bank spends one day a quarter in a branch office, cashing checks and taking deposits to learn what's on the mind of his customers.

• *They are genuinely curious.* They want to know why a process is performed, and why it's done a certain way. In the search for hidden problems, their favorite question is "why?" Why do we perform this activity? Why here? Why at this time? Why with that tool? Sometimes, they also ask: "Why not?"

• *They are personally and professionally committed to learning and teaching quality improvement concepts to others.* This is a tough new reality. Many managers feel as if they are already overloaded with work. "I'm too busy," they say. "I've got people to manage." And my answer to that is "Yes, you do, and your management of people includes teaching them how to operate the tools of quality improvement."

Continuous Improvement

The strategy of the future is intertwined with an endless loop of continuous quality improvement. Improving our processes will give us better quality—and lower costs. And if our managers can teach process improvement to others, then quality will improve throughout the company, and bottlenecks, brushfires and impediments will diminish or cease to exist. Inventory will shrink, defective parts diminish, institutions built around waste and scrap wither, costs fall, and profits soar. And we will have more time to devote to suppliers and customers—anticipating their needs and having the products our customers need, when they need them, at a price that is very competitive.

What a strategy! Am I dreaming? Absolutely not. I know we can all achieve these results. And that's good news. The bad news is, so can our competitors. The pace of change is accelerating. In this global economy, there is no time to coast, and no place to hide. To succeed, we must move more quickly, anticipate customer needs, and reach for goals we didn't dream were possible. The future is yours to shape. Will yours be a world-class company? Will you be a world-class leader? I believe both objectives are within your grasp.

Chapter 19

Quality Service

by Robert W. Schrandt, Vice President of Customer Service, and John P. McLaughlin, National Customer Administration Manager, of Toyota USA

The Toyota Touch reminds us that our relationship is with the customer, not with the car, and that people are not things.

TEN years ago, our dealers had great success under the Vehicle Restraint Agreement that limited the number of vehicles Japan could ship to the U.S. and thus created a seller's market, since vehicles were in high demand and easy to sell. Unfortunately, in this market, dealers had a take-it-or-leave-it attitude about putting the customer's needs first. Also, the industry experienced rapid increases in vehicle price, resulting in longer finance periods, higher insurance costs, and improved vehicle reliability.

As the market shifted, we saw a need to build a solid business plan on a foundation of total customer satisfaction. Competitive market conditions were squeezing profits at a time when customer expectations for quality service were increasing. We realized that we had to set ourselves apart from our competitors. Our challenge was to go beyond what others do—and beyond what others think anybody should do. This caused Toyota to change its marketing strategy from one focused on conquest sales to one focused on customer retention.

The Toyota Touch, the foundation of Toyota's customer satisfaction, is a commitment to excellence, quality, and professionalism that creates a special relationship between our customers, dealers, and Toyota. It is caring for people based on communication, cooperation, and consideration. We found that not all of our management was fully committed to the spirit of the 3 C's. As we started program development and review, many barriers were erected and turf battles developed among departments. It took a lot of support and commitment from top management to get everyone moving together.

Our customer satisfaction activities are based on the premise that if you aren't listening to your customers, you won't have the business attributes needed to succeed. And, if you aren't using this information to create change, you may as well not listen.

Seven Solid Components

Toyota saw a need to build a solid business plan that encompasses a total commitment to customer satisfaction. The seven components of this plan are as follows:

• *Top management leadership.* To have a customer-focused company you need a high level of commitment and leadership from top executives who must clearly and consistently communicate the importance of customer satisfaction and ensure that it is part of the company's overall business plan.

We knew that without a high level of commitment and leadership from top management, we would not succeed. Top management involvement ensures that operational departments understand the company's commitment. It also sends a very important message: Customer satisfaction is critical to our success, and it must become an integral part of our daily activities.

Top management's first commitment was to change our corporate attitude toward customers. We needed to focus on the customer, not just the product. We needed to ensure that the quality of our service matched the quality of our products. Our president directed the top management team to draw up a blueprint for an "umbrella" business philosophy, to encompass all our activities impacting customer satisfaction. We had too many departments going in different directions, trying to address the same problem. The goal was to get everyone heading in one direction to produce consistency in concepts and applications.

To get everyone involved, we developed a Corporate Committee to give policy approval for all elements of the Toyota Touch; a

Management Committee to formulate, review, and integrate specific programs; and a Task Group to review and develop specific activities.

• *Voice of the customer.* To get "voice of the customer" information, we formed a corporate Customer Relations department that reports directly to top management. Their charge is to proactively communicate with the customer. They gather information from the customers, who are the best source of information on quality, and communicate it to operational areas. The departments are then responsible for developing and implementing action plans.

Toyota has two proactive ways of collecting the voice of the customer. First, the Customer Assistance Center utilizes a toll-free 800 number to encourage customers to call, to communicate that they really care about customers, and to rectify problems more expeditiously. Each year, 40 full-time people in the CAC handle some 300,000 customer calls and assist customers with problems or concerns, serving as a direct link between the customer and dealer or corporate headquarters.

Through this link, we find many customers who, though dissatisfied to some degree, might never have bothered to contact Toyota. Another advantage of the 800 number is when customers know we're only a phone call away, they feel the company really cares about their satisfaction. As a result, we can save valued customers who otherwise might have said "goodbye."

Second, the Customer Satisfaction Survey measures the customer's perception of their sales and service experience and vehicle quality. This survey provides us with a better understanding of the customer's real feelings about the product and the dealership. We send the satisfaction survey to all retail and lease customers to gain information about the sales and delivery experience and product quality; and we mail the Toyota Service Survey to selected warranty customers to learn about the service experience and product quality.

Our dealers know this also, and are motivated to "do the job right the first time" and take care of the customer's needs. This results in the dealers having a more positive attitude about the customer, since they now better understand customer concerns.

• *Measurement and feedback.* Effectively reporting "voice of the customer" information empowers all people in the company to do their part in ensuring total customer satisfaction and keeps Toyota focused on the customer in everything it does. Both index and customer comment information, derived from the customer satisfaction survey process, is reported to Toyota dealerships, field offices, and manufacturing. The survey process helps to ensure that the sales and service people act as professionals and that the product actually meets the customer's expectations.

With systems in place to collect information from the customer, we then use the feedback to gauge our progress and performance. The reports that we send to the dealers are not factory essays on how we think our dealers treat customers but are based on what the dealers' own customers think. The survey results are used as diagnostic tools to provide ongoing customer feedback to identify product or dealership strengths and weaknesses. This means the survey information can then be used to recognize outstanding dealer efforts or focus on areas of improvement.

These surveys not only put the dealers in touch with their customers, they put us in touch with the customer's evaluation of vehicle quality. Monthly, we send the product quality data to our manufacturing and engineering groups, both here in the U.S. and Japan. These groups then analyze and use this data to make timely ongoing improvements in the product and manufacturing procedures.

• *Customer satisfaction improvement programs.* Helping dealers achieve their customer satisfaction goals is a critical part of Toyota's overall customer satisfaction plan. Toyota has developed several programs designed to help dealers improve their level of customer service. If a call cannot be resolved by our CAC, it's assigned to the appropriate dealer as an "Action Dealer" contact. The contact information is sent directly to the customer's dealer via a direct computer link up. At the same time, the information also goes to our field offices for their information and follow-up.

The dealer then has two working days to contact the customer and 15 days to resolve the problem. Our average resolution time is currently six days, down from 27 days before this system.

If the customer's still not satisfied, we inform the customer of our third-party arbitration program. We don't want to drop an issue if the customer still believes it's our responsibility. We promote customer satisfaction by offering an additional service of dispute resolution to them at no cost—providing customers with an impartial, non-affiliated, third-party organization to equitably resolve their complaints.

• *Recognition.* Motivating dealers to improve is another important aspect of Toyota's plan. Virtually all of Toyota's incentive programs include customer satisfaction indexes. The President's Award,

Toyota's most prestigious award, relies heavily on customer satisfaction indexes to determine winners.

To ensure that everyone maintains their focus on customer satisfaction, we set annual performance objectives for each of our indexes. Our goal is to motivate dealers and to help them focus on improving customer satisfaction at the grassroots level. To do this, we have several programs that impact all areas of the dealer's operation. One of these, the Bottom 20 Dealer Program, turns the heat up on poor-performing dealers. Once dealers are notified about a low standing, they are asked to send a personal reply outlining specific actions they will take to improve their satisfaction rating. Another program, Dealer Consultation, targets high-volume dealers who have low customer satisfaction indexes.

Salesperson turnover is a major problem in our industry. A high degree of turnover indicates a lack of career commitment by salespeople and a poor dealer attitude toward training. To address this problem, we established the Toyota PRIDE sales certification program: *P*rofessionalism, *R*espect, *I*ntegrity, *D*edication, and *E*xcellence. We follow up after the sale and service, and if any customer is not satisfied, we take action. Our research shows that if we follow up with the customer after their sales and service experience, their overall satisfaction as measured by our indexes is a full 20 points higher. To get the attention and support of our dealers, we developed several recognition and incentive programs. We include customer satisfaction criteria in all of our dealer recognition awards, and in various incentive programs.

• *Customer satisfaction committee.* The Customer Relations department communicates "voice of the customer" information to the Customer Satisfaction committee. This executive Customer Satisfaction Committee serves as the major conduit for communicating "voice of the customer" information throughout the company. We use this information to make company decisions and improve teamwork. The committee is driven by input from customer relations, operational department involvement, monthly meetings, and top management involvement.

Since this committee is run by top management, senior executives keep involved and informed on important customer satisfaction issues. Operational departments then examine this information and accept ultimate responsibility for customer satisfaction. Monthly meetings are held to stay focused on customer service and satisfaction and to enhance planning, which results in actions that produce real progress.

The information provided to the committee by the Customer Relations department has dramatically influenced and reinforced Toyota's philosophy toward customer satisfaction and its impact on our sales objectives. From our research, we conclude:

1) Satisfaction starts with excellent product quality. If customers are not satisfied with the product, they are less likely to be satisfied with the sales and service experience.

2) It continues with the sales and delivery process. Customers who have a positive sales experience are more likely to have a positive service experience, return to the dealership for service, and purchase from the dealer again.

3) It is cemented in the service experience. Customers who have a positive service experience are more likely to have a subsequent positive service experience, continue servicing their car at the dealership, and purchase from the dealer again.

4) Dealers with satisfied customers are more successful because they are more profitable, they have higher salesperson retention, and their customers are more loyal.

• *Corporate culture.* Customer satisfaction can't be just another program, it must be a part of the corporate culture. It is a process that takes time and perseverance. The results of our customer satisfaction efforts have been gratifying. Despite a very difficult market, we have made significant gains.

We attribute this increase to the commitment we made 10 years ago to make customer satisfaction an integral part of our business plan. We service customers before, during, and after the sale. Our challenge is to remember that our relationship is with the customer, not with the car. Dealing with people is more difficult than dealing with things. However, it's often tempting to deal with people as if they were things.

If we take care of the customer, the customer will take care of us. We have made total customer satisfaction the cornerstone of our business plan and part of everything we do. Satisfying customers' needs and expectations is our prime goal and the focus of our marketing strategy.

If we begin with 1,000 Toyota customers and satisfy them in their sales and service experiences, we can expect over 871 of them to return to the same dealer. If dissatisfied, only 22 will buy another Toyota from the same dealer. These numbers help everyone understand the cost of dissatisfaction.

Customer satisfaction can't be just another program—it must be a part of your corporate culture. It must involve all areas of the organization, and provide a means for checking and monitoring activities. Only when we track satisfaction over time can we see the results of our efforts. Our surveys show that our customer satisfaction activities are a major reason for our sales success.

Customer satisfaction is challenging, and does not come cheaply or easily. It takes teamwork and commitment. Customer satisfaction promotes customer retention and generates positive word-of-mouth comments, essential for future success. Customer satisfaction means listening to the voice of the customer, determining areas that need improvement, and developing action plans that have the commitment of the whole company.

Chapter 20

Continuous Improvement

by Al Tolstoy, Vice President of
Bell Cellular, Western Region

When we decided to become known for quality service, we got very serious about vision and values, skills and systems.

TECHNOLOGICAL breakthroughs and increasingly knowledgeable, demanding customers have combined to create a new revolution in most service businesses. If value is the consumer ideology of the 1990s, then quality service is the way to acquire, satisfy, and retain customers—in short, it becomes the key determinant of business success.

Bell Cellular provides cellular telecommunications services to more than a quarter of a million subscribers located in Ontario and Quebec. We compete in an industry that is only in its seventh year of existence, but one that has undergone dramatic changes characterized by "quantum leaps" in transmission quality, network coverage, sophistication of the cellular phone, affordability, and the range of service features available to the customer.

In 1988, after three years of explosive growth, our executive team had to define a strategy for the next phase, growth and maintenance. We determined that our competitive advantage couldn't rest on technology or price alone. Industrial secrets don't last, and product evolution occurs so rapidly that technological advantages are short-lived. Engaging in a price war wouldn't work without risking the quality of our product, our ability to expand (providing cellular telephone service is capital-intensive), or our responsibility to our shareholders.

Quality Differentiates Service

We decided to differentiate based on service quality. Our objective was to become *the leading service organization,* a commitment we've renewed every year since 1988. Realizing that a determined competitor could overtake a stationary service level, right from the start we made continuous improvement the core of our customer service ethic.

The leading service organization is first and foremost a company that relies on its basic product and support services to deliver quality. But it also must go beyond that and offer an added touch, an intangible extra the customer experiences during every contact with the company. The added touch is the product of considerable effort, measurement, and management planning. It is the outcome of a carefully crafted strategy intended to understand and anticipate the customer's expectations during each and every contact with Bell Cellular.

Reflected in our corporate signature, "Above and Beyond the Call," our approach to service has always been a drive to anticipate and exceed rising customer expectations. The real key to success has been creating an environment where Bell Cellular employees are willing and able to take personal responsibility and initiative to make things better for the customer, the company, and the communities in which we do business.

Three Core Areas

Our service quality and continuous improvement initiatives are based on interaction among three core areas:

• *Vision and values:* A clear statement of corporate purpose and strategic intent that is communicated clearly to all team members, initially, consistently, and repetitively. Each new employee receives two days of orientation during which the core values of the company are presented and explained. Right from the start the critical process of employee acceptance begins by reinforcing the values by actions that encourage feedback, defining the context in which interactions with customers and co-workers occur, and equipping the employee to become an effective agent of change.

• *Skills development:* Continuous upgrading of technological, interpersonal and team skills that ensure the corporate vision becomes reality. Skills development improves business relationships and contributes to a positive work environment. Coaching and team problem solving skills training embeds the ethic of continuous scrutiny, analysis, and self-directed improvement into the day-to-day work practices of employees. The result is a better-equipped, more satisfied and highly motivated team determined to improve quality at all levels.

• *Systems:* Patterns of work that are efficient, simple, and focused on the customer. Our business plan includes specific, measurable quality objectives. Continuous improvements result from a straightforward process consisting of three linked steps: 1) Listening to customers—we monitor customer satisfaction *and* potential customers' needs through an intensive research process involving monthly surveys, focus groups, and other measures; 2) Measuring performance and sharing results—continuous improvements become habitual when employees are regularly informed of corporate goals and results and when they see that it is possible to make changes through working smarter, innovating, and relying on teams; 3) Responding quickly—process changes can be effected quickly in response to customer signals, following appropriate analysis; likewise, innovations can be introduced without a lengthy or complicated planning cycle. Our ability to seize the moment through innovation and realigned work practices means that customer satisfaction, based on their perceptions of quality service, remains high.

Benefits Are Real

Here are two examples of how continuous improvements in service quality worked for Bell Cellular customers:

• We discovered through surveys and letters that some of our customers felt we took too long to produce bills. They expressed concern about incurring late payment charges because the bills were arriving too late. The department responsible for issuing bills swung into action with little prompting from senior management. They organized a task force, completed detailed process diagrams, and developed innovative ways to shave four days from the monthly billing cycle. This improvement was implemented to the approval of our customers, who equated quick turnaround time with quality service. The savings in interest and production costs to Bell Cellular was several hundred thousand dollars—money that flowed right to the bottom line.

• One of our customer service reps had an idea that produced a triple win. In retrospect, the idea was simple: designate an easy-to-remember number that our customers could use to dial the nearest detachment of the Ontario Provincial Police (OPP) from their cellular phones, regardless of their location. In collaboration with the police, we wrote the system software that routed calls for assistance to the nearest OPP detachment. The service was exceptionally well-received by traveling customers.

The OPP number gave the customer a new service that immediately increased the utility of their cellular phone. It affiliated the company and the product with safety and security, two advantages of cellular service desired by many customers. And by showing employees how good ideas can be brought to life, it reinforced a working environment conducive to continuous improvement.

Lessons Learned

By focusing on continuously improving service and quality, we have learned some things that we believe are valuable to any business.

• *Change is inevitable and must be harnessed as a source of competitive advantage.* There is no real alternative to embracing change, particularly in competitive, high-technology industries. While it may be occasionally comforting to look to the past for inspiration and solutions, the future is where quality service must be delivered to customers.

• *The power of properly trained, motivated, and encouraged employees is most often the critical difference between companies where quality service is a thriving part of the culture and others where it's just an empty slogan.*

• *Continuous inquiry and evaluation are essential to building a service-oriented culture within a company.* Bell Cellular conducts monthly customer satisfaction surveys, and seeks ongoing feedback from employees who understand this information is used constructively to uncover problems needing solutions.

• *Measurement is vital.* The commitments with real meaning are those that are reflected in measurable change. Once again, Bell Cellular is taking steps to critically examine all of its processes, then benchmark them against those used by the best companies in the world. Our aim is to use both incremental and breakthrough approaches to continuously better the service we offer, until we set the benchmarks that others use.

• *Continuous change flows from a corporate culture that encourages and rewards prudent risk.* The best proof of the existence of such a culture is the strong sense of ownership and pride that, running through the entire organization, has led to a long series of process and service improvements. Nothing can stop people who believe they make a difference.

Chapter 21

The Challenge of Continuous Improvement

by Robert L. Stark, Executive Vice President of Hallmark Cards

Excellence is a process best maintained by treating everyone as the customer and seeking constant improvement.

WITHIN the past ten years, most American businesses have experienced significant changes in markets and competition. Responses to this confusing cyclone of change, however, have hardly been consistent.

Some companies waited so long to respond that they had to scramble for survival, necessitating dramatic measures: mergers, government bailouts, massive layoffs, major restructuring.

For others, survival was impossible; changes, if any, came too late.

Some businesses, facing such circumstances, overreacted. Fearing the worst, they moved quickly and dramatically, and later questioned the wisdom of their own actions.

Watching such activities brings to mind an old adage about frogs. Put a frog in a pot of boiling water, and he'll jump out to save his skin. Put him in a pot of cold water, then gradually raise the temperature, and he'll die.

Plenty of American businesses met the fate of the cold-water frog, while others misjudged the temperature and jumped too soon. The trick is to stay in long enough to clearly understand the changing temperatures and then act accordingly.

Assessing Hallmark's Options

Several years ago at Hallmark, we realized the waters were warming up. Our markets were changing, and competition was getting tougher. Like others in similar circumstances, we began to assess our options.

Certain considerations put us in an enviable but challenging position. First, despite increased competition, our company was strong and profitable, freeing us from the necessity of moving too hastily. Because of our position, however, one of the primary challenges was to get much of the organization to understand the need to change. Communicating the need for change in a clear and straightforward manner became our first priority.

We were, and are, fortunate in having a high level of employee trust. Hallmark employees are exceptionally loyal, thanks in part to a strong benefits package that includes employee ownership of nearly a third of the company. Profit-sharing also meant, of course, that our employees had a high stake in whatever program was adopted. They would work hard for its success, but would scrutinize it carefully.

Also, in an era when many companies were downsizing, we had the challenge of honoring a long-time commitment to maintaining employment.

Last, and probably most important, was a corporate culture that has always placed a high value on excellence. Our challenge would be to refocus this emphasis in a way that would help us better address the marketplace.

Peeling the Onion

With these given, work began on a plan. Early on, we made the decision to adopt a three-part program. Like peeling an onion, we would start on the outside and work our way in—from marketing strategy to organizational structure to operating practices. In the end, the changes would profoundly affect our way of doing business.

The first step was developing a marketing strategy in tune with changing times. Where once we had a homogeneous consumer in a homogeneous channel, our market was now segmented, and our consumers were more diverse. The retail environment where they shopped also had changed, and a greater number of companies were competing more fiercely for their business.

Our new marketing strategy recognized that serving a multitude of consumer needs in a timely way must be the driving force of our business. We also would need to enhance the retail focus of the company and provide even more innovative products and services. This would ultimately result in many more items in our product offering, which already numbered in the tens of thousands.

When development of the marketing strategy was well under way, studies began that would lead to a new organizational structure. The object was to restructure the organization to bring it in line with the new strategy, reduce bureaucracy, and allow managers to manage full-time. Another major goal was to reduce the time required to bring a new item to market.

Focusing on the Journey

Even before the new structure was in place, the search began for operating practices that would lower costs, increase efficiency, and reduce lead times throughout the organization. This third part of the program, the one at the very heart of the strategy, would have to sustain and support the marketing plan. It would be the modus operandi that would carry us into the future.

Temptations arose immediately, particularly the temptation to measure our success by the amount of activity we were able to generate—the number of quality circles formed or the number of people trained in participatory management.

The task we took on, however, was to implement a program of continuous improvement. Not only did we need to get everyone to understand the necessity for significant changes in operating practices *before* it was readily apparent that such changes were necessary, but we also had to convince them that the need would *always* be there— a tall order indeed!

The answer was found in corporate values, in the long tradition of excellence at Hallmark. Excellence would be redefined not simply as a goal, but as a *process*. The emphasis would shift from the destination to the journey.

Treating Everyone as a Customer

Picking up the customer-centered focus of our marketing strategy, we determined to treat *everyone* as a customer, whether they be outside the company or inside it.

Inside the company, the new organization worked well with this idea. Product areas had been broken into business units, each with clearly defined authority and responsibility. These units became the link between the external and internal consumers. Other divisions within the company, from purchasing to manufacturing, were charged with the responsibility of providing the best possible services to the next links in the internal chain.

Because of Hallmark's longstanding corporate commitment to job security, it was necessary to implement innovative ways of dealing with the results of increased efficiency. We used a panoply of programs, including load-leveling, retraining, and attrition to smooth the transition.

Outside the company, the customer-centered approach has led us to develop more and better programs to serve the thousands of retailers who sell our products. For example, we've increased our research efforts to get an even faster reading on ever-changing consumer tastes, attitudes, and needs.

In the final analysis, anything we're doing that is not required by our customer is a hindrance to productivity because it's probable we shouldn't be doing it at all. Getting closer to our customer is a way of eliminating unnecessary activity, as well as adding work that matters.

Excellence as a Way of Life

Is the Hallmark program working? Certainly the results to date have been very encouraging.

• High employee involvement in developing more efficient operating procedures has already saved us millions of dollars.

• Cycle times have been shortened, inventory levels reduced, and new product introductions increased.

• Company sales and earnings are up; importantly, we have maintained our values and continue to be voted one of America's top employers.

But to suggest that we can in any way relax our efforts would be to misinterpret the main message—we intend to strive for *continuous* improvement. We believe there are three basic requirements to maintaining such an attitude of excellence:

• clear understanding of where you are, where you want to be and how you intend to get there

• commitment and participation of all employees

• clear communication of goals and results.

Our experience tells us that any corporation doing this can better weather the marketplace vicissitudes and competitive changes, accommodate the necessary changes and avoid the fate of the cold-water frog.

Chapter 22

Market-Driven Quality

by Stephen B. Schwartz, Senior Vice President of
Market-Driven Quality at IBM

*In our quest to make market-driven quality a
way of life, we have learned certain lessons
and identified seven milestones.*

IN early 1990, during my tenure as head of one of IBM's most successful lines of business, Chairman John Akers asked me to help him
make what we call *Market-Driven Quality* (MDQ) a way of life at IBM.
For two years now, I have been the senior vice president who is responsible for quality at IBM. The fact that John wanted me to report directly to him speaks volumes about our serious commitment to quality.

Although IBM traditionally has been dedicated to excellence,
our decision to institutionalize quality was a renewed response to our
customers and a changing global market. We realized three things: 1)
we were heavy with resources and structure; 2) we were not nimble or
responsive enough to customer needs; and 3) unless we provided high-
quality solutions, we simply would not survive. Intense global competition meant we could no longer get by with only incremental, "best
effort" improvements in quality. We needed finite, breakthrough goals.

So in 1990, MDQ became the marching order for implementing
our strategy of satisfying our customers with the finest products, services, and support. We set aggressive quality improvement goals—10
times by 1991, 100 times by 1993, and near-perfect, Six Sigma levels
(3.5 defects per million) in 1994—bold challenges.

Quest for Quality

Over the last two years, we have boiled down the lessons we
have learned in our MDQ journey into seven milestones.

• *First, we made customer satisfaction the number-one measure of our success.* We want to be the best at creating customer value in the markets we serve. As John Akers likes to say, we want "delighted customers." This might seem to fly against the traditional business axiom that financial results come first, but we believe that if we succeed in creating delighted customers all else will follow—revenue, profits, and market share.

• *Second, we made sure that our commitment to MDQ flows directly from our basic values.* This is important for identity and continuity. Early in IBM's existence, our founder, Thomas J. Watson, Sr., outlined three basic beliefs that have made IBM what it is today: to provide the best service to our customers, to perform with excellence in every undertaking, and to treat every person—customer and colleague alike—with the utmost respect. Our commitment to MDQ in the 1990s embraces a reaffirmation of those values that have served us well over the years.

• *Third, we developed our MDQ efforts in a context of our own world-class practices and the total quality management programs of more than 50 other companies around the world.* This type of benchmarking, within IBM and with industry-best companies, remains central to our quest.

• *Fourth, we identified six elements of MDQ and positioned MDQ as the implementation plan for our business strategy, as the way to get our jobs done better, and as the way to meet our business objectives.* These are the six elements of our MDQ framework: 1) to exercise leadership, a prerequisite for any quality improvement effort; 2) to define and understand market needs; 3) to eliminate defects; 4) to reduce cycle time; 5) to measure progress; and 6) to empower our employees.

Defining markets means analyzing the niches ripe for our products and services and directing our development efforts there. We also have moved out of certain markets that we believe no longer reflect our core strengths. For example, in 1991 IBM set up Lexmark International, an independent company to handle typewriters and office printers, rather than remain a direct player in this business. We are re-learning the basic truth that the reason we're in business is to satisfy the needs, anticipate the future requirements, and exceed the expectations of our internal and external customers.

MDQ is especially apparent in the areas of defect elimination and cycle-time reduction. This means reducing the time it takes to do everything from returning phone calls, to delivering a report, to developing and manufacturing products. It also means doing it right the first time. We've made giant strides here. I'll cite just three examples: 1) Our Programming Systems Development Laboratory in Cary, North Carolina, reduced the error rate 10 times for every new product shipped in 1991; 2) Our New York Brokerage branch office team reduced service call requirements to a major customer from 13 transactions to one, from 18 people to a single automated process; and 3) In Fujisawa, Japan, IBM employees have slashed the reject rate for storage device components to only four per million.

As for measurements, we have established five—customer satisfaction, quality improvement, employee involvement, market share, and financial results—in that order. Already, we can perceive substantial relationships between these measurements and specific responses designed to improve them. For example, most IBM branch offices in the U.S. have formed teams to meet regularly with customers to discuss how we are meeting their current wants and needs, and to brainstorm about possible future requirements and solutions.

By empowering employees, we mean the creation of an entrepreneurial spirit to give everyone a sense of ownership. A cultural shift is needed. Managers and their teams are encouraged to replace management by control with management by support. It takes time. After two years, about a third of all our people, including managers and executives, not only understand MDQ but also have changed the way they do their day-to-day jobs. Another third understands MDQ, but has not figured out how to apply it on the job. The last third does not think MDQ applies to them. These are top-performing people who work long and hard and find it hard to believe that they are not already performing with quality. The truth is that they are, but only to a point. That point passed by a decade ago when the PC changed our industry and working lives forever by putting the computer on nearly every desk. Today, being good is not good enough. Tomorrow's winners will be good people putting out greater effort—not by working harder or longer, but by working in definable, repeatable, and continually improving processes.

• *Fifth, we focused on process improvement—examining the progression by which tasks are accomplished, finding the best methods, recording them to repeat what works best, and continually fine-tuning them and updating them.* We are training our people not to confuse our insistence on increased skills and excellence with the processes that leverage their professionalism. A focus on processes and their continual improvement permits us to get better and better.

During the past two years, thousands of process improvement teams at the grass-roots level at IBM have already begun to see results of their efforts. In addition, we have identified 15 processes that encompass the businesses we are in and the activities we perform. Examples would be capturing market information, receiving customer feedback, or determining product requirements and manufacturing processes. Each process has an owner and a team to implement and manage it. And, as IBM evolves into a spectrum of businesses with independent authority and accountability, processes will enable these businesses to interrelate, communicate closely, and remain clearly and identifiably part of the IBM family.

Improvements from this concentration on process improvement are beginning to show. We have had a 35 percent average reduction in cycle time. In France, improvement in the distribution process raised customer satisfaction by seven points. In the U.S., process improvements in answering the phone in our branch sales offices significantly raised customer satisfaction in nine months.

• *Sixth, we required assessment: every IBM site and function must assess its progress against criteria established for the Malcolm Baldrige National Quality Award.* We're not out to win awards (though we're delighted if we do). We are out to take a good look at ourselves. Unless we measure how we're doing, we will not know how to do things better. We have examples of success here, too. Our people at our Rochester, Minnesota, plant produce midrange AS/400 computers. They had good reason to think they were world-class. But when they performed their first self-assessment using the Baldrige criteria, they fell far short. Though they did good work, they found they had no process in place to describe how they did it. The Baldrige criteria helped them define how they went about their business so that they could improve their processes and replicate the improvements.

Rochester won the Baldrige Award in 1991. At the same time, Rochester revenue per employee grew to 40 percent above the industry average and AS/400 computers enjoyed the highest customer satisfaction among midrange products in, among other places, one of the toughest marketplaces in the world—Japan.

• *Seventh, we developed four supporting activities to reinforce our MDQ initiatives, processes, and assessments.* These activities are education, communications, personnel programs, and information systems support. The IBM organizations that are furthest along in their quality journey are doing their education up front. At the outset, we

asked every employee and manager to attend two days of MDQ awareness education. Management teams attended two days of training in
which they learned to lead through support rather than by control. We
also discovered that having employees attend leadership classes with
their managers is very effective in implementing that transformation.

Our communications support has sounded a consistent drum-
beat on MDQ throughout the corporation. We have a special quality
logo that appears in publications, on correspondence and awards, and
at meetings. Every publication, every speech, every video, and every
internal television program reinforces the message. The effect is
cumulative and powerful.

Worldwide, we are learning the vocabulary of quality and its
central place in our working lives. We've updated personnel programs
with policies that reward and publicize the people and teams who
innovate, delegate, and take prudent risks to respond to customers
quickly and effectively. IBM has traditionally been a meritocracy,
rewarding employees for individual achievement.

We've also modified that. Our counseling and appraisal system
now includes not only a quality component, but how the individual
participates as part of the team, with compensation based on the success of the team as well as on the success of the individual.

Finally, our information systems support reflects MDQ principles by providing the hardware, software programs, and support to
enable IBMers to do their jobs and communicate among one another
more effectively. In short, we're doing for our own people what we've
been doing for customers over the years.

Quality has become a common language of international business. The words of this language are not just the reliability and
price/performance of a product. Quality speaks to every aspect of customer satisfaction—how fast a product is delivered and installed, its
usability, its networking capabilities, the availability of support, the
efficiency of service, the clarity of bills, and prompt responses to telephone inquiries.

Those who speak here of market-driven quality know that it's
not just a series of slogans or buzzwords: it's a complete and ever-
growing language that describes the way we do business. It's not
something we do on the job—it is our job and our way of life, a never-
ending journey that takes us closer to the Shangri-la of perfection. We
may never reach that ideal goal—but striving for it will delight our
customers, and assure our future success.

Chapter 23

Staying the Course

by Barry Sheehy, Principal of The Atlanta Consulting Group, and James D. Robinson III, former CEO of American Express Company, and President of J.D. Robinson Inc. and the Marcellus Corp.

Having staged a stunning quality and productivity comeback, America could blow it now by getting bored.

THE American quality movement is clearly at a crossroads. The recovery in quality and productivity, which has been nothing short of remarkable, is in danger of being derailed. Why? Because we've grown bored with the process and our persistence has waned. This boredom is reflected in the press more than in management ranks, but the end result is the same. We are starting to take our eye off the ball. Worse still, we are starting to drift off in search of something fresh and exciting; a new miracle cure—preferably something fast, painless, and inexpensive. There is no such remedy.

If you listen carefully, you can hear the cadence of the "quality is boring" message. What you hear sounds like this: "Deming and Juran are old geezers. Masaaki Iami is dull, and nobody can understand Taguchi; besides the Japanese economy is in trouble, and quality hasn't done much for the Nikkei index." Headlines in the popular press tell us, "Quality Movement Half Baked." Pundits are popping up everywhere, earnestly assuring anyone who will listen that Quality Improvement is yesterday's news.

So What's Not to Like?

It's one thing to say quality is boring or hard to do, but another thing altogether to say it doesn't work, which is a theme now starting to emerge. The "quality doesn't work" message doesn't refer to *quality* so much as *Total Quality Management*. But what is TQM? It's a management methodology for adding value to your product or service as perceived by your customers. This is done primarily (but not exclusively) by stripping out waste, rework, and errors, and by improving work processes. This requires you to invest in your products and services and employees and to stay very close to your customers.

If you accept this as a reasonable definition of TQM, you must then ask which part of it doesn't work. Is it the part about *adding value* to your product or service, or the part about *eliminating waste*, or the part about *improving work process*? What about the requirement to *invest in your products, services, and employees* or *staying close to customers*? Which of these elements of TQM strike you as being unsound? Probably none, because there is nothing wrong with any of these objectives. The principles and goals of TQM are inherently laudable. So if TQM isn't working, it isn't because the definition or objectives are wrong. Perhaps then, it has something to do with the implementation of the process.

TQM is a difficult process to implement. It takes time, effort, resources, and discipline. It often requires significant change in the way an organization conducts business. Change of this magnitude is never easy; a lot can go wrong and often does. But because something is difficult to do, doesn't mean it isn't worth doing. Frankly, the option of ignoring quality simply doesn't exist in a global economy. You must either compete or perish. If you can't "make it work," someone else will. Quality is the foundation of competitiveness and is becoming more important, not less important, in an integrated, world economy.

In any case, we're doing better at implementing quality improvement than we give ourselves credit for. It's time to set the record straight and sort out fact from fantasy.

Seven Myths

Let's examine a few of the anti-quality myths which are doing the most damage.

Myth 1: Most quality improvement efforts have failed. This is simply not true. Most serious quality improvement efforts have been successful, if you define success as improved customer satisfaction and long-term financial results. The government's report on Management Practice, the Conference Board Study, and the QPMA Study all came to similar conclusions regarding the success rate of quality improvement programs; according to these studies, about two-thirds of quality improvement efforts have produced beneficial results.

However, if you shift the criterion for success from improved customer satisfaction to improved competitiveness, the success rate drops below 50 percent, still a good batting average when it comes to change. But what is the source of this dropoff in performance? Competitiveness involves more than just quality; competitiveness is heavily influenced by labor productivity, taxes, currency valuations, interest rates, access to capital for investment, utility of the basic product, and management competence. Quality plays an important role, but it is not the only determining factor.

To further complicate matters, the importance of quality fluctuates in relation to overall quality levels within a given industry. If your competitors are relentlessly improving their performance, then you have to run faster and faster to stay in the same relative competitive position. Your quality may be improving, but so is your competitor's; this negates any competitive advantage you may have gained from improving quality. Does this mean your efforts were wasted? Hardly! You only have to ask yourself what would have happened if you had not improved quality in these competitive circumstances.

This may explain why some organizations have gained little competitive advantage from their quality efforts, even though their quality indices have improved. But what about those organizations which have failed altogether in their quality improvement efforts? They have experienced no improvement in either quality or competitiveness. What is the source of this poor performance? You can separate these "poor performers" into two camps: those impacted by timing and those who are victims of poor implementation. Let's begin with timing: Most quality improvement efforts in North America are less than four years old. Some of these programs are underperforming and this is probably the result of poor planning and implementation; but most are not so far off course that they cannot be righted. After all, it took Toyota more than a decade to put in place its world-beating quality infrastructure. If these newly launched quality efforts are nurtured and sustained, they will eventually pay off. In short, many of these underperforming quality processes may come around if they are given a little time, leadership, and focus.

How about the basket cases? Well, these programs usually crash because they are incompetently planned and executed. Many are so badly constructed they cannot be fixed. Anyone associated with the quality movement in the 1980s can name their favorite example of a poor quality implementation. In the rush to get on the quality bandwagon, many programs were launched without plans, resources, or leadership. Responsibility was delegated to staff functionaries, measurements were not put in place, and there was no link between the quality process and the organization's business objectives. Some organizations launched quality programs while refusing to survey their customers. These "half-baked" efforts were bound to get into trouble, and it should come as no surprise to anyone that many of them have crashed. In fact, it's surprising there haven't been more failures.

Many studies have set out to examine these failures. These studies point to flawed implementation, rather than flawed methodology, as the chief source of failure. The *Ernst & Young Report on Best Practices* concluded that different improvement techniques work better in some circumstances than in others. In short, sound TQM methodologies will underperform if they are employed incorrectly. For example, benchmarking (an extremely useful improvement tool) may overpower a fledgling quality improvement process. The gap between world-class performance and the performance of an ordinary company is huge. Exposing this gap through benchmarking can prove devastating to morale. In this circumstance, benchmarking could hinder, rather than accelerate, your quality improvement effort. Consequently, benchmarking is best employed in the context of mature quality improvement programs.

Interestingly, the *Ernst & Young Report* did identify several universally beneficial methodologies which work in almost all circumstances. These include raising employee skill levels, improving customer service, and improving work processes.

Myth 2: Most Baldrige winners have fallen on hard times, and their focus on quality is the source of their difficulties. Wrong. Only one Baldrige winner has ended up in bankruptcy out of more than 50 finalists, and this was in the small business category. Some people also point to IBM as another example, but the division which won the Baldrige Award is doing exceptionally well.

The vast majority of Baldrige winners have been very successful in business and attribute much of their success to their commitment to quality. "But," say the critics, "look at Motorola or Xerox. Weren't their earnings under pressure in recent years?" The answer, of course, is yes; as were the earnings of Toyota and Sony. However, this earnings trend has more to do with the business cycle than the quality cycle. Remember, quality is a tool, an important one, but still only a tool. It doesn't banish the business cycle, eliminate recessions, or do away with normal competitive pressures, especially in a global marketplace.

Myth 3: Most business executives are growing disinterested in quality improvement. Wrong. Surveys indicate a growing focus on Quality Improvement. The recent QPMA Study and the *Ernst & Young Report* both indicate that TQM will become a more important business strategy in the years ahead. The recent Business Roundtable of top performing companies in their field were asked point-blank, "Is the quality movement a fad?" The answer was a resounding no.

Myth 4: Our renewed focus on quality has not helped our economy. This is the most dangerous lie of all. Our focus on quality has produced fabulous results for the economy. The recovery of North American manufacturing competitiveness, including a dramatic improvement in quality, represents a stunning comeback.

There is an old saying in economics that pain makes you wise, and lots of pain makes you smarten up fast. This is precisely what happened to us in the 1980s. By refocusing our energies on meeting customer expectations, adding value, and driving down costs, a whole host of companies and even a few whole industries have experienced a turnaround. This turnaround is reflected in economic statistics. Consider these facts:

• U.S. manufacturing productivity has been increasing at 3.1 percent on average since 1983. That's faster, over that period of time, than any other industrialized country. Japan, with a proportionately higher investment level, managed about the same improvement, but from a much lower base.

• The U.S. is now, once again, the world's largest exporter. Manufacturing and capital goods exports have been soaring since the mid '80s. Exports have grown twice as fast as the economy as a whole. In fact, U.S. capital goods makers export half of their total output. The U.S. share of world manufacturing exports has grown from 14 percent in the early '70s to 18 percent today.

• Overall U.S. productivity is the highest in the world and has been growing much faster than in Japan over the past decade. This is true in manufacturing—even in motor vehicles—as well as in services and agriculture.

• The U.S. steel industry, which most economists were prepared to write off a decade ago, has made a remarkable comeback. It now takes only 5.3 person-hours to produce a ton of steel in the United States, compared with 5.4 in Japan and 5.6 in both Germany and Britain. It is worth noting that it takes 6.4 person-hours per ton in South Korea, 7.2 in Taiwan, and 8.9 in Brazil.

• In 1993, the U.S. reclaimed its premier position as the world's leading producer of semiconductors. Five years ago pundits were predicting that the U.S. would be driven out of the semiconductor industry by the middle of the 1990s.

• U.S. service industries remain more productive than their counterparts overseas. In retailing, food distribution, airlines, banking, telecommunications, and a host of service industries, the U.S. productivity lead is significant. U.S. service exports have grown 500 percent since 1986, and service sector productivity will grow even more in the '90s as competitive pressures force service companies to get serious about quality and productivity.

• In automobiles, the U.S. has made an extraordinary productivity and quality comeback. On a pure operating basis (with health care and pension costs removed) Chrysler and Ford have effectively caught up to their Japanese counterparts in terms of quality and productivity.

Myth 5: In today's "value-driven" competitive environment, quality is less important than price in determining consumer decisions. Nonsense. Quality (meeting customer expectations) is the very core of competitiveness. Yes, price is important, but price is a byproduct of value or quality. *Even a price-sensitive strategy is rooted in an implicit assumption regarding the quality of your product or service.* No one is going to buy your "stuff" if it doesn't work, no matter how cheap the price.

In a highly competitive global economy, consumers expect and can get both high quality and a lower price. The competitive forces unleashed by the global economy are putting downward pressure on everyone's margins. To compete in this Darwinian environment of ever higher quality and ever lower prices, companies must ruthlessly and continuously squeeze out all non value-added costs from their work processes. At the same time, they must work relentlessly at adding value to their product or service. They must drive down costs without taking their eye off the customer—you can't trade off quality for *price* in a global economy. To survive, you must learn to manage both *costs and quality*. Interestingly, TQM provides one of the few methodologies capable of achieving both goals simultaneously.

Myth 6: Reengineering will replace quality as the next management fad. Wrong. Reengineering is a tool, not a fad, and a powerful one at that. But reengineering is a subset of TQM and not a replacement for it. Without the infrastructure, skills, and customer focus provided by a total quality process, reengineering can become a dangerous, unguided missile. This limitation was pointed out by one of the original reengineering gurus, Thomas Davenport, in his book *Process Innovation*. Reengineering involves radical restructuring of key work processes. The dangers of taking such "big leaps" without a clear focus on customer requirements are enormous. If your reengineering process is not rooted in a quality ethos, you could very easily reengineer the customer right out of the picture.

Myth 7: Quality improvement is a management fad confined to North America and Japan—no one else really cares. Wrong. Quality improvement is a worldwide economic phenomenon. Global economic forces are driving up quality standards around the world. Over forty countries already have national quality awards and standards in place. Some of the United States' most important trading partners in the Pacific Rim, Europe, and the Western Hemisphere are adopting national quality strategies. If we slow up our improvement efforts, or become bored and lose interest, we'll sacrifice all the gains we made in the 1980s; and it won't be long before we find ourselves "run over" by these more nimble, aggressive competitors.

So What Went Wrong?

In the past 10 years we've made tremendous progress in restoring our competitiveness, and the TQM message of *customer focus, minimizing waste, and disciplined Process Improvement* played an important role in this turnaround. "So why the reaction?" Well, it all comes down to a question of expectations. Quality improvement methodologies lived up to their potential, but they didn't always live up to their promise, or more precisely, the promises made on their behalf. In the 1980s, TQM was positioned by some as a "cure-all," a modern-day snake oil, capable of solving any business problem. TQM was sold as a substitute for strategic planning, financial planning, and even day-to-day management. To make matters worse, total quality was used as a marketing umbrella for reselling a host of traditional consulting and training products. In the face of such wild promises, it's no wonder some people have become disenchanted. In truth, this reaction is healthy and probably overdue. This is a "classic correction" in an "overbought" market.

However, in the midst of this "correction," we would do well to remember that TQM, Lean Production, or whatever name you give it, is probably the most important new methodology for organizing work to come along since mass production. Properly applied, this methodology improves reliability, cycle time, safety, and customer satisfaction, and dramatically reduces costs.

Section Three

The Quality Consultant's Perspective

To the dedicated quality consultant, quality is life—the be all and end all, the alpha and omega, the top concern and the bottom line. How you get it, keep it, grow it, and replicate it are their constant ruminations; consequently, the "cud" of the consultant is often coarse and pithy.

After seeing **W. Edwards Deming** in action for the first time, I dubbed him "the Isaiah of management." He was like a bold Old Testament prophet, warning leaders of companies and nations of impending doom unless they turned to the standards of quality. Like most prophets, he was right, but that didn't make it easier to hear and hearken to the message.

Even to people who were used to being spoon-fed the warm milk of public relations, Deming and his colleagues often served tough meat—reengineering of processes and of realignment of people and other resources to produce a better product and service. He was consistent, even relentless, but right, and that made might in the fight for competitive advantage.

In his chapter, **W. Edwards Deming**, consultant to management, declares that "the heart of the transformation is the power of intrinsic motivation" and that "it all starts at the top." **Armand V. Feigenbaum**, president and CEO of General Systems Company, Inc., notes that "transforming from a make-it-quicker-and-cheaper past to a make-it-better future is the single most demanding task of leadership." **Joseph M. Juran**, chairman, and **G. Howland Blackiston**, president of the Juran Institute, Inc., write: "Charting a new course requires executives to create a universal way of thinking about quality—one that applies to all functions and levels—and to exercise extensive personal leadership."

Philip B. Crosby, founder of Philip Crosby Associates and Career IV, writes: "People respond to the standards of their leaders, and they perform to the level expected of them." **Bob King**, Executive Director of Goal/QPC, makes a convincing argument that "TQM does improve the bottom line." **Richard M. Miller**, principal of Compass Consulting Group, says that if TQM is to become a way of life, "every leader must look inward and determine his or her own principles and beliefs." **James C. Shaffer**, vice-president and principal of Towers Perrin, says that "petty politics, antiquated policies, nonsensical bureaucracy, and mismanaged communication conspire to produce unhappy customers."

Patrick L. Townsend, president, and **Joan E. Gebhardt**, senior partner, of Townsend & Gebhardt, question whether quality is "a campaign that failed" and conclude that "the final outcome is far from a foregone conclusion." **David A. Tierno**, national director of Ernst & Young's Management Consulting Group, tells us how to achieve quality in professional services. And **Richard S. Wellins**, senior vice president of Development Dimensions International, wonders whether quality is "forging ahead or falling behind" and reports that "many TQM-driven organizations have trouble achieving a transformation."

The quality consultant tends to see life in terms of the simple dichotomy of forging ahead or falling behind: "You're either improving, or you're losing ground." At times, the leaders who listen to these shrill voices must grow weary and wish to cry, "enough is enough." There is such a thing as battle fatigue. And even the dedicated quality consultant might understand losing a battle occasionally, as long as ultimately they win the war.

Chapter 24

Quality Leadership

by W. Edwards Deming,
Consultant to Management

*The changes needed now in quality relate to
how people are managed and motivated—
more people must take pride in their work.*

THE possibility to improve the future under the present system of management is slight. The present system runs by the economics of *win-lose:* I win, you lose. I can win only if you lose.

We need a transformation to a new economics of win-win cooperation where everyone comes out better. There will still be inequalities; some people will win more than others, but everyone will gain. Everybody loses under the system that nourishes win-lose thinking and the race to be number one. We must abolish the merit system and systems of incentive, as they choke intrinsic motivation. We must abolish annual ratings, performance appraisals, even grades in school. We must create leaders who work to help their people, who know how the work of the group fits into the aims of the company, who focus on the customers, and who understand variation and use statistical calculation to determine if there are people outside the system in need of help.

What is the heart of the transformation? It is the release of the power of intrinsic motivation. How? By creating joy, pride, and happiness in work; joy and pride in learning. What will make for quality products and services as well as renewed leadership in the 1990s? The prime requisite for achievement of any aim, including quality, is joy in work. This will require change. When everyone has a part in the change, fear of change will vanish.

My own estimate is that today only two in 100 people in management take joy in their work. The other 98 are under stress, not from work or overwork, but from nonproductive work—churning money, battling for or against takeover, and so on. Most of the 98 have their eyes on a good rating and don't dare contribute innovation to their work.

Transformation Required

About 95 percent of changes made in management today make no improvement. Transformation to a new style of management is required to achieve optimization—a process of orchestrating the efforts of all components to achieve the stated aim. Optimization is management's job. Everybody wins with optimization. Anything less than optimization of the whole system brings eventual loss to every component in the system. Any group should have as its aim optimization over time of the system that the group operates in.

Time will bring changes that must be managed and predicted so far as possible. Growth in size and complexity of a system, and changes with time of external forces (competition, new products, new requirements) require overall management of components. Management of a system may require imagination. An added responsibility of management is to be ready to change the boundary of the system to better serve the aim.

Management and leaders have another job—to govern their own future, not to be victims of circumstance. For example, instead of taking the loss from spurts in production to meet demand, followed by losses from valleys from decreased demand, management might flatten production, or increase production at an economical rate. Another possibility is to become agile and efficient in meeting peaks and valleys in demand. For example, management may change the course of the company and the industry by anticipating the needs of customers for new products or new services.

Preparation for the future includes lifelong learning for all employees. It includes constant scanning of the environment (technical, social, economic) to perceive need for innovation, new product, new service, or innovation of method. A company can, to some extent, govern its own future.

What business ought we to be in five years from now? Ten years from now? The components of a system could, under stable conditions, manage themselves to accomplish their aim. A possible example is a string quartet. Each member supports the other three. None of them is there to attract individual attention.

An important job of management is to recognize and manage the interdependence between components, to resolve conflicts and remove barriers to cooperation. A job description must do more than prescribe motions: do this, do that, this way, that way. It must tell what the work will be used for, how the work contributes to the aim of the system. Harm comes from internal competition and conflict, and from the fear that is generated.

Competition leads to loss as people pulling in opposite directions on a rope only exhaust themselves—they go nowhere. What we need is cooperation. Every example of cooperation is one of benefit and gains to those who cooperate. Cooperation is especially productive in a well-managed system.

The prevailing style of management must be transformed. The individual components of the system, instead of being competitive, will reinforce each other for optimization and accomplishment of the aim of the system.

The first step is transformation of the individual. This transformation is discontinuous. It comes from understanding the system of profound knowledge. The individual transformed, will perceive new meaning to his life, to events, to numbers, and to interactions between people. Once the individual understands the system of profound knowledge, he will apply its principles in every relationship with other people. He will have a basis for judgment of his own decisions and for transformation of the organizations that he belongs to.

We have grown up in a climate of competition between people, teams, departments, divisions, pupils, schools, and universities. We have been taught by economists that competition will solve our problems. Actually, competition is destructive. It would be better if everyone would work together as a system, with the aim for everybody to win. What we need is cooperation and transformation to a new style of management.

The purpose of a school of business should not be to perpetuate the present style of management (competition), but to transform it to one of optimization. Students of engineering may learn the new tools and theories of engineering, but their successful application requires new methods of management. In other words, the purpose of a school should be to prepare students for the future, not for the past.

Most people today are still living under the tyranny of the win-lose style of management. The huge, long-range losses caused by this competitive style have led us into decline.

Win-lose is the wrong philosophy, and as a business strategy it often merely seeks to choke the competition. Although it was an effi-cient tactic in an ever-expanding market, the principle of *I win only if you lose* has run out of steam. We need to learn to live and work in the world that now envelops us. We must, if we wish to survive, change to the principle of win-win. Compete, sure, but in the framework of cooperation first so everybody wins. Business survival is dependent on transformation to the new economics of win-win cooperation.

Route to Transformation

Transformation is not automatic. It must be learned and led. If executives are to successfully respond to the myriad changes that shake the world, they will need to undergo a transformation to a new style of management.

The route to take is what I call *profound knowledge*—composed of four interrelated parts: Appreciation for a system, knowledge of variation, theory of knowledge, and psychology. The system of pro-found knowledge provides a lens through which we can understand and optimize our organizations.

1. Appreciation for a system. A system is a network of interdepen-dent components that work together to accomplish the aim of the system. A system must have an aim. Without an aim, there is no system. The aim proposed here for any organization is for everybody to gain—stockhold-ers, employees, suppliers, customers, community, and the environ-ment—over the long term. The performance of anyone is governed largely by the system that he works in. The greater the independence between components, the greater will be the need for communication and cooperation between them. Also, the greater will be the need for overall management. The obligation of any component is to contribute its best to the system, not to maximize its own production, profit, or sales, nor any other competitive measure. Optimization for everyone concerned should be the basis for negotiation between any two people, between divisions, between union and management, between compa-nies, between competitors, and between countries. Everyone would gain.

2. Knowledge of variation. There will always be variation between people, in output, in service, and in product. What is the variation trying to tell us about a process, and about the people who work in it? Management requires knowledge about interaction of forces. Interaction may reinforce efforts or nullify efforts. Management of people requires knowledge of the effect of the sys-tem on the performance of people. Knowledge of dependence and interdependence between people, groups, divisions, companies, and countries, is helpful.

3. Theory of knowledge. The theory of knowledge helps us to understand that management in any form is prediction and that a statement, if it conveys knowledge, predicts future outcomes, with risk of being wrong, and that it fits without failure observations of the past. Rational prediction requires theory and builds knowledge through systematic revision and extension of theory based on comparison of prediction with observation. Information, no matter how complete and speedy, is not knowledge.

4. Psychology of change. Psychology helps us to understand people, interaction between people and circumstances, interaction between customer and supplier, interaction between teacher and pupil, interaction between a manager and his people, and any system of management. People are born with intrinsic motivation, with a need for relationships with others, with a need for love and esteem, with a natural inclination to learn, and with a right to enjoy their work. Good management preserves these positive innate attributes.

In the transformed organization, teams, departments, divisions, and plants do not compete. Instead, each area makes choices directed at maximum benefit for the whole organization. In an optimized system, everybody benefits—stockholders, suppliers, employees, and customers.

Quality Starts at the Top

The common mistake is the supposition that quality is ensured by the improvement of process alone—that operations going off without blemish will ensure quality. Good operations are essential, yet they do not ensure quality. There are four prongs of quality and four ways to improve quality: innovation in product and service; innovation in process; improvement of existing product and service; and improvement of existing process.

Quality is made in the boardroom. A bank that failed last week may have had excellent operations—speed at the tellers' windows, few mistakes in bank statements. But the cause of failure was bad management, not operations.

A good question for anybody in business to ask is *What business are we in?* To do well what we are doing? Yes, but this is not enough. We must keep asking *What product or service would help our customers more?* We must think about the future. What will we be making five years from now? Ten years from now?

The absence of defects does not necessarily build business. Something more is required. In the case of automobiles, for example, the customer may be interested in performance. He might include under performance not just acceleration but also how the car behaves on ice, how the car steers at high speed, how it rides over bumps. Does it jump and skid on a rough road? How do the air conditioner and heater work?

The customer may also be interested in style—not just the appearance of the automobile, but legibility of the levers that the driver may try to read. Comfort of passengers may be important. Performance and style, whatever these words mean in the minds of customers, must show constant improvement.

Everyone is in favor of improving quality, but many people misunderstand quality, as evident by looking at some of their suggestions for improving quality. Just add automation, new machinery, more computers, gadgets, hard work, best efforts, merit system, MBO, MBR, rankings, inspections, incentive pay, work standards, specifications, and motivation.

What's wrong with these suggestions? The fallacies are obvious—every one of them ducks the responsibility of management. Quality is determined by top management. It can't be delegated. An essential ingredient, profound knowledge, is often missing. There is no substitute for knowledge. Hard work, best efforts, and best intentions will not by themselves produce quality or a market.

The quality of the output of a company can't be better than the quality at the top. Quality is made by top management. Job security and jobs are dependent on management's foresight to design products and services that will entice customers and build a market; and their foresight to be ready, ahead of the customer, to modify products and services.

Present Practice vs. Better Practice

The prevailing practices of management cause huge monetary losses and huge waste whose magnitudes can neither be evaluated nor measured. These losses must be managed by replacing faulty present practices with better practices.

Present: Have no constancy of purpose. Engage in short-term thinking with emphasis on immediate results. Think only in the present tense. Keep up the price of the company's stock. Maintain dividends. Fail to optimize over time. Make this quarter look good. Ship everything on hand at the end of the month (or quarter). Never mind its quality.

Show it as accounts receivable. Defer till next quarter repairs, maintenance, and orders for material. **Better**: Adopt and publish constancy of purpose. Do some long-term planning. Ask this question: Where do we wish to be five years from now? Then, by what method?

Present: Rank people, salespeople, teams, and divisions; reward at the top, punishment at the bottom. Have a merit system with annual appraisal of people, a form of ranking. Compensate people with incentive pay and pay based on performance. **Better**: Abolish ranking. Manage the whole company as a system. Make every component and every division contribute toward optimization of the system. Abolish the merit system in your company. Study the capability of the system. Study the management of people. Abolish incentive pay and pay based on performance. Give everyone a chance to take pride in his work.

Present: Fail to manage the organization as a system. Think of the components as individual profit centers. Everybody loses when individuals, teams, and divisions in the company work as individual profit centers, not for optimization of the whole organization. The various components thus rob themselves of long-term profit, joy in work, and other desirable measures of quality of life. People lose hope of ever understanding the relationship of their work to the work of others; they do not talk with each other. **Better**: Manage the company as a system. Enlarge judiciously the boundaries of the system. See that the system includes the future. Encourage communication. Make physical arrangements for informal dialogue between people in the various components of the company, regardless of level or position. Encourage continual learning and advancement. Form groups for comradeship in athletics, music, history, a language, etc., and provide facilities for study-groups.

Present: Manage by objective (MBO). Set numerical goals. Manage by results (MBR). Take immediate action on any fault, complaint, delay, accident, or breakdown. **Better**: Study the theory of a system. Manage the components for optimization of the aim of the system. Work on a method for improving a process. Understand and improve the processes that produce defects, faults, etc. Understand the distinction between common causes of variation and special causes to understand the kind of action to take.

Present: Delegate quality to someone or some group. Buy materials and services at lowest bid. **Better**: Keep accountability for quality with the top management. Estimate the total cost of use of materials and services—first cost (purchase price) plus predicted cost of problems in use of them, their effect on the quality of final product.

Leading and Managing People

Transformation in any organization will take place under a leader who possesses authority of office, knowledge, personality, persuasive power, and tact.

How may he accomplish transformation? First he has theory. He understands why the transformation would bring gains to his organization and to all the people that his organization deals with. Second, he feels compelled to accomplish the transformation as an obligation to himself and to his organization. Third, he is a practical man. He has a plan, step by step. But what is in his own head is not enough. He must convince and change enough people in power to make it happen. He possesses persuasive power. He understands people.

One is born with intrinsic motivation, self-esteem, dignity, cooperation, curiosity, and joy in learning. These attributes are high at the beginning of life, but are gradually crushed by the forces of destruction. These forces cause humiliation, fear, self-defense, and competition for gold stars, high grades, or high ratings on the job. They lead anyone to play to win, not for fun. They crush out joy in learning, joy on the job, and innovation. Extrinsic motivation (complete resignation to external pressures) gradually replaces intrinsic motivation, self-esteem, and dignity.

Instead of judging people, ranking them, and putting them into slots, the aim of the leader should be to help people optimize the system so that everybody will gain. The new role of the leader of people after transformation has 14 components. The leader:

1. Understands and conveys to his people the meaning of a system. He explains the aims of the system. He teaches his people to understand how the work of the group supports these aims.

2. Helps people to see themselves as components in a system, to work in cooperation with preceding stages and following stages toward optimizing the efforts of all stages to achieve the aim.

3. Understands that people are different from each other. He tries to create interest, challenge, and joy for everybody in work. He tries to optimize the family background, education, skills, hopes, and abilities of everyone. This is not ranking people—it is recognizing differences between people, and trying to put everybody in position for development.

4. Learns unceasingly. He encourages his people to study. He provides, when possible and feasible, seminars and courses for advancement of learning. He encourages continued education.

5. Is a coach and counsel, not a judge.

6. Understands a stable system. He understands the interaction between people and the circumstances that they work in. He understands that the performance of anyone who can learn a skill will come to a stable state—upon which further lessons will not bring improvement of performance. He knows that in the stable state, it is distracting to tell the worker about a mistake.

7. Has three sources of power: authority of office; knowledge; and personality, persuasive power, and tact. He develops the second and third, rarely relies on number one. However, he has an obligation to use authority of office to change the process—equipment, materials, and methods—to bring improvement.

8. Studies results with the aim to improve his performance as a manager of people.

9. Tries to discover who, if anybody, outside the system needs special help. This can be done with simple calculations, if there are individual figures on production or failures. Special help may be a simple arrangement of work, or it might be more complicated.

10. Creates trust. He creates an environment that encourages freedom and innovation.

11. Does not expect perfection.

12. Listens and learns without passing judgment on him whom he listens to.

13. Holds an informal, spontaneous, unhurried conversation with every one of his people at least once a year, not for judgment, merely to listen. The purpose would be to develop understanding of his people, and their aims, hopes and fears.

14. He understands the benefits of cooperation and the losses from competition between people and between groups.

These 14 components follow naturally in an organization guided by profound knowledge.

Chapter 25

Leaders in Quality

by Armand V. Feigenbaum, President and CEO of
General Systems Co., Inc.

*Being a quality leader has become crucial to
the economic strength and business future of
companies around the globe.*

I SEE the potential for an enormous explosion of a new American competitive discipline emerging from the economic crucible in which business, industry, and government have been immersed over the past decade. This discipline is based upon the rejection of a false business doctrine: the way to succeed is to make products and offer services quicker and cheaper, finance them cleverly, sell them hard, and manage in a way that gets the ideas out of the boss's head into the hands of the workers.

The new discipline builds on a very different doctrine: *the best way to make products and services quicker and cheaper is to make them better and the best way to manage is to encourage the abilities and know-how of every person in the organization.*

Three Imperatives

There are three imperatives to bring about the competitive transformation we need.

• *Quality leadership has become crucial to our industrial strength.* Our research tells us that nine out of 10 buyers in the major international markets now make quality equal to or more important than price in their purchase decisions. Our comparable estimate for a decade ago was that only four customers out of ten thought and bought this way. This doubling of buyer emphasis on quality in a decade is one of the biggest changes in modern marketplace history. The reason is a fundamental social and economic change of historic proportions: *the lifestyles of today's consumers and the work processes of companies now depend almost completely upon the reliable, predictable operation of products and services with little tolerance for any failures.* How can a small telemarketing company remain in business when its state-of-the-art telephone system breaks down every other day? Warranty or no warranty, an unreliable product breeds a customer looking for another supplier—foreign or otherwise.

• *Domestic industry and education must become international, and national government become more focused on international commercial support skills.* Three out of four products made in America are now targets for strong import competition—and these numbers will only increase because quality competition has gone global. Nearly all American non-defense manufactured products will have import vulnerability this decade. American services are rapidly becoming similarly vulnerable. To protect their position in their home market, companies must now design, build, and sell their domestic product lines and service offerings with the potential also for supremacy in the international marketplace, even though there isn't yet much import competition or interest in exporting. And they must do this quickly.

• *Transforming from a make-it-quicker-and-cheaper past to a make-it-better future is the single most demanding task of leadership today.* In the last decade, the quality role of the senior manager was to be number one cheerleader, with fireworks displays of executive speechmaking, together with an emphasis on establishing a group of quality improvement islands without bridges—what I call partial quality control. The quality role of senior managers today is far more important and far more performance-driven. It is to have the personal know-how to develop the quality playbook and to be its quarterback on the field.

Six Traits of Quality Companies

To fill this demanding role, executives must recognize six characteristics of companies practicing the new competitive discipline and know how to apply the human-based quality process systems technology to achieve the competitive transformation. This technology involves the design and installation of total quality systems to improve quality and reduce costs in both manufacturing and services. These systems are based upon the systems technology of total quality control (TQC) and total quality management (TQM).

• *The rigorous objective never to miss in producing the important customer results.*

• *The emphasis on establishing stretch quality improvement goals on the basis required to assure number one competitive leadership, never on the basis of just doing better than last year.*

• *Superior use and empowerment of human resources at all levels, union and non-union employees, middle management, and front-line supervision.*

• *An emphasis on blindsiding the competition with innovative quality management process approaches that get there with better results first and continue to pay off over a long period.*

• *Recognizing that a customer who is happy with you means a six or seven times greater likelihood of return sales than a customer who is just satisfied with you.*

• *An emphasis that what you measure right, you manage right, and the quality of measurement is the key to the quality of leadership.*

Companies with these characteristics make quality a way of focusing the company on the competitive discipline of serving the customer—whether it be the end user or the man and woman at the next desk or work station. They make quality the way of achieving customer satisfaction, human resource leadership, and low costs.

Quality Leadership

Quality leadership isn't primarily measured in terms of quality defects—it's measured in terms of the total customer perception of quality. The quality of the product the customer receives is simply one important part among many in a total service support effort. Consumers demand reliable, predictable products and services with little tolerance for the time and cost of failure.

Quality leadership depends on accelerating the increase of things gone right that buyers want, not merely reducing the things gone wrong. The characteristics of companies that are quality leaders are remarkably similar. A world-class company:

• *Never misses in producing important business results.* It delivers better business performance than its competition quarter after quarter, year after year. There is a lot of debate, of course, about whether this quarter-to-quarter pressure is a good thing. But a world-class company thrives on this heat.

• *Establishes aggressive business targets and then stretches those goals as necessary for competitive leadership.* The stretch performance is never an ambiguous, quickly forgotten goal. It's established as a realistic target that is far more demanding than that of the competition—and is relentlessly achieved.

• *Supports its goals by progressively better use of its existing resources—especially its human resources.* In a world-class company, good management means *everyone* focuses obsessively on continuously making quality, cost, and delivery improvements that build better customer satisfaction.

• *Blindsides the competition with innovative management approaches that establish better results first, and then continue to pay off over time.* The "key" to quality leadership is an emphasis on being first in "*in*visible-to-the-competition" improvements in areas like product development time cycles.

• *Sells the company itself as strongly as it sells its products or services.* A world-class company concentrates on being good and getting credit for it. An important purchasing factor is what customers perceive about the company's management and work force and about the company's belief in its own product and service quality.

• *Realizes that what you measure right you manage right.* This strength is a key to why a world leader can identify and prioritize important business improvement areas of its internal resources and in its industry. With measurements in place, action for quick improvement can be taken.

Urgency for Quality

We can't improve productivity or profitability without first improving quality. And that requires executives to rethink and often to restructure their whole approach to management.

In my judgment, there are three keys to accomplish total quality: 1) meaningful quality research—not just dependence upon the loosely connected string of quality anecdotes that has diminished the credibility of some forms of quality education; 2) genuine organization-wide quality implementation—not just the fireworks display of quality awareness programs that has characterized some corporate quality programs; and 3) rigorous verification of quality results—not just some casual observations.

The challenge we face is to build bridges among these various research, execution, and verification islands. In earlier years, the lack of this integration has been a principal reason why important fields from the early human relations work through to some aspects of operations research and information management have tended to quietly die and be buried without autopsy or become another separate silo on a university campus or department in a corporate staff. This is why queasiness about total quality continues to exist in parts of the very university, business, and government institutions to which total quality can bring the largest contribution.

High-Quality Products

We tend to forget that standards of product quality are customer determinations and that quality today means something different than what it meant 10 years ago.

The marketplace's growing response to product economy, reliability, and safety is changing the definition of quality. That change is reflected in the consumer's return to the basic concept of quality as the true value per unit of price. Success in the marketplace depends on consistently anticipating and meeting these quality expectations.

To satisfy these expectations, business must recognize that the purchase price is only the beginning of a product's cost, and that buying decisions are based increasingly on total life-cycle costs (initial cost plus maintenance) of new products.

Another crucial management consideration is that, as production rates increase, companies must be prepared to achieve progressively higher levels of quality. The number of dissatisfied customers increases dramatically despite the apparently minimal failure rate.

In today's market, this exposure offers potentially high risks of product liability claims and even product recall. And we can see that the costly impact of negative customer reaction does not necessarily result from high failure rates, but instead from the total number of dissatisfied customers. It is clearly no longer enough for management to devote its attention to getting the product to market without considering the quality needed to assure continued market success. Poor quality never disappears once it leaves the plant.

Low-Quality Costs

Many of us have been conditioned to think of business mainly in terms of price, production, and sales, with quality often an incidental factor. Because quality-related activities are often fragmented and departmentalized, and because quality control in the past often rested on inspection, testing, and certain analytical techniques, quality costs became difficult to control.

But when total quality systems are installed—a strategic, corporate-wide approach encompassing everything from customer expectation to product design and production—the cost of quality can be managed as an integral part of corporate accounting.

We have measured quality costs in this manner for many years and found that 65 cents of every quality dollar is likely to be spent on failure costs, including scrap, spoilage, and reworked material. About 25 cents goes for appraisal costs of inspection and testing. Only 10 cents is spent on prevention costs—on addressing the practices that allow defective parts of unsalable units to be designed, produced, and sold in the first place.

Our experience shows that most companies are already spending enough on quality. In fact, 10 cents or more of every sales dollar billed in many firms today is spent on quality. Too much, however, is misused and wasted on failure and appraisal costs, and not enough goes to assure product quality the first time around. The total-quality approach has demonstrated that it can produce a return on investment that not only reduces quality costs by a third or more, but makes new funds available as either greater profits or cash flow for investment in company growth.

Peak Use of Existing Resources

In addition to high-quality products and low-quality costs, companies need a third component in their total-quality equation to compete effectively: the peak use of existing resources.

Successful firms are responding by assessing the value of productivity not simply as output, but as more salable, good-quality output per unit of input. This changing concept of productivity is highly significant. Many production operations that reported 85 to 90 percent efficiency by traditional non-quality-oriented standards were discovered to be at best only 55 to 60 percent efficient when measured against customer- and market-oriented barometers of productivity.

An immediately available resource to close this productivity gap can be found in the lost capacity prevalent in even the most organized plants—the facilities and labor force needed to rework unsatisfactory parts, maintain buffer stocks, replace recalled products, or retest rejects. We have found that from 15 to 40 percent of total productive capacity can be wasted on these activities. Effective quality systems can eliminate the problems that the lost capacity exists to handle, and can redirect the wasted money, manpower, and energy into development and sales. Simply put, good quality and productivity mean the most effective use of existing corporate resources.

The challenge of achieving quality must be faced positively, even aggressively. To compete successfully, corporate leadership must recognize that quality is now a strategic business goal. This means establishing corporate-wide priorities for quality achievement and budgeting the resources needed to meet those priorities.

Rethink and Restructure

Implementation often requires management to rethink and restructure its approach to quality. Our experience shows that 80 to 90 percent of the quality problems that need to be solved lie outside the province of traditional quality-control departments. To be effective, new company-wide quality systems must be organized as primary managerial, economic, and technical responsibilities involving key individuals in the engineering, production, and marketing chain. In this context, quality systems become an operating structure for harnessing the manpower, the machines, and the information needed to meet the rigorous new market requirements of corporation and consumer alike—consistent customer satisfaction with quality and reasonable quality cost.

So formidable have these requirements become that quality-minded and profit-minded have become fused into a single goal, revolutionizing the emphasis on production and market expansion that dominated management thinking in the past. Inflation and its impact on consumer expectations have forged the concept of quality into a fundamental management principle. The enterprises that prosper in the years ahead will be the ones that apply it well.

Implementing Total Quality

What would you call a company that has adopted a "we'll always fix it for you" basic quality policy in dealing with its customers? Honorable? Yes. Good intentioned? Probably. Failure-driven? Absolutely.

In many companies a "hidden organization" exists in the factory and office which results from the failure of the firm to do the job right the first time. This wastes from 15 to 40 percent of total productive capacity. There is no better way to improve productivity than to convert this hidden organization to productive use, and modern implementation of quality systems provides the most effective and practical way to do it.

As the American consumer continues to place increasing demands on American products and services, businesses need to be ready to respond to customer demands. After all, quality is what the customer says it is. Clearly the answer to meeting these needs lies in the implementation of quality systems that address the consumers' needs.

Before business can effectively address these needs, the following must first take place:

• CEOs and COOs become the number one quality implementers, not the number one quality cheerleaders

• Chief financial officers apply their financial skills to evaluating a company's cost of quality and help an organization to improve it instead of thinking of the next creative leveraged buyout financial technique

• The title "Professor of Quality" joins the ranks of the finance and marketing professionals at leading business schools

• Consumer needs are addressed as quality becomes a fundamental way of managing a company.

Quality is today's most powerful but toughest-to-execute corporate strategy for simultaneously achieving both customer satisfaction and lower costs. The basic premise of business success for many companies in the 1970s and early 1980s was to make products and offer services quicker and cheaper; sell them hard; and finance them cleverly.

Today, making products better is the way to make them quicker and cheaper, but the business habits of the past die hard. Changing a company from a make-it-cheaper-and-quicker past to a make-it-better future is one of the most demanding corporate tasks of management.

Implementation of a quality control system requires management integrity and commitment. Many companies talk about their firm adherence to providing the best quality goods and services available. Businesses need to understand and take the necessary steps to ensure the quality standards which customers demand.

Benchmarks of TQM

Those companies which respond to customers' demands for better quality products and services must first understand the basic benchmarks of TQM if they hope to succeed in the implementation of a successful total quality system. These benchmarks include:

• Quality is not a department but instead a systemic process that extends throughout the company

• Quality must be organized to recognize that while it is everybody's job in the company, it will become nobody's job unless the company's quality process is correctly structured to support both the quality work of individuals as well as the quality teamwork among departments

• Quality must be perceived in this process to be what the buyer says it is—not what an engineer or marketer or general manager says it is.

• Quality is an ethic and that widespread quality improvement is achieved only through help, participation, and zealotry from all the men and women in the company and its suppliers

• Quality improvement is continuous and requires the application of both new and existing quality technology ranging from quality design techniques to computer-aided cost measurements—not merely dusting off a few traditional control techniques. Quality is a continuous process and one which will significantly grow as businesses realize that the key to their competitive advantage lies in the implementation of quality systems.

When implementing a total quality system, it is important to remember that it takes a relentlessly disciplined methodology to establish and maintain a system—just as it does for finance, marketing, and production.

Three-Phase Approach

Once a company understands the basic benchmarks of quality it is ready to undertake the necessary phases to implement a total quality control system: analysis, planning and programming, and construction and implementation.

1. *Analysis:* Determines the strengths and weaknesses of existing work, teamwork and work process activities and their control throughout the organization based upon comparison to the best industry standards we have developed through over 20 years of international experience. This takes place with complete customer personnel teamwork participation and with emphasis on development of organization-wide total quality understanding and commitment.

2. *Planning and Programming:* Necessary improvements shown by the analysis to have the top priority for the business with special attention given to urgently needed improvements and achieving a positive cash flow. This takes place with the development of in-line understanding and organization-wide "buy-in" for the improvement plans.

3. *Construction and Implementation:* Design, develop, review, and implement the necessary improvements, integrated with existing organizational strengths into a complete system with measurements and controls. This takes place with the development of job-related, organization-wide total quality knowledge, skills, and attitudes.

By following this integrated approach, businesses have learned and experienced firsthand that quality is today's best investment in competitiveness. The return on investment results from strong total quality programs are excellent. Principal reasons include:

• Higher sales results in today's market from very high quality perceived by buyers.

• Improvement in quality costs—the full costs of quality programs. These quality costs today account for 10 to 20 percent and much more of the total sales dollar in some companies—nonetheless, the importance and practicality of quality cost measurement as a major quality improvement tool is still not well understood in some of these companies.

Quality and cost are a sum, not a difference—complementary, not conflicting, objectives. Quality implementation is the only competitive resource tool that businesses can rely on in their effort to win and maintain marketplace and economic dominance. The task that lies before business is to produce products and services that meet the customers' demands. This will require the production of essentially perfect products. Difficult? Yes. Impossible? No.

Chapter 26

Universal Approach to Managing for Quality

by Joseph M. Juran, Chairman, and G. Howland Blackiston, President of Juran Institute, Inc.

The quality crisis requires a new direction—a unified, universal approach that's integrated with your strategic plan.

THE crisis in quality won't go away. Competition in quality will continue, and so will the impact of poor quality on society. Societies now live behind protective quality dikes.

We need to chart a new direction in managing for quality. Here are just three reasons.

• Traditional ways of dealing with the quality crisis are inadequate; in fact, our adherence to those ways helped create the crisis. A new course must be charted, requiring some major breaks with tradition.

• Charting a new course requires executives to create a universal way of thinking about quality—one that applies to all functions and levels—and to exercise extensive personal leadership and participation.

• Since most senior executives have limited experience and training in managing for quality, they must be educated and armed with a new approach—one that can be readily implanted into the company's strategic business planning and not be rejected by the company's immune system.

A Unified Approach

A company that wants to chart a new course in managing for quality must create an all-pervasive unity. Everyone will know the new direction and will be stimulated to go there. Creating such unity requires dealing with some powerful resisting forces. These forces are, for the most part, due to non-uniformities:

• multiple functions in the company—product development, manufacturing, office operations, etc.—each regarding its function as something unique and special.

• multiple levels in the company hierarchy, from the CEO to the nonsupervisory worker; these levels differ with respect to responsibility, prerequisite experience and training, etc.

• multiple product lines: large and complex systems, mass production or regulated products; these product lines differ in their markets, technology, restraints, etc.

Such non-uniformities are realities in any company, and they constitute serious obstacles to unity of direction. These obstacles can be overcome if we can find a universal way of thinking about quality—a thought process which fits all functions, all levels, all product lines.

Quality Trilogy

Managing for quality consists of three basic quality processes: quality planning, quality control, and quality improvement. These universal processes are interrelated.

Each of these processes is universal; it is carried out by an unvarying sequence of activities.

Quality Planning. Quality planning creates a process for meeting quality goals under operating conditions. The subject of the planning can be anything: an office process for producing documents; an engineering process for designing products; a factory process for producing goods; a service process for responding to customers' requests.

Quality Control. The responsibility of operations is to run the quality process at optimal effectiveness to meet quality goals. But due to deficiencies in the original planning, the process typically runs at a high level of chronic waste—waste that the planning process failed to plan out. Because the waste is inherent in the process, the operating forces are unable to get rid of it. Instead, they carry out "quality control"—keep the waste from getting worse. If it does get worse, they bring in a fire-fighting team to determine the cause. Once the cause is determined, and corrective action taken, the process again falls into the zone defined by "quality control" limits.

Quality Improvement. In due course, the chronic waste falls to a much lower level—a result of purposeful action taken by upper management to introduce a new managerial process into the system of managers' responsibilities—the quality improvement process. Quality improvement is the process for breaking through to unprecedented levels of performance at levels of quality distinctly superior to planned performance. This process is implemented in addition to quality control, not instead of it.

This trilogy is not new; in fact, we see some interesting parallels to the financial processes of budgeting, cost control, and cost reduction for profit improvement.

Evaluating Performance

When senior managers evaluate their performance in the basic processes, generally they rate themselves
- low in quality planning
- high in quality control
- decidedly low in quality improvement.

Incidentally, the high marks in quality control only suggest that they are meeting established goals traditionally set to perpetuate past performance, the root of the quality crisis.

During visits to companies, we have found a recurring pattern of priorities and assets devoted to the three processes, and the prevailing pattern is not consistent with the managers' assessment of their own effectiveness. That assessment would suggest that they should put the control process on hold while increasing the emphasis on quality planning and especially on quality improvement.

To illustrate the need for raising the priority on quality improvement, we cite three baffling case examples.
- Several years ago the executive vice president of a large multinational rubber company made an around-the-world-trip with his chairman to visit their major subsidiaries and secure inputs for strategic business planning. They found much similarity with respect to productivity, quality, etc., except for Japan. The Japanese company was outperforming all others by a wide margin. The Americans were

mystified as to why. They had toured the Japanese plant, and to their eyes the Japanese were using the same materials, equipment, and processes, and yet they were making more and better products from the same facilities.

• A few years ago I conducted research into the yields of the processes that make large scale integrated circuits. To assure comparability, I concentrated on a single product type—the 16K random access memory (16K RAM). I found that Japanese yields were two to three times the Western yields despite similarity in the basic processes.

• The managers of American steel companies report that their cost of poor quality (just for factory processes) runs at about 10 to 15 percent of sales. Some of these steel companies have business connections with Japanese steel companies, and the respective managers exchange visits. During these visits, the Americans learn that in Japanese steel mills, which use comparable equipment and processes, the cost of poor quality runs at about 1 to 2 percent of sales. Again, American managers don't know why. Some don't even believe the Japanese figures.

My explanation is that the Japanese, since the early 1950s, have been improving quality at a pace far greater than that of the West. In numbers of quality improvement projects completed, the Japanese pace has exceeded that of the West by an order of magnitude, year after year.

A New Course

We must change our priorities with regard to the three quality processes. This change in priorities represents a new course. Underlying this new course is the quality trilogy. As a universal way of thinking about quality, the trilogy offers a unified approach for multiple purposes, including training in managing for quality, and strategic quality planning.

Training. Many American companies are breaking with tradition. In the past, their training in managing for quality was limited to managers and engineers in the quality department. They now extend such training to all functions. Since this is a sizeable undertaking, companies set up corporate task forces to plan the approach. These task forces run into serious obstacles as they attempt to design and establish many different training courses to fit specific functions, levels and product lines. What they need is a universal training course that will apply to all audiences, but with provision for special case examples as warranted.

The universal approach based on quality planning, control and improvement meets that need. Training courses consist of sequences of steps. These sequences apply to all functions, levels, and product lines.

Quality Planning:
• Identify customers, both internal and external
• Determine customer needs
• Develop product features that respond to customer needs
• Set goals that meet needs of customers and suppliers
• Develop process to produce the product features
• Prove process meets quality goals during operations

Quality Control:
• Choose what to control
• Choose units of measurement
• Establish measurement
• Establish standards of performance
• Measure actual performance
• Interpret the difference
• Take action on the difference

Quality Improvement:
• Prove the need for improvement
• Identify specific projects for improvement
• Organize to guide the projects
• Diagnose to find the causes
• Provide remedies
• Prove remedies are effective under operating conditions
• Provide for control to hold the gains

Strategic quality planning. The quality trilogy parallels the American approach to strategic business planning. Companies are already experienced in business planning; they are comfortable with the concepts of financial budgets, cost control, and cost reduction. We can benefit from that experience by grafting the quality trilogy onto the existing business planning structure, thereby reducing the risk that the implant will be rejected by the company's immune system.

To formulate and coordinate the activity companywide, set up a quality planning council, consisting of corporate officers; the chairman is the CEO or an executive vice president. The council establishes corporate quality policies, goals, and plans; provides the resources needed to carry out the plans; reviews performance against plans and goals; and revises the managerial merit rating system to reflect performance against quality goals.

Setting goals. Traditionally, goal setting has been heavily based on past performance. This practice tends to perpetuate the sins of the past as failure-prone designs are carried over into new models. Wasteful processes are not challenged if managers meet the budgets, which assume that the wastes are a fate to be endured. All this must change. Goals for parameters affecting external customers must be based on meeting competition in the marketplace. Goals for parameters affecting internal customers must be based on getting rid of traditional wastes.

Infrastructure. Much of the infrastructure needed for strategic quality planning has long been in place to serve the needs of divisions, functions, factories, etc. This structure must now be revised to meet strategic quality needs; for example, many large corporations, which traditionally delegated matters of quality to autonomous divisions, now require corporate review of divisional quality goals, plans, and performance reports.

Resources. Resources are needed in several areas to carry out plans and meet goals. To date, companies have shown a selective response to this need.

• Training. Here the response of companies has generally been positive. Companies have invested heavily in training programs for special areas such as quality awareness, statistical process control, and QC circles. To go into strategic quality planning, however, will require extensive training in the trilogy—how to think about quality.

• Measurement of quality. Because of the quality crisis, American companies must set goals based on measurement of market quality on an unprecedented scale. For example, some companies now have a policy that new products may not go on the market unless their reliability is at least equal to that of leading competitive products. Such a policy cannot be made effective unless resources are provided to evaluate the reliability of competing products.

Beyond the need to expand quality-oriented marketing research, other aspects of measurement also require resources: establishing the scorekeeping associated with strategic quality planning; extending measures of quality to the non-manufacturing processes; and establishing means for evaluating the quality performance of managers, and fitting these evaluations into the merit rating system.

• Quality improvement. Here we have some puzzling contradictions. An emerging data base tells us that quality improvement projects provide a higher return on investment than virtually any other investment: in large organizations with sales of $1 billion or more, the average quality improvement project yields about $100,000 of cost reduction and requires from $5,000 to $20,000 in resources to complete a project. These resources are needed to diagnose the cause of the problem and to provide the remedy. The return on investment is obviously attractive, and yet many companies fail to provide the resources and hence fail to get the results.

A New Role

Strategic quality planning will require companies to create, for the quality function, a new role—a role similar to that of the financial controller. This new role will likely be assigned to quality managers and will involve the following duties:

• assist management in preparing strategic quality goals.

• set means of reporting performance against quality goals.

• evaluate competitive quality and market trends.

• design and introduce needed revisions in quality planning, quality control, and quality improvement.

• conduct training to assist company personnel in carrying out the necessary changes.

For many quality managers, the new role will involve a considerable shift in emphasis: from technology to business management; from quality control and assurance to strategic quality planning. But such is the wave of the future. Those quality managers who accept that responsibility, if and when it comes, can look forward to the experience of a lifetime. They will be participating fully in what will become the most important quality development of the century.

Renaissance in Service Quality

Historically, quality in service has lagged behind quality of product. For example, many service organizations lend themselves to a sort of monopoly. The challenge of competition is insignificant or completely lacking. The regional hospital, for instance, is usually not in competition with another hospital in the same area; and until recently, telephone communications were dominated by one giant service company. Other services such as mass transit, armed forces, and municipal agencies are government supported or financed, and this also thwarts a competitive challenge. And in many service industries, the emphasis remains on quantity—not on the quality of service. In addition, whereas our manufacturing industries have been on the receiving end of overseas competition, our service industries have been spared this threat.

American service industries are beginning to respond to several driving forces that are contributing to a renaissance in service quality. These forces include deregulation of certain industries; regulations in response to public demands; mandatory budget-balancing laws; the need for increased productivity in services; increased consumer expectations; and decreased consumer tolerance for poor quality.

In days gone by, there were no power failures, no communication breakdowns, no delays in air travel schedules. That is simply because there was no electricity, no telephones, and no air travel. Life is no longer so simple. As technology has developed, it has become increasingly vital that we protect ourselves against potential damage. That protection is quality, both of goods and services.

Like the dikes that protect the Dutch from the sea, our quality dikes protect us against those things that are bigger than anything else, including the much publicized Japanese quality revolution. This driving force, perhaps more than any other, is stimulating the way service industries are thinking about quality. We live dangerously behind the dikes of quality.

Choice of Strategy is Critical

The choice of quality strategy is critical to a company's ability to make significant improvements in the quality of their products and services. While there are many options to choose from—including quality circles, exhortation and slogans, statistical quality control, quality departments, and massive capital expenditures—we at Juran Institute have found that companies making the greatest progress in quality improvement have adopted an ongoing, structured, project-by-project approach.

We have also observed that companies carrying out improvement projects on a substantial scale are becoming the quality leaders.

A notable example of a service company making large-scale quality improvements is Florida Power and Light. In the five years between 1981 and 1986, they completed more than 1,400 projects, greatly improving the quality of their service to their customers, while at the same time reducing their costs by many tens of millions of dollars. Their approach to quality improvement has been revolutionary, not evolutionary.

Other examples of the project concept include the following:

• At First Tennessee Bank, customers were waiting 40 minutes at teller windows. Bank managers, desperate to reduce the wait, observed that there were regular, predictable surges of customer arrivals within and between days. Using desired maximum customer waiting time and statistics on the customer arrival patterns, they developed a model to identify the number of tellers required for a given time period and service standard. By rearranging the teller staffing patterns to match the periodic traffic intensity changes, bank managers reduced annual costs approximately $1.5 million and reduced customer waiting time to less than eight minutes.

• An AT&T customer service support center group, together with a group of design engineers, formed a team to study ways to improve the design quality of private service orders. Within two months, their work resulted in a 47 percent jump in error-free design rates. The quality improvement team cut the cost of rework and produced cost savings of over $120,000 per year.

• In the National Marketing Division of IBM, a team undertook a project to study canceled orders. The result was a dramatic reduction (from 13 percent to 3 percent) in products shipped and then canceled prior to installation of the products. Another IBM team took on a project to discover ways of increasing multiple sales of electronic typewriters. The result was a 182 percent increase in multiple typewriter sales.

• An improvement team at the Internal Revenue Service identified major causes of the tax return processing errors. Most errors were the result of incorrect keystrokes made when some of the information on the taxpayers' returns was converted into multiple digit code numbers by IRS employees. The project teams identified ways of reducing the number of code digits, or in some cases, eliminating the need to enter code digits. This effort resulted in over one-half billion fewer keystrokes, revisions to new tax forms and better overall quality of service.

From these and other case examples, we conclude that 1) project-by-project quality improvements result in large savings and impressive returns on investment; 2) a revolutionary rate of improvement requires many more completed projects than an evolutionary rate; and 3) the project-by-project approach can be applied to many service industries, processes, and functions.

Organizing for Improvement

Executives seeking extensive quality improvements should be leaders in establishing a new structure and process by:

• *Creating a Quality Council.* Since the Council directs and coordinates the company's quality improvement efforts, membership is prerequisite to all else. Company executives should serve on the Council and participate personally throughout the quality improvement process—approving the strategic quality goals, reviewing progress, giving recognition, and serving on some project teams. Often top management's participation in the quality improvement efforts determines the rate of success. In fact, every successful company-wide quality program we know of has enjoyed the active participation of top executives.

• *Making quality improvement part of the business plan.* Project-by-project improvement must be accepted as a new managerial activity of the company. It is to become as much a part of managerial life as meeting the budget and developing new services. Indeed, to make lasting quality improvements, the company's strategic business plan must be enlarged to include quality: goals, responsibility, resources, and evaluation.

• *Setting goals.* Goals for improvement should be set, and progress should be measured against those goals.

• *Providing training in quality.* All managers at all levels must be trained in the quality improvement process and in associated skills and tools (such as group dynamics and problem solving). Upper managers, in particular, must know how to think about quality; how to manage for quality; how to lead their company's quality efforts. In most companies, this training must be done on a much wider scale than has been done in the past.

• *Allocating resources.* Upper managers should make available the resources necessary to carry out project-by-project improvement. This takes such forms as time for teams to work on improvement projects, facilitators to aid the teams, diagnostic support for data collection and analysis, a review process for monitoring progress, a means for publicizing the results, a system of recognition for specific achievements, and revision of the merit system to include performance relative to quality improvement.

• *Starting small, then scaling up.* Begin with bite-size projects that can be completed in less than four months. A project should be significant but manageable. Keep it focused and simple. Consider starting a quality effort in one division using a team of willing managers. Their success will often stimulate reluctant mangers. With well-publicized results from early projects, it then becomes easier to scale up to a company-wide quality effort.

• *Remembering external customers.* When choosing quality improvement projects, don't overlook the external opportunities. Take the initiative to carry out marketing research; find out what is important to your external customers. This is much different than responding to customer complaints. Such research will help identify improvement projects that will directly respond to your customers' needs.

• *Forming interdepartmental teams.* The most significant gains result from projects carried out by interdepartmental teams, not intradepartmental teams. We find that in large companies (sales over $1 billion), the average intradepartmental project yields around $5,000 per completed project, versus an average gain of $100,000 per interdepartmental project (a 20 to 1 ratio). The most significant improvement projects can only be addressed by crossfunctional teams of managers.

Because the driving forces are sometimes subtle and the environment relatively crisis free, many industries are slow to embrace a formal quality management effort. It may be that things will have to get much worse before they begin to get better. Life behind our quality dikes is becoming increasingly precarious. Our society demands that those dikes hold up. We rely on quality to protect us from our technological world. This driving force will not go away.

Chapter 27

Growing Quality Leaders

by Philip B. Crosby, founder of Philip Crosby
Associates, Inc. and Career IV, Inc.

*Show people how to prevent problems, not
just fix them. Educate, train, and support
those who do the work.*

FOR 40 years, I have waged war over the way quality is managed in
business. I have emphasized prevention as opposed to detection and
fixing. As a result of my campaign, many organizations have capitu-
lated, the philosophy of management has changed, and much of what
I have written has found its way into other people's material—the
ultimate compliment, of course.

Encouragingly, I see MBA schools deliberately trying to eliminate the "silo" concept of teaching and to embrace a much broader
agenda based on the concepts of quality management. There has been
genuine progress. Many companies are so proud of their programs
that they are writing books about it. Executives are making speeches
at quality conferences. But in many areas, there has been a decided
lack of progress. No more than 25 percent of those management teams
who did something have been successful in making quality a part of
the normal operation of the organization.

The companies that are successful in reforming their quality
posture do so by ingesting the concepts. I can tell by looking at their
financial results and the overall environment of the operation. They
absorb what I call the *Absolutes of Quality Management.* They understand that quality is not goodness—it is conformance to the requirements. As part of this, senior management recognizes that they are
responsible for causing the right requirements to be made. If the cus-

tomer, internal or external, is to receive what has been promised, everyone must know what has been promised and how to do their personal part of making it all come true.

They understand that it is necessary to prevent problems rather than learn how to implement SWAT-type corrective action. Prevention involves the specific education, training, and support of those who do the work. Top management are helpers rather than overseers. They create a climate of consideration that produces high revenues per employee.

They understand that management must insist on a performance standard of getting things done right the first time, every time. When this doesn't happen, they approach problems with the idea of learning how to prevent them from happening again, after the fix. Symbolically this insistence on being correct is called Zero Defects—the oil that causes consistency.

And, being pragmatic, this management realizes that they need to measure quality in financial terms. Emotional commitments don't last. When quality means conformance to requirements, it is possible to routinely record the cost on not conforming to requirements—everything from reprocessing paperwork to customer service counts, and it adds up quickly. The accounting people need to do this task; otherwise, no one will take the numbers seriously. When manufacturing companies see that they are spending 25 percent of revenues, and when service companies see that 40 percent of operating expense is being wasted, then they start being serious. The Price of Nonconformance (PONC) numbers appear on the monthly review overheads, and soon specific problems are being unearthed. Companies who get serious about quality management receive some serious blessings.

Aim to Prevent Problems

When your efforts are aimed at preventing problems rather than finding and fixing them, your error rates drop.

Remember: quality is the result of management policy—all the well-intentioned things we do in quality departments have little to do with it. We might inspect, test, educate, measure, draw charts, travel to suppliers, meet with customers, and try to create a system that would produce quality, and yet, our customers rarely receive what they order.

Today, every executive is very interested in quality, and many speak knowingly of quality. They compare the various aspects of the "systems" and defend their favorites with vigor and enthusiasm.

And yet, for the most part, few understand what these things mean. Consequently, very little changes. They work hard on what turns out to be the wrong problem. They don't realize that the "fix" is in prevention.

Most organizations have no intention of doing things right the first time, or even the second time. They plan for things to go wrong, and they instruct their people in that manner. They just assume it has to be that way. And so most systems that are used to improve quality are based on the concepts of "quality control." These concepts, in turn, are dedicated to the inevitability of error. Management arranges to deal with nonconformance on a routine basis by having rework of some sort. "Customer service" is usually rework with a smile. Traditional systems of "total quality" have been aimed this way and have produced the same thing.

In addition, most efforts are aimed at the end of the operation—the final 10 percent of the output receives 90 percent of the quality improvement effort. This is like trying to win a race by having "heart" despite never practicing or building up strength. It is like continually buying new golf clubs to improve a game that flounders because of a poor swing.

The drive for a "quick fix" has led management to leap into things they don't understand. "Total quality" means many things to many people. There is no common agreement, no common language.

Changes Are Needed

I have learned that people respond to the standards of their leaders, and they perform to the level expected of them. Given proper instruction and opportunity, people will produce defect-free products and services on time for their customers, both internal and external.

Now, the people I am talking about are not just the end of the operation. While they are very important, they can do very little to prevent problems. We need to include those who make policy, those who write procedures, those who buy, those who sell, those who design, those who administer—everyone must be included. It takes all those people to make an organization function properly. We depend on each other. Add to this the suppliers, from whom everything comes, and the customers, to whom everything goes.

All of these people also need to understand quality the same way. They need to recognize their personal roles in making quality happen. And they all need consistent leadership to make quality routine. None of this can happen through some "silver bullet" quick-fix operation.

• We are talking about changing a culture from being nonconformance oriented to one that routinely conforms to all requirements.

• We're talking about changing from supplying the customers with almost what they wanted to an organization that works hand in glove with the customer to anticipate needs.

• We are talking about changing from an organization that grows in an irregular manner to one that is consistent and profitable at the same time.

• We are talking about changing from an organization that takes things as they come to one that manages change and causes it on purpose.

• And we are talking about changing from an organization whose employees tolerate it to one that they belong to with pride.

In successful organizations, everyone understands quality the same way. Each is educated specifically, not only in concepts but also in tools. And they all have to fit together.

Time-Tested Concepts

Hundreds of corporations in all industries have overcome their quality problems and learned to meet the needs of their customers. They have dramatically reduced their price of nonconformance, and their employees go about work with pride.

It was hard work on their part, and the senior executives had to recognize their personal role and perform it every day. They could not turn it over to some "system" that was going to work miracles. They could not leave it to Quality, Training, Human Resources, or some other group because these dedicated people do not make policy, do not provide leadership, and do not have the right material.

So we learned to bring these folks to school, teach them how to facilitate the material, and then help them go back and assist management by teaching the concepts and tools that will turn an organization around. We learned to teach them something they could understand and explain. If something is so complex that only a few qualified people can understand it, there will be little useful fallout from it.

Over the years, we have tested our concepts to see if they are clear to everyone. Some choose to misunderstand, but the majority of the world gets along very well with them:

• When the people all understand that quality is conformance to requirement, and management has caused clear requirements to exist, then everyone knows what to do.

• When the organization is based on preventing problems rather than finding and fixing them, the error rates become smaller and smaller and then extinguish forever.

• When the policy of "we will deliver defect-free products and services on time" is clearly established, old-fashioned things like "acceptable quality levels" disappear.

• When improvement is measured by determining the costs of doing things wrong and the positive benefits of having more money to work with become apparent, then everyone will realize that quality comes from a tough policy and a well-oriented work force.

People produce success—it is the only way it comes. There are no quick fixes. When management realizes that there is no tooth fairy and quits wasting time, then they can put the problem of quality behind them and turn it into a permanent profit and productivity producing asset.

Quality Management

Quality management is entirely different than quality control. It is the difference between financial management and accounting. Quality management is oriented around preventing; quality control is aimed at measuring, containing and controlling. Quality management involves long-term company policy; quality control involves "use and do not use" decisions on a daily basis. Quality management involves corporate policy; quality control involves department procedures. Quality management is about people; quality control is about things.

To understand and implement quality management a company must recognize two things: all work is a process; and what is delivered to the customer is the result of the entire operation.

• Ecology of quality. Quality doesn't just lie with those who touch or deliver the product or service. A company has an ecology, just like a forest. If everything is not working with the same attitude for the same purpose, the whole body may die.

• Language of quality. A common language of quality has to be accepted. It applies to every part of the company. This involves the definition of quality; the determination of the system of causing quality; the performance standard that becomes policy; and the managerial measurement of quality. I call these the absolutes of quality management. And "absolute" means just that. These points have to be understood and used as stated, or your product or service will be defective.

• Definition of quality. I define quality as conformance to requirements. Management's responsibility is to see that these requirements exist; in most cases, no new ones are needed once they start to take the old ones seriously. Requirements should be formally upgraded on a continual basis as people learn how to improve the work. When we ask people to "do it right the first time," we have to tell them what "it" is. "It" consists of the requirements for the product or service and the jobs that cause them to happen.

• System of quality. Prevention is where quality originates. Quality control concepts have placed the major emphasis on appraisal, which is after the fact. We need to vaccinate the organization so that it doesn't have diseases, rather than learning how to find and fix them. This is the biggest culture change involved. The analogy here is "wellness," learning to stay healthy rather than to cure illness.

• Standards of quality. Many problems with quality emerge from the use of Acceptable Quality Levels. These statistical goals let management think that it's not possible to get things right the first time and that there is an Economics of Quality. The proper standard is Zero Defects, or defect-free, which means that each of us will conform to the requirements we agreed to meet. When management insists on defect-free work, and takes action to cause that to happen, their world begins to change for the better.

Quality control people have a problem accepting zero defects as a standard, and so they use "continuous improvement." While this sounds good, it basically means we will never actually reach the target of doing everything right the first time.

• Measurement of quality. Money is the only measurement that management relates to, and quality is easily measured in that manner. The price of non-conformance (PONC) is the expense of doing things wrong. It is rework by any name, as well as fixing, chasing, and warranting. It is excess overtime, inventory, expenses, and all the other things that are undesirable. In manufacturing companies that don't attack quality systematically, PONC is 25 percent of revenue, or more; in service organizations, it is 40 percent of operating costs, or more.

Many executives are doing something about quality; but unless they build it into the fabric of their organizations, they will not get complete and lasting results. Since any quality program can bring instant improvement, they may think the battle is won. But changing a company culture takes a while. Everyone in the organization has to work in a new way.

Quality Improvement Process

People do not start working in new and better ways by applying techniques only. It is necessary to use a management system we call the Quality Improvement Process. Here are some of the components.

• Management commitment. The process begins with management commitment in such areas as measurement; awareness; cost of quality; correction action; zero defects; error cause removal; recognition; goal setting; and more. These road markers help the company touch each base as it orients itself to the new thinking and acting.

• Management policy. Management must adopt a new policy: "We will deliver defect-free products and services to our customers, both internal and external, on time."

• Supplier quality. Suppliers must be brought into the improvement process. Purchasing has to receive only material that conforms exactly to the requirements as ordered. There will come a time under a quality management process that old traditions such as initial inspection and waivers can be eliminated.

• Corrective action. Companies need to learn how to eliminate and prevent problems, not just patch them up. Every kind of nonconformance—whether product, service, procedural, or what—can be handled by corrective action approaches.

• Statistical process control (SPC). These techniques are applicable in many production areas. We have developed software programs to support SPC efforts, and provide teaching systems that enable client companies to teach the mysteries of SPC to anyone they wish.

• Work group systems. A compact system that lets a supervisor and group develop communication skills while examining problems in the company. This is a continuing activity and becomes part of regular meetings.

• Work measurement software. Real-time results let management know what is happening on a moment-to-moment basis. A new concept of operations.

These and other components are part of quality management. Measurement of work through professional inspection and testing during the manufacturing or administrative processes is continual to ensure that everything is going properly. However, the acceptance measurement of individual entities, as has been customary in the past, will begin to disappear along with the conventional wisdom of deviations and waivers.

The idea is to have a river of work and check its purity regularly rather than building dams the water has to pass after being checked.

We have installed the concepts and systems of quality management in hundreds of companies throughout the world. But then all that is necessary for quality management is people. Those who are making the decisions about their company's quality future must understand the difference between quality control and quality management. As Mark Twain said when talking about two things that sounded similar: "It is the difference between lightning and a lightning bug." Don't let the lights go out by not taking quality seriously.

Creating Quality Leaders

Successful organizations are always run by thoughtful executives. These people uniformly have broad experience in business, and they are good at relationships. I feel that my value in this quality revolution has been to break this complex subject into concepts that fit into the thought banks of these executives. Suddenly they can see that this is just a way of managing; it is not some mumbo jumbo that only a few specialists can understand. The fact is that very few of the specialists do understand the reality of quality management.

When I retired, I wanted to see if I could help create some of the executives I admired so much. I reviewed my personal career, starting back in 1952 when I made a decision to become an executive and created a plan to make that happen. In 1959, I was a department head at Martin-Marietta; and in 1965, I became a corporate executive with ITT in New York. As a vice president of that corporation, I worked all over the world in every industry. From that experience, I realized that leaders could be made, with help, even if they weren't born that way.

The need for leadership has never been so clear. This planet-wide economy has turned everything on its head. Only the wise will survive. With this thought as my motivation, I began to see if we could package some wisdom to hurry the process along.

Those who want their organizations to be successful need to recognize people with potential and encourage them. Doing this is a talent not many have. Personally I had to change companies several times before finding senior people who were not locked into "old" being "best." They gave me a chance and it worked out for all of us.

The senior executive who is willing to help identify and educate the "young comers" is probably the same one who took time to understand the benefits of quality management done properly.

Chapter 28

How TQM Can Improve Your Bottom Line

by Bob King, Executive Director of Goal/QPC and author of *Hoshin Planning*

Effective TQM leads to improved customer satisfaction, increased market share, reduced cycle time, and lower employee turnover.

SOME articles in the business media would have you believe that Japanese and American organizations have abandoned Total Quality Management (TQM).

Of course, Japan is expanding rather than reducing TQM and, in fact, is gearing up for a major push to teach it in the schools as a response to United States initiatives in this area. TQM is producing major success in the United States: the turnaround of Xerox; Six Sigma quality (less than 3.4 mistakes per one million opportunities) at Motorola; 50 percent reduction in time to market at Hewlett-Packard; and 10-fold improvements in reliability at IBM in Rochester, Minnesota, to name a few. Florida Power & Light is expanding rather than reducing its TQM activities and has been in an expansion mode for more than 18 months.

Some of the press is guilty of sloppy reporting. But, to be fair, TQM gurus and enthusiasts are also guilty of not adequately documenting TQM results. As Marta Mooney of Fordham University has said, "There is no quality control of TQM." There are other problems. Some companies are doing Statistical Process Control (SPC) and calling it TQM. A mutual fund of so-called TQM companies did worse than the Standard and Poor's 500 in the last five years. My assessment is that the companies that were picked were not doing mature TQM. A mutual fund of assessment is that the companies that were picked were not doing mature TQM. But for the novice all of this does create some questions of how effective TQM is.

Improve the Bottom Line

How can senior executives use TQM to improve bottom-line results? I look at three issues: 1) why TQM will not go away; 2) what evidence we have of results produced by TQM in Japan and in the United States; and 3) what guidelines will help you produce a major TQM success in your organization.

1. What TQM is and why won't it go away. TQM represents a fundamental change in management based on increased knowledge of workers. The scientific method has taught us that improvement most often follows the pattern of plan, do, check, and act. Around the turn of the century, Frederick Taylor, because of low education of supervisors and workers, suggested that improvement in a business should be designed by engineers and specialists and carried out by workers. Increased education during this century has led to the possibility of all employees being involved in continuous improvement.

The methodology of transforming an organization requires instruction and practice in the processes, organization, and tools of continuous improvement. These may be organized into four major categories: Daily Management, Hoshin Management, Cross-Functional Management, and the Customer-Driven Master Plan.

• *Daily Management* is the processes and tools that employees use to improve each unit of the organization.

• *Hoshin Management* builds on the processes and tools of Daily Management and includes the processes and tools to focus on priority improvements for the whole organization. It improves vertical alignment.

• *Cross-Functional Management* builds on Daily Management and Hoshin Management. It's the basis for consistent improvements of quality, cost, delivery, and quality of organizational work life. It improves horizontal integration in the organization and is executive-driven.

• *The Customer-Driven Master Plan* is the five-year plan for orchestrating the roll-out of Daily Management, Hoshin Management, and Cross-Functional management in the organization. All of these support the strategic plan for making the company better.

Will we ever go back to a few people in the organization deciding how to make things best? Will we ever decide that only a few should be educated? Will we discover that one head is better than five or 10 or 100 in producing continuous improvement or innovation? I think not! If some people get unimpressive results from TQM because they don't know what they are doing, or because they hired a lousy consultant and got bad advice, will others who are getting major bottom-line improvements from TQM stop using it? Be serious. Of course not. TQM is here for the duration because when it is done right it successfully helps organizations make planned fundamental improvement.

2. Bottom-line results from TQM. So where is the evidence? What results has TQM produced? Noriaki Kano developed a chart indicating some of the early success in Japan. He looked at the profitability of Deming Prize winners vs. the average profitability of manufacturing companies.

These numbers show that successful TQM companies in Japan, companies that won the Deming Prize, had double the profit of manufacturing companies as a whole. This happened during the 1970s when Japan was hit by two major oil shocks. TQM use expanded dramatically. These numbers are a little old, but they represent a time when it was still possible to compare companies that were doing TQM with companies that were not doing TQM.

In summary there are four major benefits of TQM according to Deming Prize winners as reported by Kano: 1) TQM produces growth in market share; 2) TQM improves customer satisfaction by reducing problems and defects; 3) TQM reduces costs, which helps grow market share (Deming progression); and 4) TQM reduces superior design of new products and in companies that use QFD this happens in one-third to one-half less time.

In the United States, TQM progress is still at a relatively undeveloped level. It takes about five years once you understand TQM to use it to truly transform your organization. Few U.S. companies have been making serious efforts to do TQM for more than five years and the best companies today still understand only about 60 percent of how the Japanese are doing TQM. (A new reference book by Katsuya Hosotani, referred to in Japan as the best overview book of TQM, is available in the United States in English for the first time at this GOAL/QPC conference. We hope that this book, translated by the GOAL/QPC research committee, will significantly close the gap of knowledge about Japanese TQM.)

Despite the newness of TQM in this country, a study by the General Accounting Office in 1990 showed TQM to have produced very favorable results at early winning companies of the Malcolm Baldrige Quality Award.

The General Accounting Office study requested by Congressman Ritter of Pennsylvania shows that TQM has led to many improvements in U.S. companies: 1) Customer satisfaction is improved because of reduced errors and defects and because of increased reliability and on-time delivery; 2) Market share and profits are up; 3) Employee satisfaction, safety, and health are up and turnover is down; and 4) Costs and cycle time are down and productivity is up. These results happened at companies who were only 50 to 60 percent down the TQM road.

This data is powerful and significant. What we need in coming years is careful documentation by all companies of their bottom-line results from TQM implementation. Companies need to be clear about the purpose of TQM and need to measure results.

IBM has provided some leadership in this regard this year by examining the correlation of scoring on a Baldrige self-assessment and bottom-line results. Business units that scored over 500 on the Baldrige self-evaluation at IBM were divided into three groups. The high third were the gold, the middle third were the silver, and the bottom third were the bronze. They then examined each group in terms of profit as a return on assets, customer satisfaction, quality levels, market share, etc. They found a strong correlation. The better a group did on the Baldrige, the better were their bottom-line results. This is a beginning analysis effort. As it is expanded it will provide additional understanding of how TQM produces bottom-line results.

3. What we know about how to maximize TQM success. It might sound a little silly at first but TQM works better if you are doing it for a particular reason than if you are doing it for no particular reason at all. But, in fact many if not most companies doing TQM in the United States today do not have a clear understanding of what specific significant change it will make in their company. TQM is so hot today that people often simply decide to do it because everybody is doing it.

Let me give you a personal example. When we were starting our formal implementation of TQM at GOAL/QPC, we said, "We should practice what we preach, so let's do TQM." It didn't work. You need to have a sound business reason to do TQM. You need to regain lost market share, turn around losses into profits, or find another specific reason for using TQM.

It is not good enough for health care organizations to do TQM because the Joint Commission on Accreditation of Health Care Organizations thinks it is a good idea. It is not sufficient for universities to do TQM because the best companies will not hire their graduates if they are not doing TQM. There needs to be an organization-specific reason.

Before he died in 1990, Mizuno helped many companies implement TQM. At the International Quality Conference in Tokyo, he offered 15 reasons why companies sometimes fail to get bottom-line results in implementing TQM: 1) The top executive is indifferent; 2) The responsibilities of each manager for TQM are not clear; 3) The purpose and objectives of TQM introduction and roll-out are not clear; 4) The vision statement is not tied to real quality problems or to analysis of customer needs or competitor advantages; 5) The scope is limited to certain sections of the company, and so not everyone is involved; 6) TQM implementation plan lacks measures, timetables, and responsibilities; 7) Employee TQM education is limited to awareness as the QC tools are neither taught nor practiced; 8) Much paper is generated, but no real change is accomplished; 9) Activity is limited to QC circles or teams; 10) Activities are limited to daily management and Hoshin management and the organization never gets to cross-functional management; 11) Activities are limited to daily management; 12) Crises and problems are seen as an excuse not to do TQM rather than as a focus of TQM; 13) The TQM coordinator and staff are ineffective in getting TQM going; 14) The TQM effort has not been structured and managed in such a way as to accomplish growth in sales and profit; 15) There is not a common TQM language throughout the company.

Noriaki Kano has offered four pointed suggestions for successful TQM implementation: 1) Decision making should be based on facts, not guts; 2) Decisions of top management should be based on "market-in"; that means the customer must be placed first; 3) The source of corporate revenue and profit is rooted in quality, which will only be achieved by strong leadership from the top; and 4) Top management should study TQM before others in the company.

In summary, TQM works when there is a clear understanding of what fundamental change the organization is going to make and a clear understanding of how TQM will help. TQM works when it is directed and led by the personal involvement of all top management. TQM works when each employee understands the seven QC Tools and uses the PDCA cycle to continuously improve and hold the gains (Daily Management). TQM works when each employee contributes in an integrated way to the fundamental improvement of the organization (Hoshin management). TQM works when the whole organization is structured to produce significant results in quality, cost, delivery, and quality of work life with the leadership of key executives (cross-functional management). TQM works when the organization has a customer-driven master plan of how it will accomplish its fundamental improvement and carries out that plan during four to six years.

I wish you well in your TQM journey.

Chapter 29

TQM as a Way of Life

by Richard M. Miller,
Principal in Compass Consulting Group

*What we do requires that we do it totally
with a relentless regard for high quality of
product and service.*

TOTAL Quality Management is not the point. Everyone wants high quality. People get satisfaction from doing something well, or creating something of high quality. People want to receive high quality in the products or services they purchase.

Management is the issue. All businesses have management. It can be good or bad. Good management is often perceived as one that is successful. Yet there are many poorly managed firms that get by "successfully." Unfortunately, there is no definition of what constitutes success. However, we are not interested in getting by; we are interested in "good management" and high quality products and services.

To understand management that achieves high quality, consider the totality of what gets done, who does it, and how it gets done. Clearly, management cannot be effective piecemeal—a little good management over here, not so good over there, and bad in one area or another. Likewise, it is ineffective to make parts of the product good, some parts poor, and the remainder bad—and that goes for service as well. A surly confrontation can overshadow all the prior good service a customer had during an engagement. The quality of management or the quality of a product or service is only as good as the weakest link.

The point is—what we do requires that we do it "totally" with a relentless regard for high quality of product or service, having a high quality of management throughout the enterprise. High quality of management means managing the quality of what is done.

W. Edwards Deming made it very clear that good intentions, hard work, positive mental attitude, highly motivated people, having high tech equipment, in the finest working environment, all doing their best, is far from adequate to produce the quality of product or service needed to survive. He went to great lengths to demonstrate the need for leadership from people with substantial knowledge—of people, systems, philosophy, and variation—emphasizing the dignity of the individual.

Joseph M. Juran goes into finite detail to spell out the mechanics and technical details required of the leaders, and the organization, to improve the quality of output needed to survive.

Philip B. Crosby presses the need to change the way business does things, management's responsibility and integrity, and the need to focus on perfection with various requirements and axioms that must be addressed—or else.

Given an inclination to want to do better and trying to succeed, managers endeavor to respond to all this expertise and demonstrated excellence—only to find these dogmatic solutions are unclear, and alien to their lifelong experience. Furthermore, taken at face value they seem to cause confusion, frustration, and cynicism. Each program flashes, burns, and then fades out, leaving the participants weary of one more program imposed upon them—knowing full well there will be yet another fad in the future.

The problem is we try to perfect one or two elements of management and expect success. We are "sold" the parts and expect the whole. Consider all the elements of management.

Consider the most tangible element of the quality cycle—the product or service. Is it good or bad? How good or bad is it? It is never as good as it could be, even though it may meet the customer's needs. After all, isn't that all the customer asked for? There will always be a better way to do something—easier, with less waste, less time, and less cost. Someone will find it and take the customer. Good enough is no longer good enough.

How do we know quality? If we cannot measure it, we cannot compare it to anything else, or determine how good it is. We must learn scientific methods of analysis, measuring what we do, and tracking how we do it, to determine what to fix, where, and how. Deming, Juran, and their students have developed tools of quality improvement that have proven to be very effective in creating dramatic improvements in the quality of the product or service, cutting waste and costs, and increasing customer satisfaction.

Three Action Elements

To make significant, sustainable improvements, every business and industry must have a high capability in the use of scientific tools of quality improvement.

Vision & Leaders
- Fundamental Values
- Principle-Centered Paradigm

Tools of Leaders
- Management and Planning Tools
- Quality Improvement Tools

Skills of Leaders
- Knowledge of People
- Dealing with Their Needs

• Tools of leaders. Often there is so much attention on basic processes and the use of the quality improvement tools, that management is at a loss to determine what needs to be improved, why, and by whom. Without an effective scientific methodology of issues identification, prioritization, client needs, and management decision making, action takes place either autocratically or chaotically. In either case, considerable energy is misspent.

The random analysis of many activities frustrates senior managers, who have trouble determining the value of what is going on. This also conflicts with middle managers' efforts to control their units so they can execute their perceived responsibilities. The solution is to have the ability to use the "Tools of Management and Planning" to determine where to effectively apply the Q.I. tools. The ability to determine the right things to do. But, there is more.

• Skills of leaders. People make quality. That fundamental has not been challenged. What is controversial is how to make people make quality. People make quality when they want to, assuming they have the management support, knowledge, empowerment, and resources necessary—and every one of these pieces must be in place—all the time. All the tools and processes in the world will never take the place of leadership skills and knowledge. "Management" must learn the difference between leading and managing. People must be led—not managed. People hear and see what leaders say, do, and don't do. When these are out of "sync," or any one is missing, nothing will make or inspire people to do well. People see and hear not only what management does, but they "read" what is seen and not heard, and interpret it by its worst implication.

Fear, in its many forms, is present in every person in every work place—at all levels. Every leader and manager must develop substantial knowledge and capability in the area of communicating and dealing with people. They must have a better understanding of why people (don't) do what they (don't) do.

• Vision and leadership. At all levels, regarding all things, everyone must consider why they are doing what they are doing. Furthermore, their "how" is based on their own belief system of principles and values. Significant conflict arises in this area, which is critical to creating a quality organization. Would anyone "give 110 percent" if what they were doing "might be OK," but they didn't believe it was right? Would the end justify the means?

We learn the flaw in this thinking every time we try it. People must feel good—be proud of what they are doing—to be able to do it well. Every leader must spend the time to look inward and determine his or her own principles and beliefs. From this foundation they develop the values from which they lead. To effectively lead and develop a successful enterprise, they must facilitate the people in the organization to look at their collective "foundational values" based upon a "principle-centered paradigm."

Regardless of the time spent developing this issue, this is the basis upon which all decisions are made. In an organization as in an individual, stress and sickness result from conflicts at this level, appropriately labeled disease. Some of the most obvious symptoms are conflict, distrust, hypocrisy, insecurity, and fear.

Finally, the fundamental "tools" used to establish the "why" are the vision and mission statements. It is preposterous to believe that anyone can have "the" vision of the company. A good leader is responsible to develop a "vision with leadership," but never in a vacuum, or involving only a few people. To energize a company and "enroll" the people requires great skill in developing a vision that captures the visions of the employees. People that focus on their vision become inspired, empowered, and committed to the enterprise that represents it. They feel, "This is where my vision will become a reality." Considerable effort must be expended to draw out the collective vision of the participants—and to make it relevant to the enterprise where they contribute their skills.

It is through a well-articulated, realistic, courageous mission that the vision can be applied or adapted. An exciting, ethical vision will enroll people to make the mission theirs so the company can succeed. Everyone must understand "what we do around here." There may or may not be a good reason to change how things get done. But there must be a consensus of what and why, with a commitment to engage the effort and resources for the long haul to make it happen.

The above cannot be done overnight, and does not have to be. People get inspired by the challenge and the "journey" if it is sincere, supported by all of management, and the culture is created to support it. It must start at the top of the organization and be worked down through the ranks. Integrity, trust, honesty, and openness must come first—then education, knowledge, and wisdom.

What does a company that has TQM look like? It is a company that has a constancy of purpose, with clearly shared vision, a specific capable mission, with leaders and managers that have well-developed leadership skills and a knowledge of people, trained and capable in the use of the tools of management, planning and quality improvement. Regardless of the level of attainment of all of this, it is a learning company that places a high priority on training and continual improvement.

Chapter 30

Push for Quality Service

by James C. Shaffer, Vice President and Principal
of Towers Perrin

*If you want quality customer service, you
will need to push for some things and against
other things in your organization.*

WORKING people throughout this country have had it! They're
tired of being called lazy, sloppy producers of shoddy products. They
don't get up in the morning itching to be rude, brusque, curt, or abra-
sive. They want to design, produce, and deliver quality products and
services. They want to take pride in their work.

But many are part of organizations where petty politics, antiquated policies, nonsensical bureaucracy, and mismanaged communication conspire to produce unhappy customers. And so people are
pushing back against the garbage that prevents them from being their
best. Sensing this revolt, enlightened leaders are capitalizing on the
employee frustration to achieve fundamental change. The revolt is
happening at all levels.

• *Chief executives who can't sleep at night because the organization won't move fast enough.*

• *Line managers who want more responsiveness from the sales
force and quicker turnaround time on pricing decisions.*

• *Workers who constantly must find ways to cheat the system or
jerry-rig the machine so it meets the prescribed tolerances.*

• *Critical staff people who constantly fight rigid procedures
manuals to make a common sense decision for a line employee.*

• *Secretaries who can't get the report to the customer on time
because the copy machine won't work.*

These frustrated people are pushing back to remove friction that prevents them from delivering quality to customers.

Employees know customers want quality and will pay for it. Leaders know that people want to produce quality, take pride in their work, and go home feeling a sense of self-worth. But both bump into an infrastructure that impedes rather than facilitates the customer-employee partnership.

Identifying Friction

Identifying friction is relatively easy—it requires listening hard to customers and to employees.

• *Listen hard to customers.* To become customer-driven, begin by listening to your customers. Analyze what drives customer satisfaction and then eliminate the friction that causes less-than-perfect customer scores. For example, in one insurance company, we identified 72 different potential encounters between the company and its customers—their insurance agents. Careful analysis revealed that only six of these encounters drove the agents' satisfaction levels with the company. Using cross-disciplinary teams, the company began eliminating the friction that was causing less than perfect encounters with the agents.

• *Listen hard to employees.* Employee perceptions are any organization's reality check. Employees know about problems before customers do. They often know the organization is having a hard time before senior management knows. And why shouldn't they? They know if the equipment works, whether the product going out the door is defective or not, if the warehouse is empty or full, and when customers aren't satisfied. Remember the Challenger disaster? The employees knew the O-ring couldn't handle the cool temperature. They said so, but the right people didn't listen. Remember the recent under-the-city flood in Chicago? Employees knew about the potential leak, but nothing was done to prevent it.

Frank Perdue, Maryland's legendary poultry processor, once told us about a young man named Keith who eviscerated chickens in the Salisbury processing plant. "Keith knows more about his 25 square feet of space than anyone else in this company," Frank said. "So, if I want to know anything about that 25 square feet of space, I just go ask Keith." There are many Keiths in the business world.

Data from customers and employees should be mapped to create a pushback process that's conducted strategically.

Five Things to Push Against

Eliminating friction requires unrelenting focus and superior execution. In advance of rigorous analytical planning, you can begin to push back against the following obstacles to achieving long-term competitive advantage:

• *Inconsistent communication when the organization doesn't "walk" the "talk."* Many organizations say one thing through their publications and presentations, but say other things through their actions. Inconsistent messages confuse and distract people and diffuse valuable employee energy.

• *Reward systems that don't encourage customer-focused behavior.* Many organizations are still saddled with pay schemes that reward the wrong things. They often emphasize "meeting the production numbers," or a person's position in the company, or the number of people supervised or how long a person has been with the company, none of which necessarily have any correlation with the value the person adds to the customer.

Most people want to please customers, but old-fashioned reward systems impede their ability to do so. We were asked by a company to help find out why customer service people were "so brusque and abrupt with customers," in the words of the president. Knowing the customer service people would fully understand the problem and its causes better than anyone else, we asked them why they were being "so brusque and abrupt with customers."

"That's easy," one said. "We don't *want* to be rude. We want to make customers happy. But, we get paid for every telephone call we complete. Our supervisor gets evaluated on the number of calls we make. So, between the pressure she put on us and the pressure we get from our own pay plan, we end up being brusque and abrupt. And we don't like it."

• *Car-wash training.* This happens when people are sent off to be trained, presumably attempting to undo in a few hours years of bad habits, and then the "trained" people are sent back into the same environment that nurtured the old behavior. It's like taking your car to the car wash on a rainy day. You scrub it, dry it, buff it, and then drive off, only to get it dirty again immediately. The current total quality fad (versus sincere attempts to improve customer satisfaction) is one example of car-wash training. In search of a quick fix, quality directors pore through catalogues and order training solutions before identifying whether poor training or lack of training is causing customers to complain about their products. This misdirected attack on the quality problem led one employee in an electric power plant to say, "I'll be glad when we get finish with this TQM stuff so we can get back to worrying about product quality and customer service."

• *Rigid, stove-piped structures.* These foster turf-consciousness and functional parochialism at the customer's expense. Layers, level-consciousness, and rigid functional boundaries impede decision-making, dampen innovation, reduce speed and agility. Organizations need to be on fast-forward. Permitting excessive structure is equivalent to hitting the pause button.

We informed the vice president of human resources for a Fortune 500 company that Mary, a member of his staff, would add immense value to an upcoming meeting with the company's leadership. He seemed troubled. "Well, I agree Mary would be valuable to the discussion, but you see, this is a meeting of vice presidents and Mary is only a director. Having her at the meeting might make some of the guys uncomfortable."

We had a ready solution. "That's easy, just make Mary a vice president, then everything will be okay," we said only half tongue-in-cheek. Unfortunately, many companies don't find much merit—or humor—in thinking new ways.

• *Measurement systems that focus on the wrong things.* If customer satisfaction is important, measure it. If service is important, measure it. Measure what's important and push back from measurements that aren't important to the customer. Perdue measures quality, service, and reliability, not "birds per man-hour," as one employee calls it.

Measure against what you should be, not what you used to be. Those numbers are dead. You can't do anything about them. You can't afford to manage from the rear view mirror. Enlightened leaders enable the pushback process by shaping an externally-focused, customer-driven vision and providing resources and removing obstacles to achieving the vision. Then they get out of the way and let their people work the magic.

Chapter 31

A Campaign that Failed?

by Patrick L. Townsend, President, and Joan E. Gebhardt, Senior Partner,
of Townsend & Gebhardt

*After a decade of "quality," we now hear reports, informal and for-
mal, of quality efforts failing to produce desired results.*

AN increasing number of executives are saying, "Well, we tried
quality and it didn't work. What's next?"

It's the wrong question. When taking a close look at the perceived
"failure" of quality processes, either in terms of budget impact or
longevity, asking "Why is that?" rather than "What's next?" is far more
helpful in determining the forces which cause an improvement effort to
stagnate. Shortcomings can almost always be traced directly to one of
two situations: senior managers who trusted outsiders before trusting
their own people, or senior managers who invested money rather than
ego. In short, quality requires guts, and too many executives come up
short: too many prefer to be cheerleaders, watching from the sidelines,
rather than being leaders and getting out on the field themselves.

A Short History

Quality consultants have frequently been collaborators in creating disappointment. A look at the history of the quality movement in
America can help to explain why.

Following World War II, if American manufacturers could get whatever they made into a box, they could find someone to buy it. Making life even easier, the American market was, for all practical purposes, a closed market since no foreign country was in any shape to export to the U.S. Americans didn't make and sell real good stuff but, then, what they bought from other Americans wasn't all that good either, so everybody broke even. Even if the near-term obsolescence of an object wasn't always "planned," it was accepted.

Efforts at quality were limited to "quality control" or "quality assurance." Both involved a minimum number of people with very specific tasks; both focused on the manufacturing segment of the economy. Many firms and individuals now billing themselves as "quality consultants" and "quality consultant firms" were in business during this period, but most used words like "productivity" and "efficiency" rather than "quality."

Things changed in the 1970s. First came the Japanese products, then came the oil shortages. Suddenly Americans were aware that things that worked weren't necessarily ruinously expensive, and that they lived in a world of limited resources, making America in some ways a "have not" nation. While folks were trying to absorb those ideas, the NBC White Paper "If Japan Can Do It, Why Can't We?" catapulted Dr. W. Edwards Deming into superstardom.

Suddenly, quality was hot. Quality consultants, experts, gurus, and authors were equally hot—and ludicrously unprepared. This situation was exacerbated when service companies began to decide that they, too, could use this "quality thing." For their problems and challenges, often more difficult than those faced by manufacturing, the quality community was even less prepared.

Several quality consultants decided that the answer to "If Japan can do it, why can't we?" was, "We can. And we'll do it exactly like the Japanese." This led to some changes in the way work got done (quality circles came to America, for example), but it overlooked differences between the Japanese culture and the American culture.

Undaunted, consultants proceeded to peddle wonderfully expensive systems to companies that should have known better, if for no other reason than that the systems being touted didn't pass the common sense test. Quality improvement requires the active input of every employee on the payroll. Most quality processes recommended by consultants do not.

What to Ask

The question that any CEO should ask a prospective "quality consultant" is, "What percent of my employees will be actively involved, participating in the quality process on the first day?" With only one caveat, the only acceptable answer is the logical one: "All of them, including you." The one caveat is the size of the company. Due to a lack of resources or time constraints, the answer may be, "Well, the first day will see 100 percent of this division active, but only a fraction of the whole organization. However, here is the schedule for when 100 percent of the organization will be actively engaged."

Yet, this rarely happens, mainly because such a question forces the company leadership to examine its own relationship with subordinates. To implement a process in which every person in the company is on an active team means that senior management must, in advance, come to grips with the idea that they have been hiring adults—and that these adults are capable of creative thought, not just of following yet another set of requirements. These stipulations may appear somewhat facetious, but the fact is that launching a 100 percent process means forfeiting the "right" to micromanage quality improvement.

Too few executives are willing to concede that right. The late Dr. Deming maintained that at least 85 percent of all problems in an organization could be traced to the management. This is due, in large part, to the fact that the only ones making any decisions are managers. To implement true change, this cycle must be broken. To this day, however, the main objection heard when the idea of implementing a 100 percent process is suggested is that management won't be able to assign a sufficient number of projects. That observation is absolutely right. This means that every quality team must be given the authority to make decisions equal to the responsibility of the team and its members. With that mandate, there will be far too much simultaneous activity to allow micromanagement. The fact that management can't think up things for every team to work on, and yet, if left alone, the teams think of plenty to work on, is just one indication of which body of people knows the most about what needs to be done.

Is the continuous involvement of every person on the payroll really possible? The answer is "yes—if senior management is up to the challenge."

Consider the two winners of the Malcolm Baldrige National Quality Award in 1993. At first glance, they appear to have little in common. One, Ames Rubber Company, is a small manufacturer of hard rubber rollers, employing 445 people in Hamburg, New Jersey. The other, Eastman Chemical, has 17,750 people spread over five states, Canada, and the United Kingdom, making chemicals, fibers, and plastics for 7,000 customers throughout the world. Yet, they both have every person on the payroll on at least one quality team—with many employees in both companies on two or more teams. And they are both highly profitable.

A well-implemented, 100 percent participation, quality process not only makes an outrageous amount of money but also makes the employees and the customers feel better.

Take a look at the experience of the Paul Revere Insurance Group in Worcester, Massachusetts. In 1982, before they began their 100 percent participation *Quality Has Value* process, they held 11.8 percent of the market share in their primary product—good for second place in a wildly competitive field with dozens of players. By 1992, the share was up to 18.4 percent, they were in first place and pulling steadily away. The company has enjoyed several consecutive years of record profits; customer satisfaction and employee morale have also been high.

It is time for senior managers to take the lead in returning the power that they have slowly usurped from their subordinates over the years. True, an active, 100 percent employee quality process is much tougher to implement than the standard top-down, incremental approach, because it requires an emotional as well as a rational investment of time, ego, effort, and resources. And, too often, setting 100 percent as a goal is seen as an invitation to a lifetime consulting contract, which it definitely is not. While consultants have an important role to play in helping to establish training programs and facilitating discussions, the entire training period can be relatively short. It shouldn't take more than six months for a company of 3,000 people to move from an informed commitment to act to the launching of a multi-faceted, bottom line-impacting, quality process.

Whether plunging into a new quality effort or rejuvenating an old one, executives need to ask, "Who can we afford to exclude?" The only answer that makes any sense is, of course, "No one."

When an executive begins calling for "change in the corporate culture" or "change in the way we do things around here," the first question silently asked is, "And how are *you* going to change what *you* do?" If the response is, "I'm going to change the way you do things" or, worse, "I'm going to hire some people to tell you what to change," the project is doomed—regardless of how expensive the consultants, how elaborate the program, or how lavish the roll-out.

This is especially true if the change is aimed at improving quality. Quality improvement requires the personal, constant, and consistent involvement of top executives. In fact, the word "commitment" may be too weak; "obsession" may be more accurate.

A willingness to sign checks (usually large) for consultants and to make an annual speech (usually short) does not constitute commitment, much less obsession. Talking with employees at all levels, casually and formally, about quality; funding the classes and the structure needed to sustain a viable quality process; and being personally involved in the day-to-day operation of a unique quality process—that is what is needed.

There are, at least, three reasons why leaders might choose to do something that requires them to critically assess how they do their own jobs, to transfer considerable portions of the power they exercise down the chain, and to radically realign their own priorities: money, money, and more money. Quality makes money.

Secondary reasons include the preservation of jobs, the creation of jobs, the positive impact on the morale of all employees, and the simple fact that a quality process is not only wonderfully satisfying, it can be a great deal of fun.

All of these benefits are readily available so long as top management focuses tightly on quality—not on productivity and not on cost-cutting (these are by-products of a quality process).

The Quality Process

Executives must take responsibility for the definition, implementation, and continued activity of the quality process. It begins with personal development and learning. Having a group of executives attend an expensive school, while useful and perhaps even necessary to ensure a certain minimal knowledge level, is not enough. In the eyes of people who rarely go on a company-sponsored trip and whose favorite in-house training class was canceled last month for lack of funds, attendance at such schools can be viewed as recreation. Such attendance has the added disadvantage of being a "one shot" occasion, when what is needed are new habits.

That is why a series of in-house meetings featuring discussions of books and articles on quality has greater impact. Talk with some of the experts in the field. Send different executives to courses taught by experienced trainers whose books or articles are studied in the sessions. Ask each executive to report to or even teach his staff what he learned to speed the group learning process.

The object is to reach consensus at the top on whether a quality effort is appropriate or not. The boss cannot make the decision in isolation and storm ahead; if the top management team, acting as a team, hasn't decided that this is where they want the company to go, the results will never approach full potential.

Once a decision to proceed is made, the top management team should establish a Quality Steering Committee (under any name) to translate theory into action. A good rule of thumb here is that this committee be composed of either the number one or the number two executive from each division or major department. The committee's task is straightforward: to define a quality process that will formally enroll every member of the organization in the effort to continuously improve the organization. Funding must be made available; money well spent on a quality process is money wisely invested.

Meetings of the Steering Committee must have high priority. The definition of "tomorrow's company" must have precedence over all but the most calamitous problems of today. For reasons of style and substance, hold the meetings in the most noticeable conference room with religious regularity. Attend yourself. If employees are hearing (at least through the grapevine) all about this "new quality process" in the company's future but then see that the executives aren't making it to the Steering Committee meetings, they will excuse themselves immediately.

Another valuable action that has elements of both style and substance is the regular inclusion of a discussion of the quality process in every top management meeting. Ideally, it will be the first item on the agenda (so that it doesn't fall off the end of the schedule in a rush to finish). Once the habit is set, the executives can carry the procedure to their own staff meetings. At this point, it might be time to notify the company newspaper to begin publicizing the process company-wide.

Company executives (not outside consultants) should decide what elements actually go into the makeup of a company's quality process. Certain concepts are common to virtually all programs, systems or approaches. These need to be adopted. The specific techniques appropriate to implement these concepts must be adapted to the particular corporate culture at hand.

One key decision to make up front: who will be formally enrolled in the process when it is finally launched? The only logical answer, and the one that is most difficult to implement, is "everybody." Any lesser response invites the questions: "Why are you leaving them out? Are they already perfect? Or are they too stupid to improve?"

"Everybody" includes top executives. Whatever rules the company sets for participation in improving quality, they must apply across the board. When it comes to quality, everybody on the payroll has equal responsibility. If employees are required to attend classes on quality or to be members of a quality team, that applies to every employee from the CEO to the newest hire.

While the Steering Committee is progressing with its work, all of the company's executives can begin laying the groundwork for the new process. They can test some concepts. And talk about them. All the time. Much of what needs to be done can be categorized as communications and leadership.

One of the most valuable concepts can best be described as "listening down." Normally, business people are taught to listen up and proclaim down, reflecting the assumption that superior knowledge is always higher up the corporate ladder. Listening down, acknowledging the existence of a great, largely untapped, pool of knowledge on lower rungs of the corporate ladder is an integral principle of a successful quality process. Executives should start early, learning and actively practicing this new form of communication.

Listening down requires getting out and asking questions of real people, to include a large number of that most maligned of working classes, middle managers. It is precisely this kind of personal involvement that will insure that a quality process will retain its vigor, and its financial benefit to the company.

Talk about quality at every opportunity. Take part in training classes, either as a regular speaker or as a drop-in. This invites people to ask questions and make comments about the quality process with support for the company's training program.

Executives should be formally involved in thanking employees throughout the company. The simplest and most complete system is to first define a program of recognition, gratitude, and celebration that is structured so that most employees can earn recognition; and second to involve top management in every award presentation or congratulatory celebration, big or small. These award ceremonies, often no more than 10 minutes long, afford the executives the chance to ask successful employees what they have been doing. The information gained will be clearer, and more useful, than most of what remains in official company memos after they have been carefully worded and even more carefully screened. Regular, and frequent, trips throughout the company to say "thank you" also increase the executives' visibility and underscore their commitment to the idea of creating and maintaining an environment in which continual improvement is the norm.

Informed, active commitment to quality is the responsibility of top management. It will be even more critical in the future as an ever-increasing number of competitors challenge companies in both the manufacturing and service segments of the American economy. Soon, just getting better won't be enough. The question will become, "Who is getting better faster?" Only organizations whose leadership is personally and obviously involved in the quality effort will have the flexibility and drive necessary to take full advantage of the talents of every person on the payroll.

Leadership and Quality

Most executives would agree that involving all people on the payroll in the continual improvement of products and services is a commendable idea. So why doesn't more happen? Figuring out how to do it can be difficult. Actually doing it is more difficult still.

An emphasis on quality can be the glue that holds an organization together as it reshapes itself, first to survive and then to compete in an increasingly difficult world. An effective quality process gives value to the input of every employee; it moves a company away from a we/they structure in which one group thinks while the other, larger, group does the work.

A quality process is carefully crafted to take advantage of 100 percent of the work force and encourages employees to automatically take responsibility. Such processes all have one thing in common: they are run by a top management who considers the task to be a leadership role—not merely a management problem. Leadership is necessary because a quality process will require giving power to employees. The pushing of authority down the system to the appropriate level (i.e., where it is commensurate with responsibility) takes self-confidence. Only the self-confident can lead; the insecure are doomed to be managers forever.

One of the first acts of leadership called for is the informed, active, and obvious involvement of the top management team. Much has been said (in virtually every publication in print) about the need for commitment from the top. In truth, however, that bromide is insufficient. To agree that "this quality thing" is worth a try and to demonstrate commitment only through authorization of checks and an annual speech is the act of a manager. The commitment to change followed by informed, active, and obvious involvement is leadership.

Top management must then define the company's quality process. This task cannot be delegated. Consultants can be brought in, but only for specific periods and with the requirement that they leave their knowledge behind when they depart. They may be used at the beginning of an effort to define a process (to act as "research" resources) and to train the company's trainers to teach company employees particular skills. The quality process that an active top management group defines for their company, however, will doubtless be unique, which is highly desirable. Each organization, composed as it is of unique individuals and serving its own particular set of clients, is, in fact, different from any other.

Some principles, however, are fundamental to successful processes. Among these are: 100 percent involvement based on a belief that the personnel department has been hiring adults all these years; a structure which formally enrolls every employee in the effort and a method which encourages and implements ideas; and a varied program of recognition, gratitude, and celebration. By building a structure that enlists every person, a new and valuable basis for communications is established across all internal barriers. There is a reason for discussion, a common experience shared by everyone from the CEO to the most recently hired person—everyone is trying to make their piece of the action run better.

A readily accessible idea tracking system can also furnish fodder for communication. This is particularly true if ideas from the company president are on view to company employees. By displaying ideas to every employee, the president lets the company in on the problems executives are addressing. Frank Dodge, president of McCormack & Dodge, recently logged several ideas on the tracking system, well aware that in the following weeks, he would receive many suggestions from employees at all levels about the ideas his team were considering.

Three major objectives are accomplished. First, some suggestions are useful. Second, when changes occur, there are few, if any, surprises. Third, employees know that they have a part to play in the evolution of the company.

In addition to being informed and active, leadership must also be obvious. At Paul Revere Insurance Group, President Aubrey K. Reid and his top reports have taken part in over 1,500 recognition ceremonies for Paul Revere's Quality Teams during the first five years of their *Quality Has Value* process. Whenever a Quality Team earns any recognition, Reid or one of the senior vice presidents are there to talk with them, to say "thank you," and to present various gifts.

Companies with thriving quality processes are already making substantial changes—breaking down the barriers through leadership and communication. The final outcome is far from a foregone conclusion.

Chapter 32

Achieving Quality in Professional Services

by David A. Tierno, National Director of Ernst & Young's Management Consulting Group

Quality is the best way to beat the competition. And service quality is best achieved through a four-step process.

ONE of the most challenging and important problems any company faces today is differentiation. This is true for companies that sell products as well as companies that sell services. When marketing professional services, however, the problem is even more acute because the "product" is less tangible.

What must a professional service firm do to stand out from its competitors? The best and surest answer is so obvious that it appears to be nothing more than a truism: Commit to quality, to providing quality services and doing quality work. An important corollary is to be perceived by its clients as a high quality firm. Achieving quality demands the involvement of everyone in the firm and an ongoing commitment of time, energy, and resources.

If we examine why quality is absolutely necessary, what quality means, how we can produce quality work for clients, and how we should manage for quality, we may better understand why the successful professional service firm will be committed to quality, and will want to be perceived as a quality firm.

Quality: The Unqualified Necessity

A firm that commits to quality and consistently provides quality services enjoys many competitive advantages: it can more easily foster client loyalty and maintain successful client relationships; it can develop high employee morale and retain and reward employees; it can control costs, charge premium fees, and earn substantial profits.

Without quality, a firm may face such dire consequences as: losing clients to the competition, being forced to discount the fees for its services, finding that errors are commonplace, finding that time-consuming rework is a recurring necessity, spending inordinate time responding to client complaints, and suffering from high employee turnover rates.

Even when quality is recognized as an absolute necessity, it remains difficult to define. An intangible itself, "quality" is a term used to describe services that are also often intangible. By discussing quality, I hope to make it more tangible for professional service firms as well as for their clients and prospective clients.

Over the years, the definition of quality has evolved through at least four stages.

Transcendent definition. David Garvin, Harvard Business School's expert on quality, calls this the oldest definition of quality. It simply holds that quality is something we can recognize at sight but can never quite articulate or define. While true to a degree, this view of quality can lead to problems in actual practice. Any professional may, for example, expend much of his own effort and the client's resources to achieve a high degree of technical elegance, whether the product be an intricate legal argument or a lavish architectural design. While meaningful to the professional, this level of quality may be of little value to the client, and therefore inappropriate.

Product-based definition. This view of quality stressed a product's distinguishing attributes. In management consulting, for example, this resulted in an overemphasis on the quantity and packaging of such consulting "products" as reports and presentations. This led to some distortions and aberrations. There was a period in government consulting, for example, when results were measured by the sheer quantity of the documents produced: volume and quality became synonymous.

Manufacturing-based definition. This approach to quality attempted to establish quality control by first defining, then meeting a set of specific criteria. Consultants influenced by McKinsey and

Arthur Andersen began following standardized methodologies in an effort "to get things right the first time." These latter techniques are, to a certain extent, useful today. A standardized process and/or product can be a controlling factor in both the cost of delivering services and the quality of those services.

User-based definition. If David Garvin's statement "quality is in the eyes of the beholder" is true, then it makes sense for a professional who is market-driven (attuned to serving the needs that actually exist in the marketplace) to focus primarily on the needs of the customer or client. When Joseph Juran states "quality is fitness for use" and Hirotaka Takeuchi says "quality should primarily be customer-driven," they confirm this approach.

Solution-oriented Services

A professional who wants to achieve the highest useful quality for his or her client must know unequivocally what the client expects to accomplish. Anyone who serves clients knows that the client frequently knows what he wants, but may have only the vaguest idea of what he needs. One professional responsibility is to help the client understand what he actually needs as opposed to what he thinks he needs; this often requires the provider of services to spend a great deal of time up front defining the scope of the work and how performance should be measured.

As clients have become more sophisticated in their demands, services have become more refined and specific. Management consulting, for example, has become much more results-oriented. Where historically, consultants analyzed, advised, and recommended, today they must provide solution-oriented services. Where in the past clients occasionally asked consultants to help implement their recommendations, today clients demand that consultants implement functional solutions to the business problems they are retained to address. The solution-oriented consultant is, therefore, closer to providing a real "product."

Typically, the client asks for a specific solution, such as a Just-In-Time production method. Implementing a specific solution to a specific problem is considerably more difficult than diagnosing a problem and making suggestions. Implementing improvements to a particular business operation is much harder than delivering an erudite report.

Today's client, besides demanding results, is also typically concerned about cost. Because of competition in the marketplace, the client wants a good solution to his problem at a price he is willing to pay. Law firms, for example, have had to be extremely sensitive to this issue, because the high costs of litigation not infrequently render lawsuits counterproductive. (Garvin believes this issue is the foundation of the "value-based" approach to quality.)

The provider of professional services must therefore strike a balance. He must provide the solution at a price that allows him a profit, while making certain the client needs and wants this solution and perceives it as valuable. In other words, he must define the appropriate level of quality, remembering that the client may perceive personal standards of elegance as wasteful.

Standardized methodologies can help service professionals provide an appropriate level of quality consistently, while ensuring that the client receives a level of quality service that he perceives as consistent with his idea of value.

Four Steps to Quality Work

Professional service firms face a common problem best exemplified by CPA firms, whose clients are increasingly unwilling to pay standard fees for audit services. Because many clients fail to fully understand the meaning and importance of the CPA firms' opinion on the financial statements, there is a significant gap between the value the accountants place on the service and the value the clients perceive.

Many other professionals face an even greater problem: they have no objective, independent body to define service requirements and standards of performance. These professionals must define each project precisely. From the outset, the client must understand what he needs, what he can expect, and what can be achieved for the agreed-on price.

Again, it is a matter of balance. While methodologies and the delivery of services must become more standardized, each client assignment must be recognized as unique. Each client lives with a special set of circumstances, has unique needs and requirements and a corporate culture unlike any other. To meet that client's specific needs and give him the quality he deserves, the project should be customized so as to fashion a solution to the client's particular problem.

Each solution evolves, moreover, from an organic process that involves a number of interrelated steps.

The proposal. Writing a proposal is not a routine task. A proposal writer can't simply copy the last proposal or manual. Rather, the consultant and client must think long and hard about the business situation, discuss it in as broad a context as possible, and probe to reach the deepest possible understanding.

Proposals, of course, are written before there is a contractual agreement with the client, and this creates a problem. In today's competitive environment, management does not often allow much in-depth discussion of its needs before a firm is selected and the agreement is signed. This means the service professional is responsible for finding a way to validate and confirm the client's needs and requirements before charging forward in search of the appropriate solution.

The proposal is an integral part of professional services because it sets the stage for the delivery of the service and defines the project's parameters. It is the first attempt at describing the client's needs, what the service firm intends to do to meet those needs, and the expected results. The proposal is critical, therefore, to the notion of useful quality because it helps set and manage the client's expectations. If these expectations are clear from the beginning, they become the final goal toward which the professional strives, a guiding light to keep him on course, and a marker against which to measure progress.

Delivering services. To the client, what the professional does and how he does it are equally important. Professionals must, therefore, plan in three interrelated areas: 1) the process of delivering services; 2) the benchmarks used to measure progress during the project; and 3) the ground rules and protocols used in interacting with the client.

The importance of planning is best exemplified by a typical problem that most service professionals face: they often concentrate too intensely on the end result they are trying to achieve to the detriment of focusing on how they will achieve that result. They focus on a specific need, for example, installing a new accounts payable system or a new inventory system. The final result may be a system that works perfectly, so that inventory turnover is increased or stockouts are reduced. The consultant is, of course, satisfied.

The client, however, may be disappointed because he had different expectations. The client may have felt, for example, that the implementation should have included training his people to use the methodologies and techniques the project team used to develop the new system. In this case, the consultant leaves the engagement wondering why the client is not happy.

The client's disappointment can be traced back to the earliest stage of the project. From the outset, the client and the consultant should agree on the two objectives of the project: 1) implementing a new system that meets specific, pre-established criteria, and 2) training the client's personnel to use the system development methodologies and techniques.

After these objectives are defined at the beginning of the project, they must be built into the consultant's interactive work with the client. This approach should result in a clear set of procedures that allows both objectives to be met and, therefore, satisfies consultant and client alike. The key, however, which can be applied to other professionals as well, is in defining the results clearly in advance, so that they meet the client's expectations.

Ensuring reliability. The concept of "reliability" is much more commonly associated with products like automobiles, refrigerators, and vacuum cleaners than with services. Yet, as professional service firms increasingly concentrate their efforts on providing tangible "products" or results, they then must deal with a greater element of risk, a host of quality-related problems, and with the reliability of those results or "products." Product reliability can also extend into legalities related to the level of warranty the professional is willing to offer. He must manage and control the quality of the product and be able to ensure, for example, that a system he had installed operates efficiently and is easy to maintain, or that a design rendered by an industrial design firm is not only visually exciting but is also functional and can be produced within the cost parameters established by the client.

Quality assurance and product reliability in service firms relate to clearly defining objectives and managing client expectations at the outset. When the professional delivers what the client expects, according to standards on which both have agreed, then both are content.

Giving details their due. The client's perception of the level of quality is of the utmost importance. This perception develops over time and is affected by the way the professional and his firm handle details. Because mundane matters can color the client's view, the professional must be aware, for example, of how the client is treated when he calls the professional's office. If the client's phone calls are not returned promptly, he may decide the quality of the service is poor.

The client, after all, is free to use whatever measures he chooses to judge the quality of the service and the work. He may also expect the professional to maintain a higher standard than he does himself. While he may accept typographical errors in his own letters and memos, for example, he expects the professional's letters and memos to be perfect. Therefore, the actual physical appearance of anything that is delivered to the client, from a note to a presentation, must enhance the client's perception of the firm's quality.

Three Keys to Managing for Quality

To deliver high quality services consistently, the professional must make managing the quality of the service and the work delivered to clients his first priority. Those who try to concentrate on new business development to the exclusion of managing for quality are focusing on the short term. It is easier to market services if a firm or an individual consistently delivers high quality work and is perceived as giving clients significant added value.

It's also easier to sell services to an existing client than to cultivate a relationship with a new client. A professional who consistently provides high-quality work will find his clients returning to him again and again for solutions to new problems.

Delivering quality should become a way of life. The professional should approach a brief presentation for a local manufacturer and the conduct of a multimillion-dollar study for a major multinational financial services firm with the same commitment to quality. Each assignment, no matter its size or the stature of the client, can enhance or diminish a professional reputation. Everything counts— from a small brochure announcing a public seminar to the final presentation to the board of a Fortune 500 company.

Managing for quality means, first, focusing on people, second, training them, and third, providing leadership.

People, first and last. Quality begins and ends with the people who deliver the service to clients. People must be managed and supervised, trained and developed, motivated and rewarded, and supported, in turn, by management. Each person who represents the firm contributes, either positively or negatively, to the perception of the firm's quality.

If employee turnover is high, a firm can't deliver the highest quality service to its clients and, ultimately, the firm is not as profitable as it might be. Conversely, high quality work can help prevent employee turnover. People remain loyal to a firm that is perceived as being a high-quality firm, one they can take pride in. They participate in the firm's reputation and high morale.

Turnover often indicates poor quality. Though people may say they leave a firm for better opportunities or more money, they often move in the hope of having their expectations met. High turnover means a professional services firm has a problem.

Quality training means quality work. Training is not an ancillary activity. Training helps people develop the skills they need to deliver quality work. Professionals must be trained in many skill areas, ranging from technical areas to how to manage client relationships and deal with legal and business risks. If the most junior staff person is not technically competent to perform whatever is asked of him, there is a risk of undermining the client's perception of the firm's quality. With a trained and competent staff, management can deliver high-quality work consistently and profitably.

More important than training, however, is recruiting. New recruits must have basic technical skills and solid interpersonal skills. Once hired, the firm must encourage ongoing development of the entire gamut of skills.

Leadership—the source of quality. When a firm's top professionals actively manage client expectations, supervise staff work, and review all deliverables on a project, problems with clients occur rarely. On the other hand, quality and financial problems occur often when top level people are not involved in the project. The correlation is clear: quality work demands the close, hands-on participation of senior practitioners.

To produce quality work and provide quality services, staff people need the feedback—performance appraisals and evaluations—of senior professionals. Less experienced professionals need to know how well they performed and to have constructive guidance about improving their performance. To be most useful, such evaluations should occur as a project is completed and, in long-term assignments, at least every six months.

Leadership is more important, however, because it is the foundation on which any quality effort is built. A firm cannot achieve quality unless senior management is committed to doing whatever is necessary to achieve it.

Quality Perceived, Quality Achieved

If "quality is in the eyes of the beholder," then consider the perceived quality of a professional service firm. Clients' perceptions of the firm's quality depends on how the clients view the accretion of literally everything the firm does, including the interaction between any and all the people in that firm with all the people in the client firm.

A service firm's reputation, though intangible, can be measured accurately by its financial results and by such barometers as the number of repeat assignments performed for clients. Conversely, a firm that is forced to discount work regularly or that works for each client only once should seriously evaluate the quality of the service it provides and the quality of the work it delivers.

Incontrovertibly, quality must be the primary focus of professional service firms. By focusing on quality, the service professional can control factors that cause costs to increase, such as high turnover, discounts, and morale and client relationship problems. Those who manage their practices most successfully are those who concentrate on providing quality work. When service professionals get personally involved with clients and manage their expectations, profits follow. As clients perceive that a firm's commitment to quality differentiates it from its competitors, that firm will grow and flourish.

Today, many clients do not perceive that they are receiving long-term value from their service professionals, whether they be lawyers, public relations firms, or even doctors. Consider the opportunity this environment presents to a firm that consistently provides high-quality, value-added services to clients and helps them solve their problems in a spirit of personal involvement, so that the client perceives the firm's commitment to helping them achieve their goals. Clients are looking for firms that can provide the kind of quality they can depend on. When they find those firms, they will come running.

Chapter 33

TQM: Forging Ahead or Falling Behind?

by Richard S. Wellins, Senior Vice President of Development Dimensions International

Only during the past few years have organizations paid serious attention to a strategy called total quality management.

TOTAL quality management (TQM) differs from other quality campaigns in its approach. It involves an integrated, systematic, organization-wide strategy for improving product and service quality to meet or exceed customer expectations. TQM isn't a program, nor is it a specific tool or technique. Rather, it represents a shift in thinking and culture—a way of doing a job every day. Meeting the needs of customers—through speed, flexibility, superior service, and near-perfect levels of product quality—has become the critical business strategy.

A strategy as comprehensive as TQM often involves the transformation of underlying beliefs, values, and culture. It also requires changes in the way people behave. While there are many success stories, growing evidence suggests that many TQM-driven organizations have trouble achieving such a transformation.

Seven Trends

Several studies have tried to quantify TQM's success and identify practices that facilitate or hinder implementation. Further, there's a growing focus on the importance of the "human side of quality." In our study, we discovered seven major trends.

1. Total Quality Management is still an emerging business strategy. Today's culture demonstrates an amazingly low tolerance of any management trend lasting more than a few years. Where TQM articles once were euphoric, many now express disappointment. Some managers and experts are beginning to say TQM's time is past. But according to our surveys, TQM is still getting off the ground.

2. TQM does improve organizational performance. Most organizations experience moderate to high success in three areas—operational results (cycle-time reduction, higher quality, improved productivity, reduced defects); levels of customer satisfaction and retention; and organizational climate (morale, turnover, quality of work life). This is an encouraging trend, especially considering that most respondents are only a year or two into the TQM journey.

3. TQM success takes patience. Long-term commitment to TQM influences people's perception of success, especially in customer satisfaction and retention and operational results. Based on data from the multilevel survey, organizations with two or more years of TQM experience saw greater gains in customer satisfaction and retention and operational results than those at it less than two years. Organizational climate remained fairly constant regardless of length of implementation. These results support the idea that organizations willing to stick with TQM longer are more likely to reap greater benefits.

4. A significant gap exists between what's needed for successful TQM implementation and actual execution. We examined 13 factors critical to TQM's success: 1) training—ensuring that people have the skills, knowledge, and techniques needed to participate effectively in the process; 2) leadership commitment—modeling behaviors that others should use to improve overall performance; 3) customer focus—focusing on the requirements and expectations of internal and external customers; 4) alignment of systems—making all production, information, financial, planning, and personnel systems consistent with the quality improvement effort; 5) empowerment and involvement—enabling employees to solve problems and make decisions, activities traditionally reserved for senior executives; 6) communication—providing frequent, ongoing two-way information on the purpose and status of the TQM effort; 7) implementation and rollout—determining what's important, what will be done, and who will do it; 8) vision and values—having a shared concept of what the organization can become and having guiding principles for improving performance and customer satisfaction; 9) performance management and appraisal—using a consistent process for managing performance that links people's performance to the organization's quality goals; 10) measurement—using measures to assess performance, ensure feedback, and consider trends; 11) supplier involvement—creating cooperative relationships with external suppliers and vendors to improve quality, delivery, and cost; 12) recognition and rewards—using formal and informal recognition to reinforce quality initiatives and sustain quality improvement; and 13) tools and techniques—selecting and using the most appropriate methods for implementing TQM.

Unfortunately, we discovered a big difference between how participants perceive the importance of the factors versus how well they think their organizations actually practice them. Despite the importance assigned to the factors, participants reported limited proficiency. Experiencing the largest gaps between importance and proficiency were: training, alignment of systems, leadership commitment, recognition and rewards, performance management, and appraisal. All the factors are vital to successful TQM. Ignoring any one of them could be leaving out a critical piece of the TQM puzzle. Unfortunately, organizations have a long way to go toward practicing the factors in the workplace.

5. Success breeds success. Organizations experiencing high overall success emphasize the importance of the factors more than moderate or low-success organizations do. The same is true for proficiency: High success organizations do a better job on the 13 factors. Evidently, the more success an organization has, the more importance is placed on factors. The more importance it places on the factors, the better it does.

6. Demonstrated leadership commitment is critical to TQM success. The executive survey explored which organizational levels are perceived as most resistant to TQM. Corporate leaders took some responsibility for their organizations' TQM shortcomings; in fact, they laid more blame on themselves than on front-line associates or supervisors. But they still were more likely to point a finger at middle management as the biggest source of resistance. This trend suggests that organizations have a long way to go in building the support and commitment of those "in the middle." The relationship between senior executive commitment and TQM success or failure is clear. Corporate leaders either feed or starve the quality initiative.

7. TQM still is the most viable long-term business strategy. The complexity of TQM—and some of the recent negative reports about it—haven't soured organizations to the concept. Respondents ranked

TQM as the strategy most likely to have a long-term effect on their competitive positions. Workplace training and development was number two. Of the three strategies tied for third, two (improving production and support processes, and focus on teams or teamwork) are underlying components of TQM.

Organizations are beginning to realize the benefits of long-term strategies involving the "total" organization. Most respondents selected strategies that require change in culture and processes instead of ones that were more likely to be a quick fix.

What they didn't rank highly is almost as interesting. External strategies, such as governmental regulations and assistance, took a backseat to inside strategies, such as TQM and workplace training. The Malcolm Baldrige National Quality Award came in last, perhaps because of a growing realization that the award is a means, not an end.

Section Four

The Business Consultant's Perspective

To the business management consultant who has other things on the plate, quality is often an appetizer, at least initially. Later it may become an entree.

Every consultant with a memory or a copy machine is quick to pick up on the lexicon of quality. Beyond language, there lies a promised land of real results—improved products and services and more customer satisfaction, resulting in better bottom-line performance. Still, the 1-2-3 formula often fails to deliver; hence, we hear talk of quality as "a campaign that failed."

Any consultant worth his or her salt, however, knows that a superficial stab at quality is bound to fail. The only way to bring home the bacon is to last it out, see it through, stick with it. Of course, that's tough to do when senior executives are playing a concurrent game of musical chairs and worrying about sizing, partnering, merging, reengineering, etc.

That's why we see a "steady-as-she-goes" refrain coming from the lips of **Stephen R. Covey**, chairman of Covey Leadership Center. His "basic principles" approach to Total Quality suggests a long-term observance of the laws upon which quality is predicated. **Kenneth Blanchard**, chairman of Blanchard Training and Development, and his associate **Richard Ruhe** counsel leaders to measure quality through the eyes of their customers with the basic objective of meeting or surpassing expectations. **Albert J. Bernstein**, clinical psychologist and author of *Neanderthals at Work,* notes that one of the reasons why quality is hard to come by is that it's hard to measure. **Guy A. Hale**, chairman of Alamo Learning Systems, says if we hope to "close the quality loop" we need to review the "critical realities" and create a quality environment. **Philip R. Thomas**, chairman and CEO of Thomas Group, insists that good intentions aside, "quality is not enough" and that we need to close the "competitiveness gap."

Donna E. Shalala, Secretary of the Department of Health and Human Services, turns our attention to the high stakes of "quality education" and asks for more business-university partnerships. **Lawrence M. Miller**, chairman of L.M. Miller & Company, asserts that "the key to total quality is customer focus." **Buck Rodgers**, former Vice President of Marketing for IBM, reminds us that any way we cut it, "mediocrity is in trouble." **R. Art McNeil**, founder and former CEO of The Achieve Group, and **Barry Sheehy**, principal of The Atlanta Consulting Group, talk about the "seven prerequisites" and the "basic values" that go with quality.

And to end this section and book, **Tom Peters**, president of The Tom Peters Group, says that in spite of the best-seller acceptance of *In Search of Excellence,* the search continues. While there are "pockets of excellence," the sad fact of the matter is that "excellence is the exception." After all is said and done, it is the only thing that matters, especially from a customer's perspective. And that's a good note to end on—the customer's perspective. CEOs, managers, quality consultants, and other business consultants can talk, write, pitch, and present until they are blue in the face, but what matters is the customer's perception and experience of the value of the product or service.

Chapter 34

Basic Principles of Total Quality

by Stephen R. Covey,
Chairman of Covey Leadership Center

*Certain universal principles and purposes
must be observed to obtain total quality of
services and products.*

W HEN one of our governing values is total quality, we will care not only about the quality of our products and services but also about the quality of our lives and our relationships.

The paradigm of total quality is continuous improvement. No person or company should be content to stay where they are, no matter how successful they now seem to be. And very few people or companies could possibly be content with the status quo if they were regularly receiving accurate feedback on their performance from their stakeholders. Quality begins with an understanding of our stakeholders' needs and expectations, but ultimately it means meeting or exceeding them.

Four Areas of Total Quality

Total quality is an expression of the need for continuous improvement in four areas: 1) personal and professional development; 2) interpersonal relations; 3) managerial effectiveness; and 4) organizational productivity.

Personal and professional development. Character and skill development is a process of ongoing improvement or progression, a constant upward spiral. The personal side of total quality means total integrity around your value system—and that suggests that you are always getting better, personally and professionally.

W. Edwards Deming's principle, constancy of purpose, implies that we first *have* a purpose or mission—a statement of what we are about, a vision of what we can become. The common denominator of success is a strong, empowering, guiding, inspiring, uplifting purpose. If you have it clearly set into your mind, if you begin with the end in mind, that purpose will guide everything. It will unleash your creative capacities; because of it, you will tap into your subconscious mind and bring out of it its memory, its contents. You begin to work from your imagination, not memory. You are not limited or tied to the past, but have an unlimited sense of what is possible in the future; your mind-set is prophecy, not just history.

Continuous improvement means you are not content with some-thing being half-right or half-true. Your customers certainly won't be content. And if you are getting accurate feedback from them, you will be motivated and challenged to improve.

Many executives lack the internal security to seek and take feedback from stakeholders; in fact, they are threatened by it. And yet feedback is the breakfast, lunch, and dinner of champions. Champions are continuously getting feedback, and they listen and learn from it. They use it to improve their performance day by day. Personal and organizational improvement programs are built on accurate feedback, not on inaccurate social data. The more your self-image is framed and your security formed in the social mirror, the more threatened you are by feedback.

The key to a quality life is the secret life. Once in New York City, I attended the play *The Secret Garden.* It was particularly poignant for me that evening because my mother had just died.

The story is about a young girl whose mother and father die of cholera in India as the play begins. She is sent to live with her uncle in a large British manor. The old house is filled with romantic spirits. As the restless girl explores the grounds of the estate, she discovers the entrance to the magical secret garden, a place where anything is possible.

When she first enters the garden, she finds that it appears to be dead, much like her cousin, a bedridden boy, and her uncle, still haunt-ed by memories of his lovely wife who died giving birth to the boy. In harmony with natural laws and principles, the girl faithfully plants seeds and brings new life to the garden. As the roots are warmed and the garden cultivated, she brings about a dramatic transformation of the entire culture within one season.

When I returned home to Salt Lake City the next day to speak at my mother's funeral, I referred to *The Secret Garden,* because for me and many others, my mother's home was a secret garden where we could escape and be nurtured by positive affirmation. In her eyes, all about us was good, and all that was good was possible.

We all live three lives: public, private, and secret. In our public lives, we are seen and heard by colleagues, associates, and others within our Circle of Influence. In our private lives, we interact more intimately with spouses, family members, and close friends. The secret life is part of the other two. We could be in the middle of a crowd and ask, "What does this mean to me?"

The secret life is where your heart is, where your real motives are—the ultimate desires of your life. And this is the mainspring that motivates the other two lives. Many executives never visit the secret life. Their public and private lives are essentially scripted by who and what precedes and surrounds them or by the pressures of the environment. And so they never exercise that unique endowment of self-awareness—the key to the secret life—where they stand apart from themselves and observe their own involvement.

Courage is required to explore our secret life because we must first withdraw from the social mirror, where we are fed positive and negative feedback continuously. As we get used to this social feedback, it becomes a comfort zone. And we may opt to avoid self-examination and idle away our time in a vacuum of reverie and rationalization. In that frame of mind, we have little sense of identity, safety, or security.

The most critical junctures in my life take place when I visit my secret life and ask, "Why am I doing this?" These are times when I choose my motives. One such time occurred the first time I heard Dag Hammarskjold say, "It is more noble to give yourself completely to one individual, than to labor diligently for the salvation of the masses." That statement had such a profound effect on me that I started to say to myself in regard to my relationships with other people, "Wait a minute—it's my life. I can choose my own motives."

One of the exciting fruits of the "secret garden" is ability to choose your own motives. Until you choose your own motives, you really can't choose to live your own life. Everything flows out of motive and motivation—the root of our deepest desires.

When I get into a perplexing situation, I enter into my secret life. That's where I find not only motives but also correct principles—that's where inner wisdom is.

As you explore the secret life, you tap into self-awareness, imagination, conscience, and into the exercise of free will to choose another motive. People who regularly explore their secret life and examine their motives are better able to see into the hearts of others, practice real empathy, bestow real empowerment, and affirm one's worth and identity.

A healthy secret life will benefit your private and public lives in many ways. For example, when I'm preparing to give a speech, I read aloud a favorite sermon because it helps me to purify my motive. I lose all desire to impress. My only desire is to bless. And when I go to a public setting with that motive, I have great confidence and inner peace. I feel more love for the people and feel much more authentic.

Executives who attend our leadership training often tell me, "This is the first time in many years that I've done any soul searching. I've seen myself as if for the first time, and resolved that my life is going to be different. I'm going to try to be true to what I believe." Many people write me to say, "Your principles have made the difference. I'd never thought about some of them before, but I resonate with them." That's because these principles are stored in people's secret life.

And yet most of us spend our busy days doing our thing, never pausing long enough to enter the secret life, the secret garden, where we can create masterpieces, discover great truths, and enhance every aspect of our public lives.

Interpersonal. Total quality on an interpersonal level means making constant deposits into the Emotional Bank Accounts of others. It is continually building good will and negotiating in good faith, not in fear. If you create an expectation of continuous improvement but fail to deliver on that expectation, you will see a buildup of fear and negative energy.

Emotional Bank Accounts can evaporate fast—particularly when expectations of continuous communication and improvement are violated. If communication doesn't take place, then people begin to tap into their memories and into their fears and spin off negative scenarios and start planning based on those scenarios.

In interdependent enterprises such as a marriage or a business, past deposits will evaporate unless people are continually making new deposits in their partner's Emotional Bank Account. With old friends, we don't need to make many new deposits because we have few expectations. We can pick up where we left off and achieve instant rapport. Moreover, with old friends, we rarely deal with interdependent jugular issues, only pleasant, happy memories. But in a marriage, family, or business, we deal with jugular issues day-by-day, and these require constant new deposits into the Emotional Bank Account. If we aren't giving 12 hugs a day to some people, we will soon have a withdrawal state because our deposits are essentially evaporative in their nature.

Interpersonal quality means giving those 12 hugs a day—physical hugs, emotional hugs, verbal hugs to the people around us—so that those deposits are constantly being made.

Managerial. Managerial quality is basically nurturing win-win performance and partnership agreements—making sure they are "in sync" with what is happening inside that person and what is happening inside the business. These Win-Win Agreements are subject to renegotiation at any time—hopefully on a synergistic basis, not a positional bargaining basis, and open to all the dynamics and vicissitudes of the market. So there is a sense of two-way openness.

Win-win thinking creates teamwork. Win-lose thinking creates rivalry. Rivalries are common in established systems as departments develop a life of their own, and their own survival mechanisms. Rivalries are very natural when people have limited resources; they perceive their professional world as a limited pie, and they gradually develop win-lose approaches. They sit and talk about "those guys over there" and about what they are going to do to get more internal resources for building their empires.

Our fiercest competitors are right inside our own divisions or departments. And who needs internal competition when we have plenty of it out there in the market?

We need internal unity to get win-win cooperation, loyalty to the mission, constancy of purpose. Win-lose competition is fueled by bad-mouthing other people behind their backs. If you have a problem with somebody, go to them, discuss the problem with them, talk it through, and then get into team building. It is disheveling to the culture to have rivalries.

Most people search for quality in techniques, practices, and processes; they don't realize that quality requires a whole different explanation of the role of management. All great breakthroughs are breaks with old thinking. Breakthrough thinking comes from not continuing to look through our pair of glasses at our work—it is to take our glasses off and to examine the lens.

Management looks through its pair of glasses and does its work, but leadership looks at the lens and says, "Is that the right frame of reference?" Management works in the systems to make them work. Leadership works on the systems. Leadership deals with direction, with vision, with purpose, with principles, with top line, and with people building, culture building, Emotional Bank Account building, and strengthening people. Management deals more with control, logistics, and efficiency. Leadership deals with the top line, management deals with the bottom line. The hand can't say to the foot, "I have no need of thee." Both leadership and management, effectiveness and efficiency, are necessary.

Few people give as much emphasis to the people side of what W. Edwards Deming says as they do to the technical side. But how do you develop the concept of a leader as a source of help? How do you remove fear, remove barriers, and build cross-functional teams and personal self-worth? The human side is the heart of it because people are the programmers—they produce everything else.

People must know that they are being managed by principles and are entitled to due process. You can't manipulate people's lives and play with their rice bowls arbitrarily without making massive withdrawals from their Emotional Bank Accounts. If you must cut costs to remain economically viable and competitive, see that it's done according to due process; otherwise, you can become overdrawn immediately. And once fear gets into the culture, everyone wonders what is going to happen to him or her.

Once the executive vice president of a large company told me, "I've been scared twice in my life—first when I ran up the beaches of Iwo Jima after seeing two-thirds of the first wave killed right in front of me."

"And the second time?" I asked.

"Coming to work here just this morning."

"How so?"

He said, "You never know what the old man is going to do. Twice I've seen him capriciously move in on people and disrupt their rice bowls. That created such a fear in me that I have never forgotten it. And I can't get over it. I never know when I might be hit."

If you violate a key principle even once, that one event will affect the quality of your relationship because people never know when you might lose it again.

Management's job is empowerment, and empowerment means "Give a man a fish, you feed him for a day. Teach him how to fish, you feed him for a lifetime." When you give people principles, you empower them to govern themselves. They have a sense of stewardship. You entrust them with principles to work with; guidelines to work within; resources to draw upon; win-win performance criteria to be measured against; consequences and rewards to work for. When you empower people, your paradigm of your role changes. You become a servant. You no longer control others; they control themselves. You become a source of help.

If you want to influence and empower people, first recognize that they are resourceful and have vast untapped capability and potential. Understand their purpose, point of view, language, concerns, customers, and boss. Be loyal. Don't do other things that undermine the emotional ties. Maintain credibility. By empowering people, you increase your span of control, reduce overhead, and get rid of unnecessary bureaucracy.

Empowerment takes an Abundance Mentality—an attitude that there is plenty for everybody and to spare, and the more you share the more you receive. People who are very threatened by the successes of others see everyone as a competitor. They have a Scarcity Mentality. Emotionally, they find it very hard to share power, profit, and recognition.

Organizational. Proactive leadership springs from an awareness that we are not a product of our systems or environments. Those things powerfully influence us, but we can choose our response to those things. Proactivity is the essence of real leadership. Every great leader has a high level of proactive energy and vision—a sense that "I am not a product of my culture, my conditioning, and the conditions of my life; rather, I am a product of my value system, attitudes, and behavior—and those things I control."

Deming continually emphasized that quality starts at the top—that the leadership of the organization must be intimately involved in the process to see that the quality paradigm is translated into the minds and hearts of people. He noted that the quality crisis is more fundamental than technique and that the solution calls for a new paradigm, a new way of viewing our roles, and a transformation of management operations. Quality is not always doing things better—it's doing different things.

The heart of organizational continuous improvement is problem solving around stakeholder information. Most organizations do problem solving around financial data and analysis. But the best organizations are constantly getting information from all stakeholders—all those who have a stake in the welfare of the enterprise—and they listen fully and then develop solutions based upon that diagnosis. This is why they are in a constant state of improvement. If our improvement paradigm is one-time, seasonal, or unsystematic, we are not moving toward total quality.

In financial accounting, everyone is trained in the eight steps: gather data, diagnose data, set up objectives, identify and select and evaluate alternatives, make a decision, implement the decision, study the results against the objectives, then go back to gathering data. In human resource accounting, we often stop at gathering data—one step.

Stakeholder information systems are rare. Sure, management will gather data occasionally through some survey, but that only arouses expectations and creates disillusionment unless the exercise results in change. And the next time they attempt to gather information, they encounter cynicism. The quality in those organizations is hit and miss, often determined by whether individual employees are committed to quality improvement.

Real quality improvements happen when management begins to resolve problems around stakeholder information. Most organizations don't even have the tools to get the data. They don't have a human resource approach to problem solving; they use a benevolent authoritarian style, and so total quality becomes a program of the company instead of the philosophy and value of every person in the company.

Procter & Gamble's first step to total quality is always to understand their consumers—to understand what they require, what they demand, what they want. That's first, and everything is driven by that. The next step is to give them more than they expect, to go the second mile, to give them service, the augmented product that wins such competitive advantage.

I recommend that every organization develop a feedback system to know what stakeholders—shareholders, customers, employees, communities, suppliers, distributors, and other parties—want and expect. If done systematically, scientifically, and anonymously, using random sampling, this information will have the same accuracy and objectivity as financial accounting. We can then see at a glance the progress we are making with our suppliers and customers.

I also suggest that every organization develop synergistic relationships with customers and suppliers. There is a place for competition, but it's not in areas where you need cooperation. If you're in an area that requires interdependent teamwork, do all you can to get rid of competition and to get synergy; reward people for cooperating and teaming, for giving their best ideas. Diversity in ideas, not just gender and race, is very powerful, especially when people respect and value the differences in perceptions, feelings, opinions, and backgrounds.

A Total Philosophy

Total quality is a total philosophy, a total paradigm of continuous improvement in all four dimensions. If you don't have it personally you won't get it organizationally. You can't expect organizations to improve when the people don't improve. To improve systems and processes, people have to mature to where they can create win-win solutions using empathy and synergy.

In our training, we emphasize the human side more than the technical side of quality because we believe that the origin and essence of total quality is empathy with the motives and buying habits of customers.

Everything is guided by feedback from internal and external customers and from other stakeholders. The key to total quality is to listen to your stakeholders, to seek first to understand, then to be understood.

Why isn't the principle of continuous improvement more fully implemented by individuals and organizations? Generally, we are not hurting enough yet. We are like the frog that stays in hot water heated one degree at a time. In a decade, if the present trends of moral degradation and economic deterioration continue, we won't govern our economic future—we will be owned, sold to a higher society. Second, we don't want to change our lifestyles. We want quality to be a program *for* people instead of a value *in* people.

Even the best companies—companies striving to achieve total quality—generally regard quality as a program, a compartment. It's not integrated in their structure, systems, and style. But total quality is rooted in timeless principles such as faith, hope, humility, industry, constancy, improvement, progression, growth, virtue, and truth. And without the roots, we won't get the fruits. Unless we center our lives and companies on the governing principles of total quality, our methods alone won't produce quality products, services, or relationships.

A Total Approach

Every executive could learn some valuable lessons from Solectron, a company that won the Malcolm Baldrige Award. The power of the Malcolm Baldrige Award is that it's not self-evaluation, but rather it is based on objective, external criteria and standards that put management and everyone else through their paces.

From my study of the Solectron corporation, I conclude that in our efforts to improve quality, productivity, and profitability, we have to work holistically. We can't just do a quick-fix program to improve communication, for example, if we have misaligned systems. We can take people into the wilderness for two days and have them do free falls off mountains to learn trust, but if they come back to misaligned systems, all our improvement efforts are undone. We can reorganize, restructure, or reengineer the company—or simply come up with a new compensation system or a new strategic plan—but if we lack a foundation of trust, again our work is undone.

Solectron designed a total approach that deals with the entire package. Their high degree of employee empowerment allows them to move away from inspection toward prevention. They anticipate and prevent problems, so that quality is designed and built in from the beginning. They learned early that to compete and win in the international arena, they had to offer world-class products and services. And so at Solectron, quality management is not just a strategy, it is a new style of working and thinking. Their dedication to quality and excellence is more than good business, it's a way of life.

They started a partnership program with key suppliers and customers to tap their resources, ideas, and talents. As a result of these partnerships, Solectron has improved productivity, performance, and effectiveness. Defect levels declined, yields increased, and on-time delivery reached 98 percent.

Solectron executives create openness and trust with all internal and external stakeholders by entering into strategic partnerships with employees, suppliers, owners, shareholders, distributors, and customers. They share with each other, and synergize around common problems. They also study their competitors and identify the best practices in different functions so that they have benchmarks to evaluate themselves by. Improvement accelerates when performance is measured and benchmarked against the best in the world.

Win-Win Agreements are made with all stakeholders. The Win-Win Empowerment Agreement is a clear mutual understanding based on a mutual-gain idea produced through synergistic interaction with other people. Much communication takes place among stakeholders. Weekly they ask their customers to rate them on quality, delivery, communication, and service and then they share this information with customers.

They have learned that quality control can't be imposed from top to bottom; they understand that quality management must cut through organization charts across departments and offices, that quality culture does not depend upon titles and job descriptions, and finally they realize they're only as strong as the intelligence, judgment, and character of their people.

What works for Solectron can work for other companies. Winning the Baldrige Award confirms the power of a principle-centered approach where quality is seen as a dynamic process, continuous and evolutionary. And quality will give any individual or organization a long-term competitive advantage. If quality is in the character of the individual and in the culture of the organization, it can't be duplicated by anyone.

Chapter 35

Total Quality Leadership

by Kenneth Blanchard, Chairman, and Richard Ruhe, an associate of Blanchard Training & Development

The quality of leadership will determine the quality of product and service and the level of customer satisfaction.

AMERICAN companies have problems with quality because most executives don't care enough about it unless they have to care because quality becomes a matter of survival for them.

There have been some brilliant successes in quality in very different organizations. Marvin Andrews, the city manager of Phoenix, Arizona, has won national awards for quality by capitalizing on employee recommendations to improve services. At Xerox, David Kearns and Paul Allaire confronted the issue of "value-added" head-on, and now Xerox provides a Total Satisfaction Guarantee. By making sales associates responsible for on-line quality operations, Sam Walton's company, Wal-Mart, has managed to soar during an economic recession. Jim Martin at McDonnell Douglas Helicopter has done the same. Bob Galvin's uncompromising commitment to the quality program at Motorola put quality at the top of every meeting agenda.

The Human Factor

Quality starts with meeting or surpassing customer expectations. Even though robots have no learning curve, even though machines don't go on strike, even though the business of providing products and services has been heavily influenced by exotic electronic and computer-based office machinery, the most critical single factor is the person who makes sure the product or process is meeting the customer's requirements. At some point, American executives and employees must realize that, no matter how prosperous business is right now, if they don't take care of the customer, the bottom line will stop growing and start shrinking.

Bankers have learned, for example, that many customers are happier dealing with automatic teller machines (ATMs) because ATMs do a better job of banking than do real tellers. Bankers have come to realize that they must focus on meeting customer needs rather than giving away free toasters for new accounts.

Health Maintenance Organizations (HMOs) are learning that although professional health care is important, efficient and effective handling of patient questions and requests is critical. Insurance companies, utilities, and real estate agencies are learning the same lesson.

If quality can be achieved, why do so many people shy away from taking action? In our opinion, it's more a lack of leadership than a lack of awareness. Leaders, not slogans, turn quality talk into quality action. Quality originates in operations, not in the quality department. Leaders have to put themselves into the action to make quality happen. If leaders remain distant from the day-to-day operations, there is inadequate emphasis on quality. Without the necessary support and reinforcement, strong beliefs dictated from the top will die at the top. People, not procedures, systems, or job descriptions, provide the outputs of every part of the organization.

But how do these people become the quality providers? Our premise of effective leadership is that there is no one best way to handle the customer, to plan, to manage, and to lead. Effective leadership is situational and based on the commitment and competence of followers in meeting the requirements of external and internal customers.

Customers are very loyal to suppliers who routinely get the job done right, who quickly take care of problems and complaints. Leaders may need to be closely involved, showing and telling what needs to be done, depending on the level of follower competence and commitment. Or, leaders may need to provide support and encouragement. Or, leaders may need to get out of the way altogether when they have people working with and for them who can and will do the job at hand. When they try to provide guidance, they slow down the work of competent followers. And customers are not loyal to suppliers who take too long to provide for their needs. They don't complain; they don't fight; they just take their business elsewhere.

Leadership, like quality, isn't an event, it's a process. Part of that process is diagnosing what people need. Another part of the process involves being flexible to provide for those needs. And finally, leaders have to contract with their people, so that all concerned are involved in determining exactly how the customer will best be served.

The quality leader is the battalion commander who isn't content to read about what's being served in the mess hall, but goes in to experience it firsthand. He assesses the circumstances and then decides what, if any, action is called for.

Quality leaders are situational leaders—sometimes involved to the hilt, but sometimes moving aside when they know their people can do the job best on their own. They push to see that the job is done right. And they do it by tapping the power of the best resource they have: their people.

As Fred Smith, chairman and CEO of Federal Express, says, "Customer satisfaction begins with employee satisfaction." Situational leadership creates satisfaction because people are our ultimate high technology. Products and processes help, but the primary quality resources are human resources. And when people come first, service, quality, and profits will follow.

Out of the Clouds

Too many managers and executives find quality to be nebulous. Simply stated, quality is what customers should get out of using a product—pride is what producers must build into making a product.

Any company can start to get a handle on quality if they focus on two key concepts: 1) the importance of customer perceptions in determining the acceptable quality of your company's products and 2) the importance of pride in building quality into your products.

Philip Crosby defines quality very specifically as "meeting specifications." The catch is that it's the customer who ultimately decides if the specifications are met, so customer satisfaction is what determines what quality is.

To design and deliver a quality product or service you have to start with the customer and his or her needs and preferences. That may be harder than it sounds since sometimes customers don't know what they want or even that they have a certain need. For example, a certain product or service might be able to save a customer money, but if the customer doesn't know that the product or service is available, it probably would not be an expressed need.

Sometimes customers know exactly what they want—AFTER they see or use your product or service. In other instances—especially regarding technical needs—the customer might clearly know what is needed, but not be able to clearly define the need in terms of specifications or product features.

This lack of clarity should not sway an organization from specifically determining the preferences of its customers. In fact, your persistence in this matter can create a distinct competitive advantage for the organization. It could even make a difference between a company's success or failure.

To find out what your customers want, an organization must consistently seek feedback, ask questions, and be willing to listen without biases. Tom Peters calls listening with as few preconceptions as possible "naive listening." Naive listening is crucial if you really are committed to learning what your customers have to say.

The distinction of starting from the customer's perspective is what characteristically distinguishes marketing from selling. Many companies work hard at offering a technically improved product with little or no regard as to if such an improvement is desired by customers. They then try to sell the product to meet every conceivable customer need. Often the match between the product and the customer need is a force fit.

Successful companies realize that pleasing the customer is a critical aspect of their business. Instead of forcing products onto customers, they strive to keep in close contact with customer needs and concerns and then develop products that meet those needs and concerns. This is the essence of marketing.

At Apple Computer, for example, senior officers of the company regularly listen in on a toll-free customer service line so as to be able to better keep in touch with customer concerns. They realize that keeping close to the customer is not a luxury, but a necessity—paramount to the company's success.

Product quality, then, begins and ends with the customer. Your job is to consistently focus on the customer in the development and production of a product or the delivery of a service. Doing so will give you a clearer perspective on what quality means for your company.

Design and Build Quality

Once it is clear what customers want, how should companies go about meeting those expectations? The most traditional approach to trying to improve the quality of products is done through the practice commonly known as "quality control." With quality control, companies focus on looking for mistakes after products are made by inspecting them and then rejecting faulty products.

Unfortunately, "inspecting" quality into products does not work very well. It is estimated, for example, that 25 cents out of every dollar made by manufacturers goes back into fixing mistakes made in production. In addition, quality control often creates an adverse relationship between inspectors, who look for errors, and production people, who try to avoid having errors caught so as to produce a maximum amount of product, as fast as possible. What is needed instead is to build quality into products.

Building quality into products involves paying close attention to the design of the product and the production process. This often requires that production processes be monitored and maintained with accepted predetermined ranges, rather than waiting for a defect to occur.

Building quality also involves developing and maintaining a working environment that supports quality at all levels of production—and the most important environmental aspect is pride.

To get employees to have pride in their work you need to closely involve them in the responsibility and process of achieving quality. In this way, producing quality is not so much a technique as it is a philosophy of operation. For it to succeed, quality requires a commitment from everyone involved.

The commitment has to start at the top in the organization and be clearly communicated and reinforced at all levels of the operation. Employees have to have an invested interest in producing quality products. They have to feel that what they do—or don't do—makes a difference.

For example, in many manufacturing plants the absolute last thing that is avoided is to stop the production line. Stopping the production line causes delays and shortages of the product being manufactured—both of which can cost the company money. Stopping production can be such a costly decision that usually only the plant manager has the authority to make it.

But by not stopping the production line, the attitude is communicated that it is more important that production continue regardless of the consequences. Machinery may be operated when it should be adjusted, for example, resulting in the production of defective products.

Now in some manufacturing plants (most notably in Japan) the production line can be stopped by ANY person working on it. A button is placed by each work station and if a worker sees a defective product, he or she presses the button, the entire line is stopped, and the problem is corrected.

Needless to say, workers at such plants take their responsibility for product quality seriously, and subsequently higher quality products are produced. These workers have a greater degree of pride in their work and the products that are produced.

So the secret to achieving quality is to involve people AND their pride. If the quality program in your company isn't inspired by pride, your people will see it as just another system to put up with—or to beat. When a company emphasizes quality the right way, organizational energy if positively focused on customer satisfaction and employee pride. Any other way is a wasted effort.

Chapter 36

Quality vs. Quantity

by Albert J. Bernstein, clinical psychologist
and author of *Neanderthals at Work*

The first task in any quality program is to decide what quality is and how it's going to be measured and communicated.

THE executive's most important job is setting priorities among speed, price, and quality—and communicating that decision in word and deed. Red Adair, the guy who puts out oil well fires, said it quite concisely. "I can do it quick; I can do it cheap; I can do it well—pick any two." That is the question management must answer.

"Hey, boss, do we do it quick and cheap and tolerate mistakes or do we pay the cost in time or money to do things well?" The actual answer is always a trade-off, but something has to be at the top of the list. Yes, I know quality is number one; it always is. What does that really mean, and how is it communicated?

This is a fiendishly difficult problem on which many companies get stuck. When a company is stuck in the mud of uncompetitiveness —with cycle time problems, cost overruns, communication problems, poor morale, and many other ills—a misunderstanding of the quality vs. quantity dilemma is often at the heart of the matter.

Tradeoffs Are Inevitable

Some executives don't understand that tradeoffs in speed, price, and quality are inevitable and need to be managed. And many managers don't acknowledge that quality, price, and speed are interrelated.

Controlling costs is the almost divinely ordained job of management. Speed and quality are seen as arising from the internal attributes of employees. If they are motivated people, they will work quickly and well. Since few companies are blessed with employees whose work ethic is sufficiently strong to keep them from goofing off any chance they get, traditionalists employ strict foremen and supervisors to see that employees keep up the pace. If workers lean on their shovels, the foreman, supervisors, and middle managers are expected to fall on their swords. This time-honored "Theory X" is outmoded, but virtually everybody practices it to some extent.

In this model, quality is usually handled in yet another place. It is called "the quality control committee," where representatives of different departments get together once a month and point the finger at each other or devise wish lists they pass to upper management so they can be told, "These are great ideas, but they cost too much."

Day-to-day quality problems are dealt with by customer service representatives who are often the lowest paid people in the company and whose job it is to explain day in and day out that discrepancies between what the customer expects and what she actually gets are either a big mistake that will never happen again, or a regrettable misunderstanding on the customer's part that the reps must cheerfully set straight. If customer complaints get to the front office, it is assumed the customer service reps are not doing their jobs.

The role of management in securing speed and quality is indirect. It consists of fanning the sparks of internal motivation into a high-performance flame. Managing speed and quality comes mostly in the form of exhortation—pep talks, motivational seminars, customer service training, and those posters with eagles on them that say "You can fly higher if you think you can." Bonuses (usually given to the highest producers) and the selection of employee of the month are also forms of indirect influence.

This model is the way business has been done since the end of World War II. It works reasonably well in an expanding economy with unlimited resources and no competition. In tougher times it is a sure prescription for the erosion of quality, because quality is seen as the personal responsibility of individual workers. Therefore, nobody with any status or power is accountable for it. The idea of management's role as setting priorities among cost, speed and quality just does not compute in this model. It's just intellectual claptrap that has nothing to do with the real world. In the '50s when people like W. Edwards Deming talked about such things, nobody in this country listened. He had to go elsewhere to find an audience.

Much has changed since Deming was exiled. Back then, "made in Japan" meant junk. Deming's name and the word *quality* seem to be on everyone's lips now. Some larger companies are actually using Deming-like ideas about statistical quality control and management responsibility. In small businesses or the local offices of the larger ones where most of us work, the traditional model is still in effect. Nobody actually talks about it as a theoretical model; it's just the way things are done.

Where most of us work, Deming is now fashionable, and all the acronyms have a Q in them somewhere. Quality is definitely in. But the way we go about getting it is suspiciously like the way we've always done things. The words are different now, but the job of management is still cost control, exhortation, and setting quotas. Cycle time and total quality are still almost totally a matter of workers' personal responsibility.

Most of the newer approaches to management that will be required for competitiveness in the next century are predicated on a different theoretical model than the one most of us grew up with. The idea of management setting and enforcing priorities with clear external contingencies is so alien in most settings it can't even be considered. Unfortunately, an environment that doesn't consider theoretical issues is stuck on one in a big way.

Why Quality Is Hard to Come By

Everybody is talking about quality. People are paying attention and making dollar decisions based on the quality of the products and services that they buy. But putting out a high quality product is merely the ante you need to stay in the game.

If everybody knows how important quality is, why are we still having problems with it? In the aftermath of the quality revolution, why is there still so much junk on the market? Why aren't we doing more about it? The reason is not that we're lazy and unmotivated. The problem is, in most companies, especially small businesses, what quality is, how to get it, and whose job it is are at best unclear and at worst points of contention.

I've run into six major problems.

• *Quality is hard to measure.* Unless you're talking about measuring tolerances on a machined gear, quality is not very easy to define, much less measure. This is especially true when it comes to the quality of services, as opposed to manufactured items. Even with manufactured items, what's good enough for one person is completely inadequate for another. Specifying what quality is and how it's going to be measured is a major managing task. It takes time and it costs money. It involves participation not only of workers but customers as well. You can't arbitrarily decide what quality is and expect everyone else to agree with you. The biggest efforts and the biggest costs in any quality program are deciding what quality is, how it's going to be measured, and then measuring it on a regular basis. If you don't do your legwork here, any quality program that you devise will be little more effective than merely telling people they should try and do a better job.

  • *Quality is seen as a product rather than a process.* We tend to think of quality as the final product of our efforts. The manufactured item or good customer service or whatever. Many companies put in quality programs only at the level of manufacturing or with the people who actually give face-to-face services to customers. What they don't seem to realize is how well these front line people do depends on the support that they get all the way up.

  How can front-line managers ensure that their people are taking care of quality when they have to spend most of their time writing reports on why they spend every dollar? Putting out a quality product depends at each level on the level above it. If people have the resources and directions they need to do a good job, then the final product is likely to be of higher quality. Many companies, however, seem to me to be built upside down. A significant part of most people's jobs seems to be providing support for the people above them. Making your boss *look* good is at least as important as making the product *be* good. Setting up this kind of structure is unconscious in almost all of us. Rank has its privilege, you know. It's the kind of system we devise if we don't think clearly about what the purpose of the system is. In order for any company to put out a quality product, the support structure must be focused at all levels on a high quality outcome rather than individual political objectives. This can only happen when quality has larger rewards than politics.

  • *Dollars and speed are so easy to measure.* The conceptual difficulties involved in a cost-cutting program or even one to improve cycle time are nothing compared with those in improving quality. Managers gravitate toward what's easiest to do. Also since companies are ultimately evaluated in terms of how much money they make, money is the most important thing to control. Companies earn money for doing something; if they don't do that thing well, no matter how cheaply they do it, they still won't earn money.

• *The "Up to our Rear Ends in Alligators" syndrome.* Quality is wonderful and everybody should have programs to improve theirs. But such programs cost money and we're struggling just to survive. Right? Short-run thinking can always be justified, but it seldom works in the long run. Improving quality is a long-run decision and there's never a convenient time to make long-run changes. They will always interfere with quarterly profits.

• *Lack of understanding of psychology.* In business, motivation is understood to come from within. Good people do good work, and you don't have to reward them for the specifics—they will just know what to do. It would be convenient if this were true, but all the work ethic training in the world will not suffice. People are motivated mostly by what is rewarded and punished. No matter how much you talk about quality, if people know you read the production figures first, they will focus on production. People will automatically figure out where the greatest rewards are and gravitate to them. If you're a manager your job is to ensure that the greatest rewards come to the behaviors that lead to quality. This is almost impossible to conceive of if you think that people with good work ethics produce good work.

• *Not realizing that fear inhibits performance.* A little fear, like the kind you experience knowing if you do a bad job someone will find out and make you do it over, will improve performance. Higher levels of fear, like thinking that if you disagree with your boss you'll be publicly chewed out and perhaps lose your job, lead to poor performance and often passive retaliation. People treat their customers and products pretty much the way their bosses treat them. Feeling taken advantage of or being unsure of how they stand with their bosses or about the continuing existence of their jobs will inevitably lead people to do worse work.

Improving quality is hard. The tasks of specifying and measuring are difficult enough. But the real sticking point is that to improve quality you have to change some of the basic assumptions we all have about the way work is done.

Chapter 37

Closing the Quality Loop

by Guy A. Hale,
Chairman of Alamo Learning Systems

There's no such thing as a "successful" quality program; impressive results may take many years to achieve.

A FEW years ago, the executive committee of a Fortune 500 manufacturing company decided to do something about improving their approach to quality. They determined to link their company's efforts with some well-known quality "guru."

After a preliminary review, several quality gurus made presentations to the committee. One was a real "hit" with the committee, and they decided to center their efforts on this guru's approach. Dozens of the company's managers were sent off to "learn about quality" with the intention of then disseminating the message throughout the organization.

After many thousands of dollars and hours were invested in this corporate-wide quality program, the executive committee reviewed the progress and found several unmet objectives. This was their scorecard:

Have Achieved

- An awareness of quality philosophies and principles
- An understanding of the critical importance of quality
- A quality steering committee with quality action teams
- An increase in measurement of conformance to standards
- A feeling that "our quality efforts are paying off"

Still Need
- A way of linking principles to business objectives
- A commitment to abandon old procedures and policies
- A way to monitor and measure the success
- A means to involve others in the quality effort
- A way to resolve difficult and recurring problems
- A realization that quality improvement is never finished
- A process for implementing continuous efforts

In spite of some impressive gains, the quality movement is still a long way from delivering on all promises. Should we be discouraged if our organizations are still far from real quality improvement? We can answer that two ways:

No—because concerted quality efforts are still very new. Quality has been a big item on the American corporate agenda for a decade, and the early programs were very limited in scope.

Yes—because many organizations still expect they will "master" quality in a few months or years. But when they take stock of their progress, they are surprised to see how much still needs to be done. Perhaps only by painful experience will executives learn that quality improvement is a never-ending effort.

The danger in false expectations, however, is that management may lose faith in quality improvement as soon as the initial results reach a plateau.

Four Critical Realities

I see four critical realities about quality improvement which warrant review.

Reality 1: Quality is complex. There is no single definition of "quality." The term relates to how well products and services meet customer needs, how much they cost to produce, how well our people resolve problems, how well deadlines are met, and on and on. Since each group and individual has its own particular "customer" and "product," quality, therefore, will have an almost infinite number of meanings and applications. Quality considerations impact strategic marketing decisions and capital investment plans just as they are concerned with how well a secretary types a letter or a service person greets a customer.

Corporate quality efforts have tended to ignore this dynamic reality, putting responsibility for quality on a steering committee or a "VP of Quality." These broad-scope management approaches are valuable only if they are aimed at dispersing responsibility for defining and managing quality throughout the organization. Even a network of teams can put limits on who is involved in quality. When the true goal is reached each business unit, department, and work group will consider continuous quality improvement an integral part of the way it does business.

Executives must also recognize that the complex, dynamic nature of quality means that lasting results will take a long time to achieve; the potential for results will never be exhausted; the success of a particular quality program can only be measured in what you are doing today and what you are preparing to do tomorrow. Companies closest to the ideal quality program are finding that the success they are now achieving is creating more momentum and enthusiasm—and the process begins to propel itself.

Reality 2: Internalize and modify. W. Edwards Deming, perhaps the most respected of the quality gurus, counseled organizations to make their quality effort their own, not a wholesale adoption of someone else's ideas. The only way for a quality program to be effective over time is for it to be tailored to the needs and objectives of each organization and group.

Deming, Joseph Juran, Philip Crosby, and their peers and disciples have made enormous contributions toward helping American business understand and improve quality. But to expect any one consultant or guru to have all the answers for your organization may be a serious mistake. Unfortunately, some organizations have tended to adopt a particular guru's philosophy "lock, stock, and barrel," without attention to which concepts and principles have validity for that company and which do not.

Another common danger is the temptation to bring in a consultant to guide the quality program, and to rely on quality "experts." Make no mistake, consultants and experts have a vital role; they are essential, even critical, in developing the knowledge, systems, and new ways of thinking that help fuel and guide quality efforts. But each consultant or firm will have its particular area of specialization or bias. No one has all the answers—and no expert can provide the practical, common sense contribution that your own people will offer as they begin to get involved in quality improvement.

Carefully select and apply the philosophies and expertise of quality practitioners as best meets the specific needs of your organization. As you progress, your own people will become the quality "experts" for your organization.

This fact will become increasingly important as quality programs mature and progress. It will be difficult to get past the initial
results of quality improvement unless there is the freedom and commitment—at all levels—to internalize responsibility for the effort and
continually fine-tune the program.

Reality 3: Tough challenges require hard skills. Most quality-
related education is focused in two areas: 1) developing awareness of
quality principles; and 2) providing statistical measuring skills to monitor conformance to control standards. Between these general (philosophy) and specific (statistics) categories of training lies a lot of ground.

Let's look first at awareness training. Thousands of executives,
managers and supervisors are familiar with one or more series of quality precepts. But being aware of what should be done does not help
managers to know how they should implement the changes required.
The answer is to teach them how to plan for managing quality—a
process we will explore in more detail below.

Measuring conformance or non-conformance using statistics is
also critical to improving quality; however, identifying problems is
not the same as solving them. Dr. Deming, chief proponent of the
value of statistical techniques and conformance measurement, indicated that "measures of productivity are like statistics on accidents:
they tell you all about the number of accidents in the home, on the
road, and at the work place, but they do not tell you how to reduce the
frequency of accidents."

Stories abound of production crews who were doing a mar-
velous job collecting data on their operation yet who had no clue as to
how to analyze the data once it was collected in order to improve systems and solve the problems at hand.

The "hard skills" that are missing from many quality efforts are
effective techniques to analyze data, determine effective solutions,
and build in procedures to prevent problems from recurring.
Brainstorming—the most prevalent technique for finding causes and
solutions—is a poor approach to improving quality. It invites erro-
neous assumptions, offers no process to evaluate which data are valid
and which aren't, and forces nearly every solution to be tested by
observation or experimentation—often costly and disruptive—rather
than by logic.

Brainstorming and simple group problem solving approaches
have produced results simply because they have filled a vacuum,
providing a process where there had previously been no direction at

all. Counting on them to carry forth continuous quality improvement is a mistake.

Reality 4: Plan, plan, plan. No well-managed company would spring a new product on the market or initiate a merger without a plan. Planning is the organization's way of managing the future to accomplish its objectives. Amazingly, however, effective and cohesive planning is commonly not a part of the implementation and management of quality improvement efforts. Yet a task as critical and complex as quality requires a level and detail of planning that matches few efforts a company will ever undertake.

The following diagram illustrates four major categories of effort involved in quality improvement:

Management philosophy and principles—the guiding precepts that define how quality will be viewed within the organization and outline the overall organizational objective and commitment.

Customer/supplier focus—the process of examining the product or service of each group in terms of whom they serve, what is needed and expected, and how those needs can best be met.

Measurement—the establishment of systems to determine how well the organization is meeting its quality objectives and how those efforts impact the company's financial performance. It includes frequent, timely feedback systems to direct the organization toward continuous improvement.

Education—the continuous effort to develop the skills essential for quality improvement within the organization.

Existing corporate quality programs typically include all or most of these components to some degree. What is missing is the central circle, a process to integrate and relate each component to short- and long-term objectives. Because there is no common planning process, it is nearly impossible for anyone within the company to determine which elements are working (and which aren't) and where the effort is going. Rather than adapting the existing plan to meet specific needs of business units or departments, each group is forced to create its own plan from scratch.

The plan itself should not be overly complicated. Long-term goals can be visionary, but the plan should focus on doable, manageable steps that over time will enable the group or organization to reach the goal.

The following figure depicts the elemental steps in the plan and the importance of leaving details to those directly involved in achieving results.

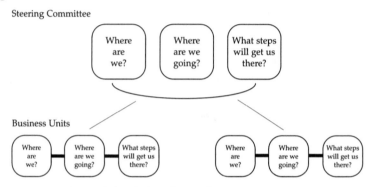

Simplified Quality Planning Process

The master plan and specific sub-plans must be considered "living" documents, continuously and regularly updated to reflect the progress and changes impacting quality efforts.

With a process and commitment to plan and monitor the quality effort throughout the organization, each manager, supervisor, and employee can begin to better understand his or her role. At the same time, top management will have a mechanism for making the organization respond to the fast-paced change and tough competition that will rule the business world for decades to come.

The emphasis on planning for steady, continuous improvement of quality is the real key to "closing the loop" on a corporate quality effort.

The progress made and results produced by many corporate quality efforts have been impressive and encouraging. The worst mistake now would be to pat ourselves on the back and rest on our laurels. We have to continually question our assumptions about what quality is and redefine the meaning of "success."

Managing for Competitiveness

If your organization does not recognize these realities and plan for a never-ending effort to improve its quality, you will someday find yourself looking in dismay at a competitor who is.

The most important contribution any executive can make to overall American competitiveness is to make his or her *own* company the most competitive organization possible.

Even under the best of circumstances, staying competitive today is more difficult than ever before. Why? Because the conditions that determine competitive advantages change at an unparalleled speed. Today's hot product is tomorrow's flop; the secure, stable market of yesterday is racked by technological advances and overseas competition.

Today a company can hold its competitive edge and stay ahead of change only through *quality and innovation.* Innovative companies keep their collective eyes and ears open to change and opportunity, and respond with ideas and action that keep them growing and profitable.

Two categories of innovation contribute to the competitive strength: 1) *continuous improvements*—innovations conceived and implemented by an individual or small group to make their job easier, better or more productive; and 2) *organizational innovations*—changes that involve different functions and levels within the company. These innovations require broad commitment and cooperation.

It's important to note, as does Tom Peters in *Thriving On Chaos*, that continuous improvements and organizational innovations have a synergistic relationship: "The reality is that millions—*literally* an unlimited number—of innovation and improvement opportunities lie within any factory, distribution center, store, or operations center. And you can multiply that by more millions when you can involve the factory and distribution center working together as a team. And multiply again when you add in involvement in innovation by suppliers and customers."

Five Keys to Quality Environment

The first goal of executives seeking to build competitive innovation is a climate that encourages, supports, and rewards quality and innovation. The challenge is to erase the common fear of being punished for rocking the boat. Executives must show, through incentives, rewards, and recognition, that they will listen to the ideas of *all* people.

Ford Motor Company achieved success when it gave a cross-section of employees the charge of designing a new car—one that would set Ford apart from its competition in customer appeal, yet be practical to build with quality. The result: the Taurus, Sable, and Thunderbird, a successful line of popular, distinctive automobiles. Ford's employees, dealers, and suppliers knew the climate was ripe for ideas.

Innovation and quality are not magic, but what Peter Drucker calls "hard, focused, purposeful work." The company that competes through quality and innovation is one that has made the *process* part of its daily operation. Success-story anecdotes do little to clarify this process or provide a model that other executives can use. However, by looking deeper into the success stories and working with innovative companies, we have identified five keys:

First, identify opportunity. Competitive innovation is proactive. Instead of waiting for threats to make innovation a necessity (by which time it's often too late), your organization can set up systems to scan for innovation opportunities.

Pure research, though important, will not by itself make a company truly innovative. Many of the most important innovation opportunities are found by individuals who are closely tied to products and customers. Most employees have a pretty good idea what can be improved at their jobs, and can learn—given the right climate and training—to recognize innovation opportunities in the changes, successes, surprises, mistakes, customer inquiries, and other events around them every day.

Second, focus on a direction. Obviously, not every idea is a winner, nor does every good idea meet the needs and objectives of the organization. Determining the general direction for innovative efforts, therefore, enables a company to quickly concentrate on those opportunities most likely to make it more competitive. Some important aspects of establishing focus and direction include clearly communicating goals and objectives; defining what innovations are *not* sought, so efforts can focus exclusively on the goals at hand; and presenting limits or constraints so that employees can be realistic in their assessment of opportunities.

Third, generate ideas. Generating ideas includes that mysterious aspect of innovation: "Creativity." Creativity is *not*, as some believe, synonymous with innovation, but it *is* an element of the innovation *process*.

Fortunately, generating worthwhile, workable ideas is not the exclusive realm of "creative-types." Anyone can participate in the exercise of generating ideas around an opportunity for innovation. We teach a number of very effective techniques—variations on the brainstorming concept—to draw out creative ideas in group or individual situations. The important responsibility of management, however, is to provide the time, resources, and direction needed for people to be creative.

Fourth, analyze and implement. The organization must ensure that these innovative ideas are captured, analyzed, and, if deemed valuable, brought to reality. A real resource-saver is for the idea generation team to refine its ideas and develop recommended solutions. Just as importantly, managers who receive ideas must analyze them objectively, rather than reject or accept them based on subjective biases (e.g., a marketing executive should not be partial to a marketing-based solution unless it is truly the *best* innovation idea). Innovative organizations use project management to guide an idea to implementation. Such management permits repeated assessment of the idea and ensures that the innovation meets its "window of opportunity."

Fifth, management support. Support is critical to the success of any organizational innovation. But support is not limited to the tangibles of money, personnel, space, and equipment; innovation requires philosophical support as well. Executives must be committed to the principle that their company must change, must innovate, if it is to remain competitive in today's changing business environment. After all, support for quality and innovation works against what has been called the "Corporate Swamp"—that tendency to squash or ignore ideas that threaten the status quo.

Chapter 38

Quality is Not Enough

by Philip R. Thomas,
Chairman and CEO of Thomas Group, Inc.

Through total cycle time, you can beat foreign competition on all business parameters—including quality.

TOO many Total Quality efforts stall a few steps beyond the inspirational stage. Others produce incremental improvements, but such results do not improve their company's competitive position. The lesson takes a while to sink in: Quality is not enough.

Quality is not enough because customers everywhere are becoming more savvy and exacting. Anything short of first-rate quality will simply not do. In a demanding climate, top quality will become a given, not a differentiator.

Quality is not enough because quality alone does not drive business. In a competitive environment, good quality is a result of orderly, simplified processes wherein resources are used to their best effectiveness, things are done right on the first try, and customer needs are met in timely fashion. Good quality occurs naturally when working people can analyze their business processes, learn quickly from experience, and use those lessons to further simplify their work cycles.

Cycle time, not quality, drives a business. To a great extent, quality is a natural by-product of shortened, simplified business processes. Companies with quality concerns should, therefore, refocus their efforts toward cutting cycle times in every sector of activity.

Measuring Quality

Every executive presumes that quality can be measured in some objective, quantitative way, but that is difficult and, in many cases, impossible. Defining quality is a bit like defining "good" art: people may not have a handle on the specs, but they know what they like. And they know it when they see it.

Not that companies shrink from the attempts to measure the quality of their products and performance. Assisted by the computer revolution, managers swim in a sea of data. But how useful are all those numbers? My experience suggests that the data-based measurements they track aren't the right ones: 80 percent are self-serving, manipulatable, and meaningless to the objective of effective response to customers. Meanwhile, information systems fudge or omit measurements that could be meaningful indicators of performance. Accepted measurements of quality almost never translate to a company's bottom line.

Here are some measurements that every company should use.

• *Customer-defined quality levels.* Any definition of quality that does not focus on the customer's perceptions is incomplete and probably doomed. Any AQL that is not expressed in parts per million is, or soon will be, uncompetitive. In fact, some leading companies are already thinking in terms of parts per billion.

• *Reliability: more than fit and finish.* Companies who understand customer expectations of reliability design it into their product before the manufacturing stage. Reliability has to be designed in, not corrected or ignored in the make/market loop.

Any manufacturer that does not use design of experiments, multiple environment overstress testing, and the like will soon find itself coping with the poor reliability syndrome.

• *How customers use a product.* Although zero defects, high reliability, and performance to schedule are motherhood issues, customer preferences are not always that simple or quantifiable. For example, easy installation, ease of use, or an item's "fun quotient" may outweigh pure quality considerations, making a more costly or less well-made item the "best" in its field. Since the customer is always right, good quality is a function of design in which customer needs and tastes are considered from the start.

• *Manufacturability.* Designers may come up with a reliable product that is too much trouble to make economically. Such a condition might take place in a company where the two loops are regarded as separate bailiwicks rather than interlocking parts of a seamless business process. Competitive, quality-minded companies know that manufacturability must be part of a product's initial design. Interestingly, ease of manufacture often translates into higher reliability. Quality means getting business processes under control from the very start. Concurrent engineering, in which production and design engineers evaluate and rate each design for manufacturability, is making headway in many leading companies.

• *Cost of quality.* The so-called "cost of quality" actually tracks the cost of unquality, the expenses incurred because of substandard products. The true cost of unquality is the collective cost to companies when business processes (not just products) fail to perform to expected standards. This includes expenses incurred by quality programs and people, such as prevention and assessment costs. It also includes materials wasted because of low first-pass yield, returns from customers, billing from customers for the inconvenience of coping with substandard products, and the like. Added together, such items commonly amount to 10 percent of sales, although 20 percent is by no means rare.

Many companies could substantially lower these costs by carefully examining their relationship with outside suppliers and adjusting their specs accordingly. A business may dictate a set of specs to a supplier that are unreasonable and counterproductive to the quality goal. Getting a reliable handle on cost of unquality requires an understanding of your suppliers' businesses.

When a company's quality is good and the goal is to make it better, more resources are usually laid on in the form of testing and quality personnel. At such times, cost of unquality actually increases as things improve. To keep cost of unquality at a minimum, companies should keep the quality team small, keep it technical, and move the responsibility for quality to the lowest possible level. Such measures are in keeping with the principle of simplifying processes and removing bureaucratic barriers.

• *Performance to schedule.* Performance to schedule is part of the mismeasurement syndrome. As a manipulatable index of quality, it almost always looks better than it is. PTS makes sense as a measurement when a company can respond effectively to customers' deadlines. The deadlines, however, must be determined by the customer. PTS is pernicious if manipulated to create the appearance of rapid, precise response.

• *First-pass yield.* Industry trackers use an interesting gauge of quality in the automotive field: returns per hundred, a fancy label for plain old first-pass yield (the percentage of things done right the first time around). Manufacturers with the lowest numbers are, of course, presumed to be the quality companies.

Your company's quality should be defined in the same terms. If your processes are in order, your first-pass yield is high and your customer satisfaction rating is almost certainly the same. Computed correctly, first-pass yield is an important internal measurement of quality and competitiveness. Computed incorrectly, first-pass yield is another dangerous, self-deceptive index.

• *Cycles of Learning.* This is the ultimate index of quality, and yet few companies have discovered Cycles of Learning as a track toward better performance. Why pass up repeated opportunities to benefit from experience? Those opportunities are even greater than they may appear at first, because Cycles of Learning have a profound effect on the celebrated learning curve.

However, learning curve thinking is concerned with incremental learning gains brought about by the repetition of the same task, not occasional insights or creative breakthroughs that could make an exponential difference in the process. That is where Total Cycle Time makes a crucial difference; it increases the number of Cycles of Learning. When equipped with a structured feedback loop to exploit the greater number of learning cycles, any company can achieve creative breakthroughs. Lower your cycle times and you will achieve more and faster Cycles of Learning. As Cycles of Learning accelerate, creative breakthroughs increase.

Cutting cycle times in half doubles the Cycles of Learning, and Cycles of Learning have an enormous impact on a company's experience curve.

Conventional measurements of quality serve two purposes: to track what is pertinent to better quality, and to revise a mindset in favor of a more competitive culture. Changing a company's habits is always laborious, so measurements should be as simple, accurate, and forceful as possible. Measurements should be simple and accurate, tightly focused on the quality issue at hand, limited to exception reporting, and should embrace hard issues such as designing for quality. Every quality effort should concern itself with reporting only what is exceptional.

How do you know when you've got good quality? Externally, you'll know your quality is good because your customers will be satisfied. Customer satisfaction is good quality, and no system of measurements that fails to focus on that is worth its salt.

Internally, you'll know you have good quality because your first-pass yield will be high. High first-pass yield is a function of simple, orderly systems and short cycle times. Accordingly, the most important indices of quality are first-pass yield, cycle time, cycles of learning, and the effectiveness of feedback loops.

When calculated and tracked properly, two conventional measurements are effective: Cost of unquality and performance to schedule.

A final measure of quality in a competitive company is the absence of quality programs and people with "quality control" titles. By nature, such people and programs are fixes for things that are not up to par. Quality is not an ongoing program—it is a system that proceeds from the business process itself and the changed mindset of those who participate in it. Think of it: a quality company making quality products without a single quality manager in sight.

Put Time On Your Side

Suppose you were asked, "What would make your company unbeatable?" How would you reply?

You would probably be very tough to beat if your business required a lot less cash to operate, or if you had leadership in customer response; rapid new product time-to-market; accelerated results, particularly in quality, cost, and productivity; and superior resource effectiveness, especially of people, equipment, and inventory.

You *can* make your company unbeatable if you know the "what" of world-class international competitiveness *and* the "how" of making it happen. In this article, I provide a brief but hopefully stimulating summary of how you can make it happen.

My conviction is that Total Cycle Time is the ultimate business weapon. Total Cycle Time is the total time it takes to get things done: to bring a new product from concept to cost-effective production; or to take an order for a product or service and satisfy that customer's need. It's the time from the *expression* of a need to *satisfaction* of that need.

Three Standard Processes

Your business can be viewed as three major business processes, each with many sub-processes.

• *Make/market process*—from receipt of an order to delivery of product or service, with typical sub-processes of order entry, planning, manufacturing, or product creation and distribution. Incidentally, we have found that between 60 and 90 percent of the cycle times critical to achieving competitiveness occur outside the manufacturing area.

• *Design/development process*—with sub-processes of product definition, resource assignment, product or service design, bringing the product or service to cost-effective availability, and then transferring to the make/market process.

• *Strategic thrust process*—in which you may want to start a whole new product or service area; it contains the sub-processes of market research, strategy development, and business execution to the point that the new area of business can be transferred into the make/market or design/development processes of the mainstream business.

Having reduced Total Cycle Time in many companies for the last 20 years, we can estimate from practical experience the actual improvements you might achieve. While very substantial qualitative improvements occur in on-time delivery, quality, cost, productivity, asset utilization, time-to-market of new products, and, by no means least, employee morale, the quantitative improvements I have experienced are shown in the following table.

Typical Ranges of Improvement (%)

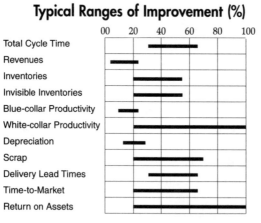

	00	20	40	60	80	100
Total Cycle Time						
Revenues						
Inventories						
Invisible Inventories						
Blue-collar Productivity						
White-collar Productivity						
Depreciation						
Scrap						
Delivery Lead Times						
Time-to-Market						
Return on Assets						

Most of these measures should be familiar to you, with the possible exception of "invisible inventory." One example is new product development in process. Invisible inventory is the cash tied up (although expensed) due to activities in process, such as development. If you spend 10 percent of annual sales on development and your development cycle time is three years, then the cash you have tied up (invisible inventory) will be 30 percent of annual sales.

It's instructive to examine your own business in light of these typical improvements and to calculate the total high and total low dollar impacts over the ranges of results. When driven by Total Cycle Time, these improvements happen together; the question is, "Where does your business fit within the ranges?"

The Competitiveness Gap

The quantification of latent performance improvement in companies ("the competitiveness gap") is the difference between what we call Baseline (your current performance) and Entitlement (the level of performance you *can constantly* realize with present or *reduced* resources).

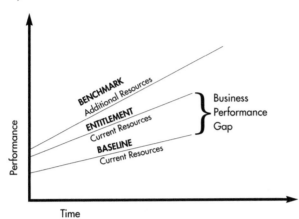

This quantification requires well developed analytical techniques plus a great deal of experience and objectivity.

Once Baseline and Entitlement are defined for all key business parameters, the transition across the competitiveness gap begins. It includes reducing cycle times in all areas; creating increased feedback through increased Cycles of Learning (defined as the work days per year divided by the cycle time); process simplification; barrier removal; and the establishment of appropriate measurements and controls.

Time requirements depend on what you are trying to achieve and how much momentum you have in your present culture; to change order-entry cycle time, for example, may take only nine months but to cut design development time in half may take three years.

Chapter 39

Quality Education

by Donna E. Shalala, Secretary of the
Department of Health and Human Services

*If Total Quality is to provide the spectacular
results it advertises, it must withstand the
rigors of inquiry common to our universities.*

W HEN the University of Wisconsin first undertook its partnership
with Procter & Gamble, those on both sides wondered whether it
could work. Someone once said it was easier to move a New England
graveyard than change habits at a university.

TQM has proved its worth in business, but the academy is not
business. Well, it is, and it isn't. Education is big business, but it's
more. Can the principles of total quality work at a university? At
Wisconsin, we began with trepidation and hope. Wisconsin is the
sixth-largest university in the United States, and one of the largest
public research universities. It turns out some of the most visible,
visionary leaders in business, science, and education, including Nobel
Prize and Pulitzer Prize winners.

And yes, our traditions, our rituals, are beloved to us. We have
some of the most brilliant faculty in the world. Convincing them that
there could be a better way to do their work could be seen as pre-
sumptuous. Why should they reinvent this wheel, which has spun for
150 years with extraordinary results?

One answer came from a senior faculty member, who, after
three days at Procter & Gamble's corporate headquarters, asked the
question: "If American higher education is the best in the world and if
the Wisconsin is world-class, why should we change what we are
doing now?" He answered his own question: "That's exactly what

they said about the American auto industry 30 years ago."

Along with many business organizations, education is running in deep sand—not losing ground, perhaps, but not making much progress, either. Recognizing the challenges, but so strapped down by a web of old procedures and conflicting demands, leaders find it hard to meet those challenges in a bold manner.

And yet, quality initiatives have resulted in important changes in the following areas.

• *Customer service.* For example, consider the most basic tenet of TQM—paying close attention to the needs of the customer. The needs of undergraduate students is one of the most burning issues in higher education. But not long ago, it had become a low priority at many colleges and universities. There were many reasons. Higher education is under enormous pressure—with less funding, more emphasis on accountability, a more diverse and larger student population, fundamental changes in what is taught and who teaches it, and an exponential growth in knowledge. Universities have a complex network of suppliers (K–12 and secondary schools) and customers (students, their families, and the businesses that hire graduates), but leaders are just applying Band-aids and putting out fires instead of envisioning a new way to improve education.

• *Graduate school admissions process.* In the past, it took an average of 99 days to give a person a yes or no. About 26 of those days were taken up in administrative offices, and the rest were spent in the various departments. Why is this a problem? A university fails to compete if it loses the best students to institutions that can make offers more quickly.

An improvement team found that most of the waiting involved a lag in getting copies of transcripts from every institution the student had ever attended. "Why do we require all these things?" the team asked. "Departments want them," was the answer. "Why?" the team asked. "The Fellowships Office demands them," we heard. "Why?" we asked again. We learned that the Fellowships Office did not want all those transcripts. We were doing work we didn't need to do, collecting information we didn't need to have, because no one had thought to ask customers the right questions. One solution was to redefine what we considered a "complete file," and stop waiting for things we didn't need. In administration, we cut the time from 26 to 3 days and saved more than $100,000 in overtime and clerical assistance in one semester. We gave departments the power to admit or reject students within five days of receipt of application. And our students, our customers, got better service.

Many professors are experimenting with curriculum, classroom methods, student involvement, and team learning in engineering, business, statistics, economics, and education administration.

• *Research grants.* We're seeing proof that total quality principles and techniques can work in settings that go beyond the "business" of the institution. One paradigm shift improved our ability to attract research grants. The department of Medical Microbiology and Immunology was not satisfied with the percentage of their grant proposals that were being awarded. When an administrator began investigating the who, what, and why of the proposal process, he learned that the lack of success actually had very little to do with the quality of the ideas.

Grant proposal submissions were coming in with only days to spare before deadline, overburdening the support staff and leaving no time for faculty and other colleagues to review proposals and add helpful suggestions. After gathering the data, the administrator created a checklist for researchers preparing proposals, and a series of reminders over a several-month period so the process of preparation would start much sooner. There was more time to compose, revise, and offer proposals for peer review. After two years, the results are clear: The proposals that were prepared thoughtfully, using the new system, were being funded at a much higher rate than the last-minute submissions. The rate for the department's success in attracting grants is rising.

• *Patent approval.* Now, a team of key people from across the university are coming together to use quality methods to improve the patent approval process on our research findings.

• *TQM in K–12.* We're keeping a close eye on the use of TQM principles in K–12 settings too. For example, in one K–12 district, third graders now spend a month refining, correcting, and analyzing a single essay until it is letter-perfect, instead of producing a dozen sloppy, inadequate efforts. They are directing their own learning, not just shoving papers marked with teachers' criticisms into their desks. They are learning to think. Each one is expected to excel, even the slowest learners.

We failed our least advantaged students most by not expecting them to soar. We funneled them off into dead-end classes. We have saved our dreams for others. What better way can we reach out to these students than with systems that tell them, "You can do this. And I won't stop until I find a way to help you"?

These are beginnings, small examples of how these methods can help us in academia. We have only begun to tap the potential.

Playing for High Stakes

The partnership with P&G was an important part of the improvement process because it let us learn from one of our major customers. Now, we share what we're learning with our suppliers, with the schools sending us our students. If we work upstream by helping K–12 schools, students will come to us better prepared for success. We need to share what we're learning with more of our customers—the companies that hire the capable, self-directed professionals we educate.

Albert Einstein said, "The significant problems we face cannot be solved with the same thinking that created them."

W. Edwards Deming's principles and methods provide an approach that has proven effective in many organizations—from business to health care to government. We need to apply these methods to education, since so much is at stake. Society depends on our success in educating our young people. Waste in industry is a shame; waste of human potential is a sin. And waste is what is built into our education system as it is currently organized.

If an industry made products and 30 percent of them didn't work, that operation would shut down in three months. It wouldn't matter how good the good products were. Yet we tolerate a similar rate of waste at institutions of higher learning. Too many students fail to meet our expectations. They drop out.

Suppose, just suppose, we could develop a process that would result in all young people meeting expectations and graduating. And, suppose we could develop a process to enable all students to do "exceptional" work. Think of how young people would grow and feel about themselves. And think of what they could accomplish. Imagine what we might do if we took a new look at education as a process—identifying what contributes to the success of each student and letting nothing block our mission.

Education is not exempt from the rising expectations of quality; in fact, education should be at the forefront—learning, researching, adapting, and teaching new knowledge. Total quality offers a combination of theories, concepts, tools, and practices which leaders in education must explore.

Business-University Partnerships

Based on the experience with Procter & Gamble, I encourage more business-university partnerships. Universities benefit in many ways. More of these partnerships are needed.

Although Total Quality came to academia through business, the knowledge began in the minds of great scholars; scholars who studied, researched, challenged, developed, and created new ideas and methods. That is the role of academics and it is as urgent as ever.

Universities are the engine rooms of new knowledge. We don't just teach knowledge, we create it. The faculty at all great universities create the theories, as well as the methods, for many disciplines through cutting-edge research.

If Total Quality is to provide the kind of spectacular results it advertises, then it must withstand the rigors of inquiry that are common on our campuses. Leaders in academia need hard evidence on the benefits, and shortcomings, of Total Quality. And they are not alone. Leaders of business and industry have indicated that they need guidance on how and when to apply quality principles in their organizations.

I believe an additional educational benefit will also accrue as a result of this process. If faculty are doing research in an area, then the curriculum will soon reflect it. The result will be students who cut their intellectual teeth on the latest thinking about Total Quality.

A resource directory would serve some of the same ends as scholarship. This directory would serve as a resource and a networking link for participating organizations—a tool providing the best known methods and linking people across distance and disciplines.

While it takes time to integrate these principles, we don't have time to try slow routes. Our students won't have second chances. Neither will our businesses. We need to pull together everything we can today to address these critical systems if they are going to survive the challenges facing them.

TQM offers the best hope. But education can't do it alone. And neither can business. In partnership, we can find common goals, shared initiative, the mutual eagerness to create, integrate, and disseminate new knowledge. That knowledge can transform our system, strengthen our society, and bring us face to face with our vision for the future.

Chapter 40

Customer Focus: Key to Total Quality

by Lawrence M. Miller,
Chairman of L.M. Miller & Company

A passionate commitment to meeting customer requirements is the key to quality and profitability.

THERE is little doubt that competitive advantage lies with the corporation able to deliver the highest quality products and services at the lowest possible cost. Quality is defined not by internal perceptions, but by the standards and expectations of the customer. Quality is conformance to customer requirements.

To achieve the highest possible customer satisfaction, every employee and manager must develop a passionate commitment to customer requirements. New products and services are also most likely to result from a focus on customer needs. Everyone, from the chairman to the newest-hired employee, must become customer-focused. Customer focus equals competitive advantage.

Creating Customer Focus

How does one create a culture that is customer-focused? The answer lies both in leadership and organization.

Leadership. The chairman of the Dun & Bradstreet corporation is Charles W. Moritz, and his leadership style provides one answer to the customer focus equation. Dun & Bradstreet is one of those rare companies that is both dominant in its markets, long established, yet still creative and dynamic. Much of the creativity is the result of its focus on the customer.

It is hard to overemphasize the power of example. Routinely, Charles Moritz personally visits customers. Not because there is a problem. Not because they may represent a large opportunity for new business. He visits customers simply to listen to them express how they feel about the products and services they receive from D&B. In the culture of this great company, the chairman considers it his personal responsibility to meet with and listen to his customers—and his behavior impacts the behavior and attitude of every other manager and employee within the corporation.

Charles W. Moritz not only listens to his customers, he listens to his own employees. Once a month he has breakfast meetings with first-line employees just to hear their concerns and suggestions. During one of these meetings, a young man asked the chairman a simple question. He said, "Mr. Moritz, I just want to know one thing. Where does my work go, and why is it important?"

The question hit him like a brick. It was so simple, yet so profound. Sometimes even the chairman of a great company can learn something from the lowest level employee. Few leaders have the humility to be open to such opportunities. He pondered this question long and hard and realized that every employee in the company ought to be able to answer this question. The work goes to a customer. Your work is important if it meets the needs of the customer. If it meets no one's needs, it is not important and it should be stopped or modified.

When employees are in touch with their customer, when they can listen to and feel the satisfaction of meeting customer needs, they not only perform better, they also gain self-esteem. The employee who asked the question was seeking the self-esteem that comes from doing something important for someone else.

Charles Moritz proceeded to institute a process whereby every employee of the Dun & Bradstreet company identified his customer and the elements of customer satisfaction. These personal actions by the chairman have done much to make Dun & Bradstreet a customer-focused organization.

Organization. The focus on customers must be carried through all of the management practices. The organization must be designed for customer focus. Each step in the management process can establish a focus on the customer.

For example, when employees are hired, is it clear that they are hired to be part of a team working to achieve some result for a customer, or are they hired to work on certain machines or pieces of paper? How many of your employees can identify their customer by name? How many have received feedback from customers letting them know how well they are doing in meeting the customer's requirements? How many are evaluated based on their service to customers? How many participate in discussions to find ways to improve customer service? Why not everyone?

Creating a customer-focused organization begins by looking at every organizational unit at the lowest level. Each employee or manager is a member of a team that does something of value for some customer. Every team creates value. If it does not create value, it serves no purpose and should be eliminated.

Critical to the concept of the customer-focused organization is the understanding that there are both internal and external suppliers and internal and external customers. The clerk working in the billing office, the group of people who supply the raw information upon which bills are created, are the suppliers. They are probably in another office within the same corporate building. It is only with an understanding of the absolute validity and importance of the internal supplier/producer/customer relationship that the highest quality service or product can be delivered to the end use customer.

The workings of a large corporation may be mapped out as a large chain, as a series of suppliers, producing teams, and customers, who in turn are producing teams for another customer. These horizontal chains represent management relationships. The future organization will be guided and motivated more by horizontal, direct customer-supplier relationships than by vertical, subordinate-manager relationships.

Many of our efforts to fix the vertical management structure are unnecessary, misguided and even counterproductive. If everyone was dedicated to serving his or her direct customer, listening to the customer's evaluation, and responding to the customer's needs, there would be far less need for the excessive overhead costs which the layers of management represent.

Supplier-Customer Relationship

In order for any team of people to do their work well, they must receive some input which they employ to accomplish their task. For example, a sales team receives new products, marketing information, and competitive intelligence, all of which are inputs that are essential to the selling task.

Suppliers. Inputs, by definition, come from a supplier. Whoever supplies the sales team with competitive intelligence may be defined as a supplier to that sales team.

In the traditional corporate culture there tends to be an adversarial relationship between suppliers and customers. Ford Motor Company had 10 or 20 different manufacturers competing for the contract to supply each component, and the decision to award a contract was made primarily on the basis of price. If the supplier failed to provide quality, or failed financially, Ford did not regard it as their problem. They simply went to another supplier. This relationship contributed to poor quality.

Ford Motor Company has since revolutionized this relationship, working closely to assist their suppliers with information, training, and joint problem solving.

To achieve high quality products or services today, every producer must work with their suppliers to help them succeed in quality. If the supplier is excellent, it will contribute to excellent output by the producer. The keys to this relationship are first, frequent and accurate feedback on quality to the supplier, and second, joint problem solving to find ways to improve quality.

Customers. Just as every team of employees and managers has suppliers, they also have customers. I believe that every employee has a right to know who his or her customers are, to personally listen to those customers, to feel the satisfaction from successfully meeting their needs, and the pain of failure. The most important positive and negative feedback, reward and punishment, does not come from managers, but from customers who use the product.

Several years ago, UAW employees at the Pontiac Fiero plant were given the names and phone numbers of customers who bought the car. On their own time they called these customers, introduced themselves as employees who built the customer's car, and proceeded to ask how the customer liked the car. They asked for general impressions and specific ways the car could be improved. From this process came 160 product improvements. But, perhaps more important, came the personal satisfaction of talking to actual end users and listening to their feedback. This changed the meaning, the purpose, and motivation of work, for these union employees.

Within a large corporation it's easy for employees and managers to get out of touch with customers and the purpose of their work. If everyone asked, "Where does my work go, and why is it important?" some would find that there is no good answer and the work should be stopped. Dozens of unnecessary reports and procedures are constantly created and complied with, simply because the customer focus question is never asked.

Sadly, the majority of employees in large corporations can't tell you who their customers are or how they are performing to customer requirements. This is one reason working in a small company is more fun. Employees in small companies are more likely to personally communicate with customers and receive the satisfaction or pain of their feedback. In a large corporation the same satisfaction can be achieved by focusing on internal as well as external customers. This is the satisfaction and pain of winning and losing, of playing the game. This is the ingredient that makes business a competitive game. Every employee should be allowed on the playing field. Huge cost savings would result if everyone asked and received an answer to the question, "Where does my work go, and why is it important?"

Ten Steps Toward Customer Focus

To create a customer-focused organization, I suggest that you take the following 10 steps:

• Identify the work team for which you are responsible.

• Meet with your team and brainstorm all of the inputs required to successfully accomplish the team's work. Agree on the four or five most important inputs.

• Define the requirements of high quality input and how you can measure those inputs.

• As a team, meet with the supplier of each input. Provide them with a graph, illustrating performance during a baseline period of supply, and explain the requirements for desirable quality input.

• Continue to provide your suppliers with periodic feedback, and jointly consider how the input can be improved.

• Define all of the outputs of your team's work and the customer who uses each of those outputs.

• Meet with each of your customers, and ask them for their requirements for a high quality product or service. Agree on a way of measuring this quality.

• Institute a process for measuring the quality of your output before it reaches the customer. Also, ask the customer for periodic feedback on your quality as they perceive it.

• Institute a process of continual team management. The team responsible for the process should meet regularly, usually once a week, to review the measures of quality performance and to problem solve ways to improve the current performance.

• Always assume there is room for continual improvement.

If you have involved all of your managers and employees in this customer-focus process, quality is assured, costs will be reduced, and competitive advantage will be gained.

Chapter 41

Mediocrity is in Trouble

by Buck Rodgers,
former IBM vice president of marketing

The challenge of today's executive is to set an example of excellence and send a clear signal that mediocrity is unacceptable.

I PREDICT that the individuals and companies who will be successful in the 1990s and beyond are those willing to adopt the kind of values, work ethics, and resolve that propelled this nation to greatness. They will demand excellence of themselves, and will not tolerate much less from others.

For too many years, we have been floating listlessly in a sea of mediocrity. We sat on its beaches and became soft and bloated. We let its tide rise up into every aspect of our lives. Mediocrity is an enemy that must not be ignored. A manifestation of complacency and lethargy, it's been around so long that too many of us have gotten used to it. Some of our younger people have lived with it all their lives.

For more than two decades, we seem to have lost our way. Vietnam unraveled us, and every part of our society suffered. Government, business, industry, education, and families seemed to break down. Right and wrong became blurred, along with our moral standards and our attitudes at home and in the workplace. Many declared that small is beautiful, and less is more; but we settled for less quality, less service, less courtesy, less thoughtfulness.

Companies that attempted to maintain their level of excellence were considered to be part of an insensitive, antiquated establishment. Watergate further damaged the image of the establishment, and double-digit inflation complicated, confused, and weakened the marketplace.

We were continually distracted throughout the 1970s by the endless conflicts in the Middle East; Khomeini humiliated us by taking U.S. hostages; terrorists murdered our Marines. We poured money into the Third World, and they hated us. When OPEC punished us with their oil embargo, it seemed that our mobile lifestyle was quickly coming to an end.

All our bad times weren't caused solely by outsiders who wanted to undo us. Some of our greatest problems have been self-inflicted. Most recently, we have seen greed and corruption on Wall Street, drug abuse in every sector of our society, and the downfall of public figures who lead less than exemplary private lives. Somewhere along the line, we forgot who we were; we seemed to lose our belief in ourselves, our power to shape and control events—our magic.

Our Competitive Lesson

The United States has been the world's leading producer of agricultural and industrial products for over 100 years. We have been the land of the entrepreneurs, the innovators, and the inventors. The whole world knew that, but our pride, like our pocketbooks, has been battered and bruised by the Japanese, who demonstrated that they can be more industrious and ingenious. Now countries we never considered capable of competing with us—especially at home—are producing products that are often superior to ours and less expensive. We can't blame the foreign entrepreneur or industrialist. It's our own fault.

We know what happened. While Japanese industrialists set their sights on American markets, the Americans had their eyes glued to short-term profit-and-loss statements. The Japanese researched, planned, and invested. The Americans were overly cautious about R&D, and failed to make meaningful commitments to education and training. In response to every economic change, these programs were turned on and off, like a spigot. American companies were more interested in the bottom line than in investing wisely in the future. The Japanese listened to their workers, listened to American consumers, and then acted on what they heard. They courted our consumers, who ignored our home-grown products.

What the Japanese had going for them was their high expectations and their commitment to success. They were determined to outperform us, and they did. They nurtured the conditions necessary to evoke that superior performance, and motivated their work force to strive for excellence and top productivity.

How the Magic was Lost

Too many people who are paid to manage companies or departments in companies became involved in internal power struggles to the detriment of those who relied on them. The managers who aimed for title, status, and power eventually found themselves in secure cabins on sinking ships.

Overly cautious leadership and unimaginative management aren't the only causes of our less than vibrant business and industrial environment. The goal of many in our work force was more pay and less work. Management accepted this condition without much of a fight, often giving in to demands that lowered the quality of products and services and increased prices.

Some unions and employee associations rejected programs that rewarded members for increased productivity. They rejected meritocracy, a system of pay for performance, in favor of across-the-board raises regardless of the quality or quantity of work done. Companies that pressed for incentives and performance increases were accused of trying to encourage competition among employees. Incredibly, in a country that flourished under the free enterprise system, competition in the workplace became feared and discouraged.

Bad management often alienated its people by being insensitive and unappreciative. In addition, employee associations and unions protected members regardless of the quality of their work or their attitude. The only ones who benefitted were employees who didn't deserve to hold on to their position.

Both management and labor have contributed to poor quality, bad service, and high prices; but their time is running out. For any company to survive the competitive pressure, excellence in service and quality of products must be a way of life.

The Customer Cries Foul

At last, the business community is awakening to the fact that it desperately needs superior performers. It settled for too less for too long. Shoddy work, negative attitudes, and sloppy work habits are no longer tolerated. The American consumers who accepted inferior products and services from these mediocre companies are also waking up, thanks to our Japanese competitors.

American business is beginning to listen. That's good news for all of us, but it's terrific news for people who recognize the change as a great opportunity and are motivated to take advantage of it. Smart business now knows it must seek out, embrace, and nurture the innovators, the corporate entrepreneurs, and the high-level producers. A company that effectively fences out creative people loses not only their ideas but also the stimulation they usually bring to every discussion and situation. What it is left with is engineered mediocrity.

Thank goodness, times are changing. American companies are waking up to the fact that they must inject excitement, enthusiasm, and creativity into the workplace.

We Need the Motivation

Our problem in the immediate future will not be the lack of opportunities, but the lack of motivated people ready and able to take advantage of them. There's no shortage of people who have intelligence and ability for success—even spectacular success—but few of them perform at the superior level I'm talking about.

Some of it is understandable. There's been too little healthy pressure put on most people to get them to stretch for their potential. For all of us, at times, the pressure to perform is tremendous. It doesn't matter what your occupation is or how successful you may be; you feel the strain—the strain of competition and expectations. You feel it in all the roles you play and in your relationships.

Let's face the hard facts: No matter how intense the pressure, no matter what the situation, you have to roll out of bed every morning and you have to perform. Like it or not, the quality of that performance depends on you. You may think you are doing a pretty good job, but I'm sure you can do a whole lot better. The secret is to escape the bland mediocrity that has trapped so many of us at work and at home.

You have to believe this: Mediocrity is in trouble! It's up to all of us to keep it there and not accept it as a way of life. You must reject mediocrity like the plague, eliminate it from your life whenever you can. The first thing you must do toward that end is to raise the level of your own performance and encourage those you care about or work with to do the same. After all, you have nothing to lose and everything to gain!

Chapter 42

Quality as Values

by R. Art McNeil, founder and former CEO of The Achieve Group, and
Barry Sheehy, Principal of The Atlanta Consulting Group

Viewing quality as values, rather than just a slick process for improving the bottom line, has many advantages.

MOST quality efforts don't meet heroic ends. There is no Armageddon, no thunderous charge to glory. They end not with a roar but a whimper. No one announces, "Our quality program is dead." Instead, the process is allowed to wind down. Starved of resources, energy, and executive attention, the it simply atrophies and dies.

Why do so many quality programs and processes die prematurely? In large part, it's because we lose interest. We seem incapable of sticking things out long enough to allow them to take root. We enter into important strategic processes without understanding what we are getting ourselves involved in. Any initiative adopted with such ease can just as easily be abandoned.

In his book *Managing on the Edge,* Richard Tanner Pascale analyzed the situation succinctly: "Perhaps our problem is pragmatism taken to extremes. If something doesn't work immediately, we abandon it for fear of having waited too long. We don't take the time to confront the deeper issues squarely."

The Greek philosopher Heraclitis believed "Man's character is his fate." What he meant was that our character and values ultimately determine our fate. Our inability to stick with any strategic process long enough to find out how to make it work represents a potentially fatal flaw in our collective character.

The failure of the process is predetermined by our inability to see it through. Each time we abandon a strategic effort, we undermine the trust and confidence of employees. This, in turn, breeds cynicism and inevitably leads to sluggish reflexes in the face of future strategic challenges. While our competitive rivals move up the quality learning curve, we find ourselves in a constant state of having to start over with yet another quick fix.

Seven Prerequisites

Can premature aging of quality process be avoided? Yes; at the very least, it can be guarded against. It all comes down to seven aspects of planning and design.

1. Educate your executive team. Before beginning any quality improvement effort, take the time to educate your executive team. Ensure they understand exactly what they are getting themselves involved in. Insist that the executive team set aside sufficient time to acquire the rudimentary quality improvement skills. The day your CEO stands up in front of a process team and doesn't know the difference between a run chart and a flowchart, your quality program is in big trouble—employees know a fraud when they see one. Don't compromise on executive participation. In TQM, involvement is commitment. If executives are too busy to learn the details of a TQM process or to acquire TQM skills, then abort the launch. Quality processes that fade away tend to be built on a weak foundation of executive skills.

2. Set realistic expectations. Nothing can be more fatal to the quality process than to set unrealistic expectations. Set a somber tone—as Deming so aptly put it, "I never said it would be easy, I only said it would be work." Your expectations of the initial phases of a quality process should be: 1) This will take several years to launch— to reach "the end of the beginning"; 2) There will be heartaches and setbacks along the way—and when these occur, you must pull the organization through the crisis; and 3) Improving quality, particularly around work processes, is hard, tedious work.

Explain the quality process in simple, understandable terms.

Explain what TQM is and is not. For example, TQM is not a magic, quick fix for all business problems. It is not a silver bullet that can make up for technological inferiority or reverse demographic trends. It will not abolish the business cycle or bring an end to recessions. Total quality management is simply a methodology for improving customer satisfaction and reducing waste through a focus on strengthening work processes, how work is done. Organizations involved in TQM are characterized by a greater focus on the customer, more employee skill training, and lots of effort to improve work process. In short, position TQM to employees in evolutionary rather than revolutionary terms. Play down expectations that "next year" the world will be entirely different as a result of the TQM process.

3. Invest in new skills. It takes a long time to execute an organization—a wide shift in thinking and behavior. The first step is to equip every employee with a new set of behavioral and operational skills. Organizations that lose interest in the TQM process usually do so long before they have reached critical mass in providing new skills. With only 20 percent of the work force trained, managers wonder aloud why 80 percent of the employees are not involved in process improvement teams.

4. Have a plan. Most quality processes fail for lack of a plan. The absence of a workable, understandable, and achievable plan is the chief reason TQM initiatives fail or never get off the ground.

Write a corporate quality plan and insist that each layer also has a plan. Make these plans part of your infrastructure. Don't allow them to be delegated down to staff functionaries. Link the outputs of your quality plan to your performance evaluation system. Re-issue your quality plan each year and begin integrating it with your strategic business plan. Every year publish an annual quality report and make this report available to employees, suppliers, and customers.

Get executives out talking about your quality process. They don't have to tell fibs; have them talk about your efforts, as well as accomplishments. Bring in outside speakers to overcome natural resistance to change. Get out and visit successful quality organizations. Attend conferences, seminars, and networking sessions. Set up quality bulletin boards, newsletters, and communication centers.

There is nothing like a challenge to bring out the best in an organization. Plan to apply for an internationally recognized quality award or standard (CABE, Deming, Baldrige, Shingo, ISO 9000, Z299, etc.). Give yourself a long ramp-up period of at least several years. A word of warning: don't become obsessed with winning. Apply to learn—winning is a byproduct of learning.

5. *Plan for a re-launch.* The ancient Greeks used to say that to ensure peace, a society must be prepared for war. Plan now for inevitable loss of momentum once your quality process is no longer new. Set up a strategy for maintaining momentum. You may even want to establish a powerful subcommittee of your quality council to plan a complete re-launch of the process. If necessary, go right back to the beginning. Remind people: Why we are involved in TQM, the consequences of not proceeding, the benefits for them, next steps, and expectations. Never take commitment for granted. Last year's mandate isn't worth a hoot today unless it has been renewed. Involve constituents in your quality process—board members, customers, suppliers, and members of the community at large. Invite these constituents to sit on quality councils and advisory boards, and participate in training.

6. *Focus early on business processes.* Quality is not a quick fix, but that doesn't mean you shouldn't target for early improvements in business processes. Waiting too long to get involved in business process improvement is a serious error. As early as possible, target two or three important business processes for improvement. Which processes? Ask your customers. Identify high leverage processes which have an important impact on customer satisfaction or the bottom line.

7. *Survey your customers.* Survey your customers as soon as possible—don't wait. Use this information to identify improvement opportunities. Tie executive compensation and performance evaluation to annual improvements in customer satisfaction.

TQM Checklist

Is your TQM effort in danger of premature aging? Run down this checklist. If you are not doing at least 75 percent of what's on this list, chances are your quality process will sooner or later run out of gas.

• Appoint a 100 percent dedicated corporate coordinator reporting to the CEO/COO.

• Put quality first on every management agenda.

• Write and publish an annual quality plan.

• Conduct visits to successful quality organizations.

• Invite speakers from other organizations to speak on quality.

• Get executives out speaking in public on your quality process.

• Put quality process (support, leadership, participation, and

results) into your performance evaluation system.
- Get some early wins/process improvements and celebrate.
- Tie quality process (support, leadership, and results) to compensation.
- Conduct public quality symposiums—get broad participation.
- Conduct external and internal quality survey—tie compensation to annual improvements in results (if possible, publish survey results frequently, i.e., monthly, quarterly).
- Conduct benchmarking against superior companies/organizations.
- Conduct third-party quality audits each year.
- Apply for quality awards or certifications.
- Get quality into your annual business report.
- Publish an annual quality report.
- Conduct an annual executive quality retreat to review last year's results and plans for next year.
- Get customers/suppliers on your quality council.

The great 18th century French general, Marshal de Saxe, once asked his gardener to plant a particular type of oak in his yard. The gardener was aghast and exclaimed, "My general! This tree grows very slowly; it will take years to mature." The general responded quietly, "If this is so, we had best get on with it."

The Values of Quality

Viewing quality as values, rather than just a slick process for improving the bottom line, has many advantages.

In their hearts, many executives don't believe quality is the key to competitiveness. They understand the concepts at a cognitive level, but their response to the quality challenge is far from instinctive.

Intellectually, executives understand the relationship between quality (doing things right the first time) and the bottom line. They can calculate cost-of-quality figures and passionately explain the evils of rework. Executives have been bombarded with articles and statistics on the market power of quality and service. One would have to live on the far side of the moon not to know there is a quality revolution sweeping through our economy. Ask any executive today, and he or she will tell you with conviction that when it comes to quality, there will be none but the quick and the dead in a world economy.

As a result of this new quality awareness, organizations are initiating service and quality improvements. Many of these efforts are limited to "smile and dial" training and "happy talk" sessions, but others are serious efforts that are producing good results. One need only look at the recovery of North American manufacturing to see some of the fruits of these quality efforts.

So what then is the problem? Isn't the universe unfolding as it should? Well, there are certainly some encouraging signs that North American executives are starting to "get religion" when it comes to quality. However, I am not entirely convinced we're out of the woods, despite these movements in the right direction.

We have made an intellectual commitment to quality, but not a spiritual commitment. Quality is still an affair of the head and not of the heart. We have adopted the quality paradigm out of economic necessity. Our goal is to save money rather than improve quality. As usual, we are focusing on the end result rather than the process. So what's wrong with that, you ask? After all, there's nothing like an economic imperative to get the heart pumping.

Economic pressure is a great motivator; in fact, the greater the pressure the better. However, as a foundation for a quality process, economics alone will not suffice. Something more is needed. A concern for the bottom line must be matched with a commitment to bigger issues. If you look at today's quality winners, you will find they are committed not only to profits but also to the future—and, by definition, the future extends beyond the next two quarterly statements.

Without this commitment to the future and the underlying values it reflects, even the most sophisticated quality improvement processes will fail. This is the quality paradox: *to make money you must be committed to more than money.*

A Set of Values

Quality reflects a set of values as much as a set of processes and strategies. It reflects a determination to do things right, a genuine concern for customers, and a deep commitment to employees. It reflects a desire to pass on to our children a society wealthier than we inherited—a world of opportunity, with good education, jobs, housing, and health care. It reflects a full determination not to meekly surrender markets to foreign competition, or to *any* competition, for that matter.

Rather than fold up tents and sneak off into the night at the first sight of competition, winners plant the colors and fight. Cummins Engines, Harley Davidson, Kodak, Xerox, and Northern Telecom, among others, have shown that companies can hold markets if they are willing to fight for them. This willingness to stand and fight reflects more than just a commitment to the bottom line; it reflects a commitment to the future—a commitment that subordinates short-term profits to long-term growth.

Quality winners look beyond next quarter's profit figures in planning for the future. This long-term focus is essential to any quality process. Quality improvement is a long-term growth strategy, not a short-term profit strategy. Think about it! If the whole purpose of the quality process is to make quick profits, what happens when the organization hits a cyclical downturn and profits suffer? We are well into the seventh year of an economic recovery—sooner or later we will have a recession. When earnings drop, the bottom line suffers and organizations look for ways to cut costs. If the bottom line—particularly the short-term bottom line—is all that counts, how many quality processes will survive the next recession?

Even in good times, I have seen organizations throw away years of work in developing a quality process when faced with only one or two underperforming quarters. Slashing staff, cutting training, eliminating improvement task forces, and beating up suppliers produces almost instant results. If you want to save a quick buck, that's the way to do it. The damage, of course, will take years to undo, as employees, suppliers, and customers withdraw their commitment and trust.

When faced with tough times, Toyota executives cut their salaries and geared up their quality program. When faced with similar difficulties, many North American car executives cut workers' salaries, laid off employees, cut training, and then gave themselves obscene bonuses. The difference between these two courses of action reflects a different set of values. Our Japanese colleague was referring to this difference in values in his provocative statement.

Viewing Quality as Values

Viewing quality as a *values* issue rather than just a *process* issue offers many advantages. If quality is simply a slick process for beefing up the bottom line, what happens when a process fails? For every three quality improvement techniques or strategies employed, one will surely fail. Techniques that work wonders in one corporation come up flat in another—it happens all the time.

If you are truly committed to the future and believe that quality represents a moral undertaking, it is easy to shrug off the failure. "So that particular technique didn't work. Let's learn from that experience and try something else. After all, the process is only a tool for achieving our larger goals, and they haven't changed. We still know where we're going and why we are going there."

On the other hand, if quality is a tool solely for making money and it fails in its first trial, there is nothing to fall back on except to try a new tool, another quick fix. If that also proves disappointing, it isn't long before the organization loses interest in the whole process.

I have seen this tragedy played in boardrooms across the nation. Imagine this exchange between a quality consultant and a Vice President of Quality inside a major corporation:

"Surely you're not serious?" asks the consultant.

"I'm afraid we are," says the VP. "This quarter's results have been awful; the whole first half looks weak."

"Is the downturn industry-wide?"

"Yes, everybody's hurting."

"But your quality process is only 20 months old, so the results are just starting to come in. You've already identified COQ improvements which more than cover your investment."

"I know. But the CEO wants to focus everybody's attention on the bottom line. He says we can restart the quality process when things stabilize."

"When will that be?" asks the consultant.

"By year end we should be out of the woods."

"So you intend to be in business next year?"

"Yes," says the vice president.

"And the year after that?"

"Yes."

"Let me get this straight," says the consultant. "You've had 20 profitable quarters since 1985. Now you expect two or three weak quarters, and then you may go on to another 20 profitable quarters?"

"Yes."

"And because of this, you're going to kill your quality process and throw away 20 months' worth of work, not to mention a couple of hundred thousand dollars in training investment?"

"What can I say? No one is more disappointed than I am, but what can I do? The CEO has lost interest. He told me he was disappointed the quality process had not produced more tangible results."

"But you are tracking your commitments. In fact, as I read the statistics, you're ahead of them."

"You know how impatient the boss is—and besides, he thinks

we can get things going again after we recover. For now he wants to concentrate on the 'real business'."

If this can happen in a strong economy, what will happen during the next recession? The answer, of course, is that those organizations committed to the future will tighten their belts, retrench, but protect their quality process the way a farmer protects next year's seed corn. Those who see quality as a quick fix will massacre their programs and walk away saying, "Now let's get back to business."

In the long run, global market forces will exact a terrible price on those who think quality is a frill.

Chapter 43

Excellence is the Exception

by Tom Peters
President of The Tom Peters Group

If you make the best products and provide the best service possible, over the long haul, you will be recognized and rewarded.

W HEN the book *In Search of Excellence* was published in 1983, "excellence" soon became a fashionable buzzword. It was an idea whose time had come. I think cynicism reigned from the middle of the Vietnam era—late 1960s—until probably 1980. And in the midst of cynicism, excellence was not the word on people's minds.

But the times changed. In the mid-'80s, people wanted to get beyond cynicism—they wanted to believe in something, and believe that they could help make it happen. By searching for and writing about excellence companies, Bob Waterman and I became instant folk heroes. Reaction to the book has been incredibly positive from people who actually work for a living—incredibly positive by middle managers, senior managers of small and mid-sized companies, and by people who work in divisions of Fortune 500.

Now, in New York, I can't move three feet without striking up several random conversations with people who would normally stab you over credit rates. Why? Because people strive to do something interesting. And I don't mean that they strive to make a good Chevrolet. If what they were doing at work is boring, they strive to be the greatest human being on the company bowling team. People want to do nifty stuff. And if it's impossible or uninteresting or not worth-while to do it during paid hours, they will do it off hours. Some guy who is hoisting steel 45 hours a week is the number one orchid collector in a seven-county area in western Pennsylvania and writes for the local orchid journal. That's not unusual. People want to be something. And if they can't be something at work, they will find an outlet somewhere else.

Waking Up the Fortune 500

Of course, *In Search of Excellence* was yawned at by many chairmen of the board, CEOs, and executive vice presidents of Fortune 500 companies. Frankly, I don't mind if these executives hate me or love me. But I am bothered by those executives whose companies are sick and yet whose complacency and apathy remain high. Those people scare me to death.

Admittedly, I have never loved the Fortune 500, although some have accused me of that. In the book *In Search of Excellence,* we were simply searching for and writing about good American companies. To say that there are some great Fortune 500 companies is not to extol the group as a whole. In fact, the real message is that *the excellent companies are the exception.* We picked 43 (of the Fortune 500) and could have picked 75, but the clear implication is that the other 425 are of a different nature. Most of the Fortune 500 couldn't innovate their way out of a wet paper bag.

I'm now more enamored of small and mid-sized companies in the sense that I think they have the greatest chance of waking up the Fortune 500. I love to tell stories about Worthington Steel because I feel that the only way we're ever going to wake up U.S. Steel, if it's wakeable, is to have a half dozen mid-sized steel companies around nipping at its heels and giving it fits.

I enjoy talking about successful entrepreneurial ventures such as Mrs. Fields Cookies, because the theory ten years ago was that if you're going to make it in the food business, you've got to be a billion-dollar company. Mrs. Fields proved that theory wrong. While she created the top half of her market, she took the other half out of the Nabisco's. I don't think America has gone crazy over cookies. I think that we have gone crazy over good cookies and are probably buying fewer Oreos. Thus, we see the Amoses and the Davids and the Mrs. Fields. And in Colorado, we see Mo Segal with Celestial Seasonings Tea Company giving Lipton fits.

I've received my share of criticism this past decade, but to me the beautiful part of that criticism is that we're being taken seriously. You don't devote a cover of *Business Week*—as editor in chief Steve Shepherd did—to attacking a book unless that book has gotten under people's skins. And so I was at least 50 percent pleased with it. I don't like getting beaten up in public and having to walk by newsstands and see "oops" all over the place, but I don't mind serious, valid, high visibility criticism as long as I feel good about what I did.

We chose companies for excellence over the long haul. *Business Week* was looking at the last two quarters. They said 13 of the companies we wrote about had problems. If you read their charts carefully, you note that they're loaded with asterisks. By our own financial criteria, only four or five of the companies really had trouble. Atari was a mistake. Kodak had a slump. But most have their act together.

Pockets of Excellence

I sense that many executives are frustrated by examples of quality and excellence because they feel that there's no way they can make their company excellent. There are a lot of frustrated people who do their own thing well within a crummy company. In our book, *A Passion for Excellence,* we talk about "pockets of excellence." In the crummiest companies in the world, one may find good product development, a good accounting department, a good factory, a good division, or what have you. And so it's possible to make your unit great within the X-Y-Z crummy company, but excellence will not diffuse from the bottom up to corporate headquarters unless you have the leadership at the top.

What troubles me is that when I meet with middle managers, they say, "We really want to get with it, but those turkey vice presidents won't let us do anything." I then meet two days later with the vice presidents and they say, "We support you a thousand percent, but those turkey middle managers won't get off the dime and get on with it." And so you have this horrible stalemate because the middle thinks that the top stinks—and the top thinks the middle stinks.

Could I make good things happen in a company? I don't know. Some people have flattered me by putting out feelers, but I don't encourage them. I don't want to be an executive—I enjoy doing what I'm doing. My role in life is to watch people do well and then write and talk about it. Secondly, I suspect there are a whole lot of people, if you go through the history of management, who have decided that because they were articulate they could be a great manager or leader. But I see no reason to believe that's the case. I have no desire to prove I'm Ray Kroc. Oh, I get an urge now and then when I see the utter simplicity of it all, but the reality is that everything I say is deceptively difficult. For example, "listen to your customers" sounds simple enough, but you need to do it every day for 25 years if you're serious about excellence.

I think you can have "turnarounds" when something extraordinary happens in a short period of time, meaning 12 or 24 months. But that doesn't mean you can sustain it. Chrysler is a good example. Has Lee Iacocca built an enterprise for the ages? I doubt it at this stage of the game.

I think Iacocca did an incredible thing, and there ought to be statues 300 feet high built in his honor because he kept some 300,000 people in their jobs and made Congress and dealers and customers and suppliers believe that there would be a tomorrow. He deserves the accolades that he's gotten, but that doesn't mean he's built a worldwide, viable, competitive car company.

General Motors hasn't exactly arrived either. I spent some time with one of their major dealers in Dallas, Texas. He told me that he's never had a visit from anybody in corporate management. GM is not exactly customer-focused yet. I think Saturn is a great thing; the EDS acquisition was a great thing; and they're doing some very innovative things in their plants—but it all adds up to about 5 percent of what's necessary.

What is necessary? I'm trying to say there are some basic components of excellence—listening to customers, acting on what you hear, providing decent service, providing decent quality, looking for every opportunity to innovate, and respecting people within the organization—and that this stuff is plausible and doable. We've taken our eye off the ball, but there are lots of role models around who suggest we can do things better.

On an individual level, the message is to make the best quality products and provide the best service possible today. Over the long haul, the odds are you will be recognized for that—maybe not in your current job or current company but someday—because the world tends to respect quality work, whether it's in cookies or computers. The only person who suffers if you don't do it is you personally.

It's All Common Sense

A lot of what I write about is common sense; in fact, one of the chapter titles in the *Passion* book is called "A Blinding Flash of the Obvious." Absolutely obvious! Story after story says if you want a superior company, go ask your customers what they want. And yet, because of the bureaucratic structures we find in many organizations, we spend seven hours of every eight-hour day working as hard as we possibly can to *not* do the obvious.

Just ask people for suggestions and you get them. For example, there's a grocery store in Connecticut that's adding a big kitchen because their customers said they'd like to have fresh home-cooked meals to take home. And then, instead of just sitting down alone with the architect, the owner brings in the cook, dishwasher, and food service manager to talk to the architect and figure out how to design this thing. What do you get? An efficient and effective facility, and moreover, one that people have bought into as their own. It doesn't exactly take genius, and yet it's not practiced in 99 percent of the places 99 percent of the time.

There has been an unintentional conspiracy to drive common sense out of a lot of our businesses. That conspiracy evolved over the last 40 years when accountants and administrative people—as opposed to factory people, marketing people, and designers—started running our companies. With the bean-counting administrative mentality, common sense wasn't required. We created these structures with no sensitivity to the marketplace, out of touch with manufacturers and engineers. I'm saying that unless we keep close to the customer, even the best companies may fail.

To improve their competitive position, executives need to look to some role models. There are good role models in every industry, and I think the Fortune 500, among other companies, should go hunting for them.

Terror of Protectionism

The greatest terror I'm living with right now is that I think there is a modestly good chance that we're going to get ourselves into a black hole called protectionism. And the goal of protectionism is to protect the weak. The people who are the leaders in most industries are not looking for protection. It's the people who are hurting the most who are crying the loudest. But heaven help us if our answer is to prop up companies that are not effective competitors.

Protectionism is the first issue that managements and unions have ever been able to agree on. In the older industries, we're seeing a most bizarre collusion between company management and union management. Both want to take the heat off. And both are looking out principally for themselves.

I have never seen a union come into a company whose management didn't dearly deserve it. People don't frivolously join a union. Look at the efforts of union organizers with megabucks behind them to organize with good companies, and you see that time and time again they're rebuffed at the door. It's my strong feeling that unions slow down the decision-making process. I am against bureaucracy; I am, therefore, on that dimension, against unions. But I predict we will have unions in Silicon Valley within five years to a modestly substantial degree because of poor management.

Some hold out hope that having more women in senior management positions will help humanize the work force, but I don't see a radical shift as women enter senior management. My observation is that women in big companies have, by and large, made it to the top by out-machoing macho males. They have really bought into the get-ahead role model and bought many books on how to do the power trip. So don't expect the work force to be more humanized as a result of women entering management. If the work force will be humanized, it's because we figure out that Japanese workers make better products because they enjoy what they're doing. And then we'll see humanization in Pittsburgh among a bunch of 52 year olds whose alternative is to lose their jobs.

I Don't Fix Companies

I would like to think that I've made a modest difference, but I have precious little proof. If there was a company that said they had changed their way because of something I said or did, I wouldn't believe it. A lot of people are talking on the same issues. Of course, there are management consultants going around talking about the scalps on their belt, "I fixed this company, I fixed that company." But that's simply not the case.

When a plant manager or company president first sees sales start to drop, he or she may start reading some books or listening to lectures. Then Tom Peters happens to walk in the door, and he or she grabs onto whatever it is you're peddling with religious fervor. If you're an idiot, you give yourself credit for it. But the reality is that

350 prior events prepared him or her to be ready to accept that kind of a message.

Moreover, I don't fix companies. Any company that I have "fixed" is because somebody had the predisposition to fix it before I walked in the door. They grabbed ahold of me as the person that they wanted to hoist up their flagpole, to justify what they already thought they ought to be doing. And that's the way change basically happens in organizations.

If you liked this book, then you'll love *Executive Excellence* magazine. Each chapter in this book appeared as an article in *Executive Excellence*. This collection is a sample of the insights on quality, service, leadership development, managerial effectiveness, and organizational productivity which appear monthly in *Executive Excellence.*

If finding time to read *Executive Excellence* is a challenge, you can simply subscribe to our new audio edition. You may order the cassette only or receive it along with the printed version. By listening to *Executive Excellence* in your car, office, or at the gym, and applying the principles, you will build excellence into your performance, products, and services, month by month.

Over the past 11 years, *Executive Excellence* has published the best thinking from executives, top-level managers, business professors, and consultants. These articles are now available on CD-ROM. With this new CD-ROM, you can search key words like "empowerment," "quality," "competitive advantage," and more. This tool will put years of learning and growth at your fingertips.

For more information on *Executive Excellence* magazine, audio tapes, CD-ROM, to receive a sample issue of *Executive Excellence,* or to subscribe to *Executive Excellence,* please call:

1-800-304-9782